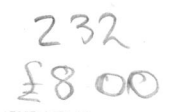

Lancashire Gunners at War

Frontispiece.

Lancashire Gunners at War

*The 88th Lancashire
Field Regiment, 1939–1945*

Stephen Bull

Carnegie Publishing, 1999

Published by Carnegie Publishing Ltd
Carnegie House, Chatsworth Road, Lancaster LA1 4SL

Copyright © Stephen Bull 1999

All rights reserved
The moral right of the author has been asserted.

ISBN 1 85936 068 8

Typeset by Carnegie Publishing, Lancaster
Printed by Redwood Books, Trowbridge, Wilts

Contents

	Acknowledgements	vi
1	The History of a Territorial Regiment	1
2	France and Belgium, 1939–1940	13
3	The Defence of the United Kingdom, 1940–41	33
4	The Malayan Campaign, 1941–1942	43
5	Changi Jail	83
6	The Railway	113
7	Coming Home	127
8	Roll of Honour, 88th Field Regiment, 1939–1945	143
	Bibliography	153

Acknowledgements

The basis of the following narrative is war diaries, official histories, and printed memoirs. For access to these the author is indebted to Lancashire County Libraries; Lancashire Record Office; the Imperial War Museum; and the Royal Artillery Institution. Yet these are merely the bones of the story: what makes this account genuinely different is the unique contribution made by the officers and men of 88th Field Regiment, Royal Artillery, Territorial Army. This is their story, and there has been no scruple made in using their recollections, retrospective notes, and, most especially, the diaries, photographs, drawings and manuscripts produced by them at the time. As far as possible the opinions expressed here are their opinions, yet amongst a whole regiment, many of whom would not return from the war, it must be admitted such opinions and experiences are many, varied, and sometimes contradictory. As far as is practical the veterans are thanked, inadequately, by inclusion in the bibliographic notes at the end of the book.

In addition I should like to thank Brigadier Ken Timbers; Mrs B. Timbers, and Major D. Rollo R.A. for their specialist inputs; John Blundell, Lancashire County Museums Officer; Sue Ashworth and Peter Donnelly of Lancaster City Museum; Jamie Wilson of Spelmount Publishing for assistance with maps; and last but by no means least, Captain 'Teddy' E.C. Dickson, one of the most self-effacing yet persistent of men, who sowed the idea, read the drafts, and nurtured the project to fruition.

It is worth noting that in the text place names, ranks, and times have been left as they were at the moment being described. Unless otherwise stated English nomenclature and titles have been preferred.

1

The History of a Territorial Regiment

There have been volunteer, or part time, gunners in the county of Lancashire for several centuries, but 88th Field Regiment claimed their descent from the volunteer units formed in 1859 and 1860, in answer to Napoleon III and the threat of French invasion. Arguably therefore the regiment's spiritual father was Robert Clarke of Preston, paymaster of the Preston Rifle Volunteers, who wrote to the Secretary of State for War to suggest the formation of an artillery corps at Preston: and, on receiving a favourable reply, went on to form the 21st Lancashire Artillery Volunteer Corps, from which the 88th would trace their lineage. In 1880 changes to organisation saw the Preston corps renumbered as 5th Lancashire, a title which they would continue to bear until the formation of the Territorial Army. In 1908, with the advent of the Territorial Force, the volunteer batteries of Preston, Lancaster, and Blackpool came together as 2nd West Lancashire Brigade. The link with the regular 'Royal Regiment of Artillery', which had an unbroken history back to 1716, was thus formalised.

The commanding officer of the 2nd West Lancashire Brigade was the old senior officer of the Preston corps, Lieutenant Colonel C.J. Trimble, best known to his friends as 'Paddy': an unconventional character whose associations with the regiment would eventually span two thirds of a century. Charles Joseph Trimble was born in Castlebellingham, Ireland, in 1856. Having studied medicine in Edinburgh he became a doctor, and moved to England where he settled into general practice at Walton-le-Dale near Preston, Lancashire. He joined the Volunteer Artillery in 1878, and also formed a branch of the Order of St John, which later helped organise ambulance volunteers for the Boer War. Apart from his more serious pursuits he was also known for his passion for amateur dramatics and singing. All in all he was the most loyal and enthusiastic of Territorials and would serve as a constant example to the unit.

The Headquarters of the 2nd West Lancashire was originally at 26 Fishergate, Preston, but as a result of the building of a new court house in the town the Old Sessions House on Stanley Street fell vacant, and in October 1911 the gunners moved into the building which would be their home until after the Second World War. The structure was of considerable historical interest, having been built to a design by the celebrated architect Rickman in 1829 to service the prison next door, to which it was joined by means of a tunnel. As originally constructed it was surmounted by a large dome, but unfortunately this architectural feature had to be removed in 1849 as it had become unsafe.

Colonel Trimble retired from active command of the brigade in 1913, but was promptly made the regiment's Honorary Colonel, or symbolic head. Despite

Lancashire gunners hauling an 18-pdr field fun through Flanders mud during the Great War. By Desmond Bettany

his years and many commitments he would serve in the Great War with the Royal Army Medical Corps, and would be decorated for saving life during air raids on the hospital at Etaples. His old command went on to no less distinction under Lieutenant Colonel T.E. Topping and the new designation 276th Brigade; whilst another old commander, Lieutenant Colonel S. Simpson helped to form, and then led, a new sister unit, the 286th Brigade. During the First World War many members of these units were decorated, including five of the 276th who won Distinguished Conduct Medals. Sergeant Cyril E. Gourley was awarded the Victoria Cross, for engaging and knocking out an enemy machine gun at close range whilst under sniper fire, and helping to save the guns.

A brief disbandment occurred at the end of the First World War, but the Brigade was reformed in June 1920. Predictably it was given yet another new title: 88th (2nd West Lancashire) Brigade, Royal Field Artillery, Territorial Army. Despite the semantic change the unit retained a continuity in its essential character; for the Commanding Officer was Lieutenant Colonel Simpson, and the Headquarters remained in the same building on Stanley Street. The Brigade now also had a history of active service, its own local heroes, and a list of names on its war memorials. The reformed unit maintained a four battery organisation. The 349 Battery at Stanley Street Preston, the 350 Battery at Dallas Road Lancaster, and the 351 Battery at Yorkshire Street Blackpool all had the old 18 pounder field guns. The 352 Battery with its 4.5 inch Howitzers was also based on the Preston Headquarters.

As was usual with Territorial units the 88th usually met for training and 'drill nights' on Wednesday evenings and weekends. The motivations of part time soldiers were, as they are now, many and various. Some enlisted solely through a feeling of patriotic duty; but there were many others who joined for social or financial reasons. The inter-war period may have been glamourous and exciting for the few, but for the many it was a period of hardship and limited entertainment. Unless he was particularly bookish, or very religious, the working man's primary outlets were likely to be the public house and the football field. The Territorial Army therefore opened up possibilities of considerable interest: comradeship, camps in other parts of the country, learning the soldiers trade, a uniform, and essentially free organised sport and games. Another attraction of the 88th in the inter-war period was its band. The most remarkable aspect of this was that it was not supported by public funds, but depended entirely on subscriptions received from the officers, and honorary members of the officers mess. The band would not be officially recognised or funded until 1955.

In the case of the 88th added interest was created by various prizes awarded within the unit for professional skills. These included a Sub Section Challenge Cup; the Calvert Subaltern's Challenge Cup, which was won repeatedly by Lieutenant C.D. Cornish and Lieutenant Denis Houghton; and the Wilson Cup for battery proficiency which was awarded yearly from 1895 to 1936. Indeed it is arguable that the 88th, like other Territorial units, took their soldiering more seriously than the regulars. In the regulars equestrian and field sports were often the main recreation for the officers, whilst it was often frowned upon to talk 'shop' in the mess. For the Territorial soldiering was the recreation, and whilst they were sometimes sneered at by the regulars as not 'proper soldiers', they were volunteers whose pursuit of military skill was not only a hobby but often a passionate enthusiasm.

It was probably also the case that the average Territorial 'other rank' was of superior intellectual material than his regular equivalent. Many soldiers had joined the regulars because they lacked other employment, or were insufficiently qualified. Territorials by contrast, were usually employed elsewhere, and were frequently skilled tradesmen for whom their daily toil alone provided insufficient stimulation. Finance of course also played its part: one member of the 88th in the 1930s was candid enough to admit that his sole reason for joining was to use his small 'bounty' to buy Christmas presents for his family who otherwise would have had none. The 88th did however have strong competition for recruits, and for public plaudits in the Preston area, as for many years the town had been closely linked with the Loyal North Lancashire Regiment; the local unit of infantry. More than one member of the 88th in the inter-war period has remarked how difficult it was to convince the populace, firstly that not everyone in khaki service dress was a 'Loyal', and then that they were as every bit as elite as the competition.

Of the officers, usually the only regular was the Adjutant, assisted perhaps

Left: Gunners G. Howson and F. Howson pictured in service dress with trumpets and bugles.

Bottom: Non-commissioned officers of the 88th West Lancashire Brigade R.A., T.A. outside their Stanley Street headquarters in the inter-war period. Note the many medals, most of them gained during the First World War.

Right: Non-commissioned officers of 352 Battery 'in action' on camp at Holyhead, Anglesea, 1928.

by a sergeant instructor or two, who were accounted 'permanent staff'. The Commanding Officers were sometimes regulars, but for the most part were officers who had seen previous war service with the Brigade. Lieutenant Colonel S. Smith D.S.O. M.C., commanded from 1922 to 1930, and was succeeded by Lieutenant Colonel J. Hudson, M.C., who was in post from 1930 to 1936. Hudson had first joined 2nd West Lancashires in 1910, and had an excellent local pedigree in that he had for many years been in charge of the Brigade's howitzer battery. Three Majors with previous war service also serving in 1930 were E. Read, R.D. Marshall, and W.E. Blackburne.

For the officers belonging to a regiment or battery often brought with it something of the atmosphere of a club. Social distinction was always of less importance in the Territorials than the Regulars, but nevertheless class difference was a factor. One gunner described Denis Houghton, who joined in 1933, as almost 'like the local squire', and stated that some gunners joined specifically to follow his leadership. Houghton was at the time a solicitor based on Winkley Street, Preston. Other Territorial officers were the scions of successful local shoe and furniture businesses.

New 'sprogs' who had no experience on striking the correct bearing for an officer and gentleman, had, in the mid 1930s, the advantage of the presence of Quartermaster Sergeant Cater at Stanley Street. This non commissioned officer had served in the Great War and exuded professionalism with his correct, smart, fit bearing, and clipped military moustache. He was also able to dispense advice on the correct modes of address and military etiquette. Another senior 'non com' who was something of a fixture in Preston at this time was Regimental Sergeant Major Thomas Higgins. The 'RSM' lived on site with his family at Stanley Street, his accommodation being the rooms upstairs, above and to the side of the old main court. The hall itself was used for drill, and for much of the time was lined with field guns for practice, and next door was a small sergeant's mess. Upstairs on the side of the building nearest to Stanley Street itself was the officer's billiard room.

Camp was undoubtedly the yearly highlight of the Territorial calender. Usually lasting about two weeks, it could be virtually anywhere in the United Kingdom which boasted sufficient space for artillery live firing. Just how vast a full size range needed to be is often not fully appreciated. The 18 pounder guns with which the 88th were equipped in the inter-war period could manage a range of 11,100 yards, or almost six and a half miles. The first version of the 25 pounder, which was approved in the late 1930s, and was sometimes called the '18/25 pounder' because it was based on the same carriage as its predecessor, could top this distance by perhaps another 1,000 yards. The width of a range had to be such that it would accommodate a battery, and allow for at least a limited degree of traversing and error in aim.

Though serious accidents were few gunners certainly had to be wary and treat their pieces with respect. Gunner Frederick Parkes, who enlisted aged 17 in 1926, recalled live firing with the 4.5 inch howitzers out to sea off Anglesey.

The peak of excitement was the 'Brigade Salvo' with all guns firing at once. Parkes remembered on one occasion that the noise and pressure was such that it actually made his ears bleed. On another firing his gun's 'spade' failed to dig into the ground and absorb recoil, and so the breech came back and smashed his nose. His third brush with disaster came when he received the word to fire and a gunner wandered in front of the muzzle. He refused to fire and landed on a charge for disobeying an order, but the other man was dismissed.

Camps attended by the 88th in the 1920s included Rhyl and Trawsfynydd in Wales. In 1933 they went to Malvern; Buxton in 1935; Tilshead on Salisbury Plain in 1936; and Richmond in Yorkshire in 1937. The next year they went to Redesdale Northumberland, before returning to Trawsfynydd in August 1939. Trawsfynydd had a somewhat dubious reputation as a small and inadequate camp, and, since practically unpronounceable to those with English as their mother tongue, was known to the 88th as 'Trousers'. The firing range here was a single valley 6,000 yards in length, which, from the mid 1920s, was used with reduced charge ammunition.

There were compensations however, for, as one gunner officer put it, 'it had a pleasantly unsophisticated atmosphere', and the officer's mess was accommodated in a charming old 'fortified farmhouse'. The Roman fort of Utica nearby reminded everyone how long there had been a military presence in this rural area, and added a touch of interest for those of an antiquarian disposition. Gunner Len Livermore of Lancaster saw the place in a far less romantic light in the late summer of 1939, recalling little but rain, corrugated iron shacks selling souvenirs, and a wet and windy day trip to Barmouth. Moreover the land round about Trawsfynydd camp itself was extremely boggy, and tall tales circulated of whole gun teams which had been swallowed up when off road movement had been attempted.

Another potential hazard for the Territorial gunner at camp prior to the introduction of motor vehicles was the fact that horses for practice were usually provided locally by civilian contractors. These animals, which were known in military circles as 'Heavy Draught' (HD) and 'Light Draught' (LD), were often actually 'Vanners' – van pullers in civilian life. The gunners and drivers often referred to the most nondescript simply as 'hairies'. The first men at camp were often the least lucky, for they were presented with a hundred or so assorted beasts, few of which had much experience as the motive power for guns and limbers; and a huge pile of tack. Much work, some of it painful, was needed to sort the horses out into gun teams and persuade them to pull the guns with a semblance of purpose. It was therefore unsurprising that the Territorial Artillery units were often amongst the forefront of those who experimented with tractors and civilian farm machinery for gun pulling.

Until the mid 1920s the 88th Brigade had relied entirely on horsed transport. First attempts at mechanisation came in 1927 when Fordson tractors were used in a gun pulling demonstration held on parts of the land now occupied by

Right: Gunners of 349 Battery on camp pose with an 18-pdr field gun and limber borrowed from another battery.

Above: Practice for the 4.5-in howitzers of 352 Battery, Malvern, 1934.

Left: Maintenance on gun breech mechanisms: Just one task of many on camp.

The much-decorated Charles J. Trimble, Colonel of 88th Field Regiment, in the uniform of the St John's Ambulance Brigade, pictured at Chorley, 1929.

Kimberley Barracks and Preston North End football ground. Several more years would elapse before the unit was completely and permanently mechanised with lorries and gun tractors, thus managing to drop the accusations that, like the rest of the artillery, it was 'poor man's cavalry'. The mechanisation of all artillery units in the United Kingdom was finally ordered in 1936, and contemporary photographs of the Brigade in training show the use of various light trucks and Austin staff cars at this time. Pictures taken at Inglewhite in 1938 show that by then the Brigade was using Morris six wheeled artillery tractors with 8 and 15 hundredweight trucks for carrying stores.

Apart from gunnery and driving camps also gave the opportunity to practice less martial skills. Baking and cooking were just two of the most obvious. At Redesdale camp 349 Battery found themselves short of a butcher. They discovered in their ranks Gunner J.E. Lyon who, though now working at Leyland Motors, had worked as a butcher in his youth.

Gunner Fielding and Sergeant Sowerby man the 349 Battery exchange, Redesdale camp, 1938.

Sergeant Buller gives recruits instruction on an 18-pdr field gun, Stanley Street, Preston, May 1938. The face of Roy Marshall, future Major General, can just be seen peeping over the group, just to the right of the instructor.

The North Camp, Trawsfynydd. This card was send home by Gunner Nelson on 6 August 1939, although the picture may have been taken rather earlier.

The officers of the 88th on camp at Trawsfynydd, 1939.

Front row, left to right: Captain H.H. Wale; Captain C.D. Cornish; Major E. Leigh; Major W.E. Blackburn; Lt Col. R.D. Marshall; Major Gregson; Captain G.M. St Leger; unidentified; Captain G. Leigh.

Middle row: Major Lumley (RAMC); unidentified; Lieutenants Gatty and Berry; unidentified; Captain D.A.S. Houghton; Lieutenants Hamilton; Priestley; Birkbeck; A.C. Dickson and Beresford.

Back row: Lieutenants Barton; Sturton; E.C. Dickson; Bradley; unidentified; unidentified; Swainson; K. Marsden; Carrington; Court; Wilkinson; Fraser; unidentified.

Lyon then became one of four cooks for his battery of 200 men, and later also served as 'Assistant Cook' at Trawsfynydd camp. Promotion to Lance Bombardier back in Preston brought with it some of the responsibility for the battery cookhouse. Amongst the mysteries he had to master were the cooking of potatoes in cut down petrol containers, and the use of the petrol powered 'hydroburner'; a device which would shoot a most alarming six foot flame along a trench to heat the pots suspended above.

The late 1930s were a watershed for the unit in more ways than one. An event of particular historical significance was the coronation of George VI and Queen Elizabeth in 1937, and the brigade had the honour of sending a detachment to take part in the ceremonial and festivities, led by Captain E.H. Leigh and Lieutenant C.D. Cornish. Perhaps more sinister were new gas masks, which made their first appearance amidst mirth at Redesdale camp, yet underlined the fact that the training might be used in earnest.

Trawsfynnyd sixty years on. A nuclear power station and a man-made lake have drastically altered the local landscape.

The Stanley Street Headquarters underwent considerable extension and modernisation, and a new drill hall, including a miniature rifle range and canteen, was built behind the Sessions House. In 1938 came a major reorganisation, which, in the army as a whole, meant centralising administration of the artillery at brigade level. The old 'Field Brigades' were therefore reduced in size, and rechristened as Field Regiments. In the case of the 88th the batteries were reorganised so that 349 and 350 were separated to become an independent command, 137th Field Regiment, based in Blackpool. The 88th meanwhile was also redesignated as a 'Field Regiment' and continued with 351 and 352 batteries, based on Preston, Stanley St, and Lancaster, Dallas Rd. The new nomenclature reflected rather more accurately the size and status of the two battery unit.

The year 1938 also saw a change of commanding officer. Lieutenant Colonel H.C.H. Eden M.C., who had the unusual distinction of being a graduate of both the Army and the Navy Staff colleges, left the regiment after a two year posting. He was replaced by Lieutenant Colonel R.D. Marshall, a Lancaster bank manager who had for many years previously been Battery Commander of 350 battery.

A good many of the officers who would serve overseas in World War Two were now in place with the regiment. These included the Adjutant Captain G.M. St Leger, another veteran of the First World War, renowned for his slow and methodical approach; and Captain P.D. Weir who had been commissioned in 1932, and had served with the Sudan Defence Force. There was also a significant group of more junior Territorial officers who lived in the Preston area, were predominantly younger, and had been commissioned within the past few years. These included the popular Captain Denis Houghton; Lieutenant E.P.K. Potter a local businessman commissioned in 1933; Captain C.D. Cornish who was a Liverpool solicitor; the Dickson brothers; and 'Reg' Bradley commissioned in 1938.

Army Form E.518

RESERVE AND AUXILIARY FORCES ACT, 1939.
TERRITORIAL ARMY.

CALLING OUT NOTICE.

To—

Name .... EADE, W. D. ....

Rank .... Gunner .... Army Number .... 902167 ....

Regt. or Corps .... 351/88TH. A. FD. REGT. R.A. (TA) ....

In pursuance of directions given by the Secretary of State for War in accordance with an Order in Council made under Section 1 of the above-mentioned Act, you are hereby notified that you are called out for military service commencing from 1 SEP 1939 19 , and for this purpose you are required to join the .... 351/88TH. A. FD. REGT. R.A. (TA) ....

at .... STANLEY ST. PRESTON .... on that day.

Should you not present yourself on that day you will be liable to be proceeded against.

BRING YOUR CIVILIAN GAS MASK.

L. H. Lund

MAJOR R.A.
Comndg. 351st. FIELD BATTERY R.A. (TA).

Stamp of Officer Commanding Unit.

Place .... PRESTON ....

Date .... 1 SEP 1939 ....

You should bring your Health and Pensions Insurance Card and Unemployment Insurance Book. If, however, you cannot obtain these before joining you should write to your employer asking him to forward these to you at your unit headquarters. If you are in possession of a receipt (U.I. 40) from the Employment Exchange for your Employment Book bring that receipt with you.

You will also bring your Army Book 3, but you *must not fill* in any particulars on page 13 or the "Statement of family" in that book, and the postcards therein *must not be used.*

[5/39] (393/2397) Wt. 21114 750M 7/39 H & S Ltd. Gp. 393 (2242) Forms E518/1

The 'Calling Out' notice, dated 1 September 1939, two days before the outbreak of war, received by Gunner W.D. Eade of 351 Battery.

2

France and Belgium, 1939–1940

For the senior officers of the regiment war must have seemed all but inevitable by the late summer of 1939. On 23 August came the first of a series of preparatory signals from the War Office under the code names of famous generals, leading up to full mobilisation and preparedness for war. The cypher 'Byng' was followed by 'Plumer', 'Allenby', and inexorably, but with little historical logic, by 'Clive'. The regiment was officially 'embodied' for active service on 31 August. Chamberlain's 'final note' to Germany concerning the freedom of Poland expired on 3 September, and so from 11 a.m. on that day 'a state of war' came to exist between Britain and Germany. In many places the build up was to an anti climax; air raids did not materialise immediately, and for civilians at least very little happened. The general perception was of 'phoney' war as Poland was devoured.

For the Territorials, and for 88th Field Regiment in particular, the story was somewhat different. The planning was that a 152,000 man 'British Expeditionary Force' would proceed to France immediately, under General The Viscount Gort V.C. The 88th was earmarked to join this 'B.E.F.', and there was much to do in a short time. Part time soldiers had to 'give up their day jobs', prepare to separate from their families for an unknown duration, and get ready all the guns, vehicles and kit necessary for modern war. It was also decided that since 88th Field was about to proceed on active service a way should be devised to leave the youngest men behind without them being entirely lost to the army. The result was that an exchange of a batch of men was organised with the regiment's old colleagues 137th Field Regiment. The 88th took some older men, leaving the youngest for 137th.

On 6 September came another significant personnel change with the arrival of a new commanding officer, destined to lead the unit to war. The new man was Lieutenant Colonel Henry Mordant Stanford: a dapper figure with a pallid face and greying hair, who was a regular officer with a chestful of medals, including a Military Cross earned in the Great War. He had been born in 1894, and first commissioned into the Royal Artillery in July 1914. Obtaining his majority in 1933, he had completed the staff gunnery course at the Royal Military College of Science the following year. His versatility was suggested by the fact that he was also qualified in coast and anti aircraft gunnery. 'Stan', as he was known to those close to him, was a practical man, who inspired confidence in his men. One of his first actions on taking up his new appointment was to examine the trucks and Morris gun tractors with which the regiment had been provided. He declared them inadequate on the grounds of lack of

Above: Gunner Richard Ainscough, aged 21, pictured with his family, Preston, March 1940. After the war Ainscough served as caretaker for the HQ in Stanley Street, Preston.

Right: Driver Tom Orritt of 351 Battery, pictured wearing the 1937 Pattern Battle Dress and Field Service cap. His left sleeve bears the driver's badge and long-service chevrons. Orritt had served as a regular overseas prior to the outbreak of war, and was respected as an experienced model by new recruits.

Left: 88th Gunners and drivers early in the war.
Back row: J. Harrison; J. Parry; T. Orritt.
Front row: E. Bamber; Williams; J. Pemberton.

stowage, and immediately had new boxes and fold down seats added so that the equipment and gun teams could be carried comfortably. For close defence each battery received two .55 inch 'Boys' anti tank rifles, two Bren light machine guns, and a dozen rifles. It was all too clear that both 'Stan' and the army meant serious business.

The deployment plan was that the vehicles and a portion of the regiment would travel to the south coast in road convoy, whilst the remainder of the personnel and baggage went by rail. Probably the first to depart was Lieutenant R. Bradley, who went ahead on 19 September and headed for the 'Road Convoy Regulating Post' at Southampton. The road convoy proper, with 253 officers and men of the regiment, plus various signallers and engineers, departed a week later under the charge of Major Gregson and Captain St Leger. Its progress via Warrington, Wellington, and Worcester, was stately indeed by more modern yardsticks, its maximum planned speed being 20 miles per hour, with an average of just 12. Breaks of 15 minutes were allowed every three hours, and the column density was to be kept down to 25 vehicles per mile, with 'blocks' of trucks and cars no more than six in strength. The scheme was intended to minimise driver strain whilst presenting a difficult target for the Luftwaffe, but it also illustrates rather starkly the state of Britain's road network in 1939, and the limited expectations of mechanised mobility. Nonetheless the road party reached Newport without mishap. They boarded ship, and docked at Nantes on 1 October: within another 48 hours everything was unloaded and ready to move.

The main body of the personnel, comprising the remaining 381 members of the regiment destined for overseas service, mustered at Stanley Street Preston in their 'Field Service Marching Order' just before 5 a.m. on 3 October 1939. When the hour struck they marched off for the station, forage caps on their heads, and helmets with red and blue artillery flashes slung on their packs. They arrived in more than adequate time to catch the 6.15 a.m. train to Southampton, and rendezvous with the steamship 'Viking' which was to transport them across the Channel. Gunner Livermore of Lancaster and several friends decided that travelling inside one of the life boats was both the safest and most comfortable option, but they were soon chased out again – perhaps on grounds of unit morale.

Early the next morning they disembarked at Cherbourg, becoming one of 20 Field Artillery Regiments with the British Expeditionary Force. Over the next couple of days the unit was again sorted out, and whilst doing so it was lodged in nearby billets. Regimental headquarters was situated at Chateau le Gresse; 351 Battery at Gesnes, and 352 at Chalons. This at least was how the War Diary described it. Gunner Livermore on the other hand had vivid memories of sleeping on straw in the out buildings of a farm, 'with a small hole in the wall and a pig on the other side'.

Advanced parties began to move forward on 7 October, and by 16 October the whole regiment had moved via Warlus to positions in the Gondecourt area, near the North Eastern frontier of France, 351 Battery established an observation post at Fort de Sainghin, whilst 352 placed another at Peronne church. Some of the guns were forward in 'harassing' positions, whilst the remainder were held back. It seemed more than likely that the regiment was about to face a major confrontation, as notice for action was put at a mere four hours. On 17 October work began on two alternative sets of positions; three forward and three battle troop positions.

Anticipation, excitement, and fear, reached fever pitch: yet despite the minor skirmishes which had already occurred in the Saar involving General Gamelin's 3rd and 4th French armies nothing happened in the British sector. The remainder of that month was spent digging in and improving the battery positions: and at the end of October a three day exercise was held, during which the new positions were occupied. The regiment trained, and dug, and trained again, thereby making their own small contribution to the 40 miles of defences, pill boxes, and ditches which constituted the BEF lines. By November the 'routine' of war had well and truly taken over. Captain Birt was posted to 352 Battery, Captain Priestley went off on a course with French gunners at Mailly. Major Lumley the Royal Army Medical Corps doctor was himself taken ill, and had to be admitted to hospital and replaced by the more junior Scottish Second Lieutenant 'Doc' Dickson, RAMC.

Getting used to the situation took some time. However at least one member of 352 Battery recalled that, despite other drawbacks, Gondecourt offered several *estaminets* where half decent food could be purchased. This made a welcome change from the 'terrible' bully beef and hard tack biscuit which had sustained them on the journey, or standing up in the barn which passed for a mess hall to eat the issue rations. 'D' Troop were at one point housed in an old school, but were later moved into farm buildings owned by a character the men knew as 'Joe Stalin' because of his resemblance to the Soviet leader. Yet this Stalin was a good capitalist, because he also ran one of the cafés; and he also had a better side to his nature. One Bombardier from Blackpool, a tram driver in civilian life even hammered away on his piano and attempted to teach his daughters to dance the Lambeth walk.

The winter of 1939 to 1940 soon turned extremely cold. Snow fell and vehicles began to freeze up, and an order came round that most were to be drained down at night to minimise the damage. Commanding officers were to personally inspect the transport and ensure that this had been done. Lieutenant Colonel Stanford protested half humorously that both his age and shape made this technically impossible. However he did what he could to keep up a state of preparedness: standing orders of that time specified that a roll call be carried out in billets every night at nine thirty, and a dispatch rider slept in each battery office in case urgent messages should arrive. Contingency plans and tables of march were also drawn up.

Gunner Livermore and his colleagues meanwhile were attending to 'contingencies' of their own. Despite straw, the welcome issue of overalls, a second blanket, and sleeping fully clothed, hypothermia still seemed a distinct possibility. They therefore clubbed together, hired a room, and took turns to sleep in it. Coffee and cognac were legitimately purchased for a penny-halfpenny before parade; whilst some of 'Joe Stalin's' seed potatoes more mysteriously made their way to the frying pan. An experiment with the cooking of snails was rather less successful: their similarity with Morecambe seafood being declared cosmetic only.

December was enlivened a little not only by a practice camp but by the visit of two dignitaries to the inactive front. Part of the regiment was inspected by His Majesty King George VI at Templemars on 6 December, whilst the Prime Minister visited Fretin Chateau ten days later. Gunner Livermore recalled much waiting, and even more spit and polish and cleaning of boots, prior to being marched out into a muddy field, after which the King drove past at some speed. Just after Christmas the regiment went to 2nd Corps training area for exercises, during which Stanford's headquarters was located at Petit Reitz, but all were returned to Gondecourt by 14 January.

That boredom and discomfort were frequently the lot of their men at the front was soon well appreciated by the friends and supporters of 88th Field Regiment at home in Lancashire. Early November saw the beginnings of an official 'comforts fund', pushed forward by Father P.J. Adamson, former Roman Catholic priest of Hoylake, Cheshire, who had recently joined 88th Field Regiment in France as chaplain. With the backing of the commanding officer Adamson wrote home to the newspapers, describing the state of the rest billets, 'usually barns without furniture, often crowded and with straw for bedding', and appealed both for funds, and useful objects. Most urgently required were furniture, utensils, tea, soap, sugar and cigarettes, but he was optimistic that more ambitious items like a piano and other musical instruments could be obtained, if the necessary support was forthcoming. There was as he put it, 'a lot of talent in the regiment' so far as music was concerned.

Colonel Trimble immediately organised an appeal with Mrs Potter in charge of collecting 'playing cards, magazines and knitted items' at the Stanley Street drill hall, and then he went on to hold a meeting at Lancaster Town Hall in order to promote a similar scheme there. By mid December Adamson was able to write to the Mayor of Preston and others involved in the collection, thanking them for their efforts and generosity. A dart board was put up in the canteen, domino sets were issued to all billets, magazines were distributed, and instruments and stage properties purchased for theatricals. Cigarettes were given free to men whom the army had somehow forgotten, their pay being 'not quite arranged'. What most excited the men seemed to be the abundance of clean dry socks, a large quantity being snapped up in under an hour of arrival.

Mid January 1940 saw a minor scare with the cancellation of leave and the arrival of 17 extra men and ten new ammunition lorries, but the general impression was one of boredom and inactivity. Lieutenant E.C. Dickson recalled endless inspections, and criticism of the positioning of his camouflage, many

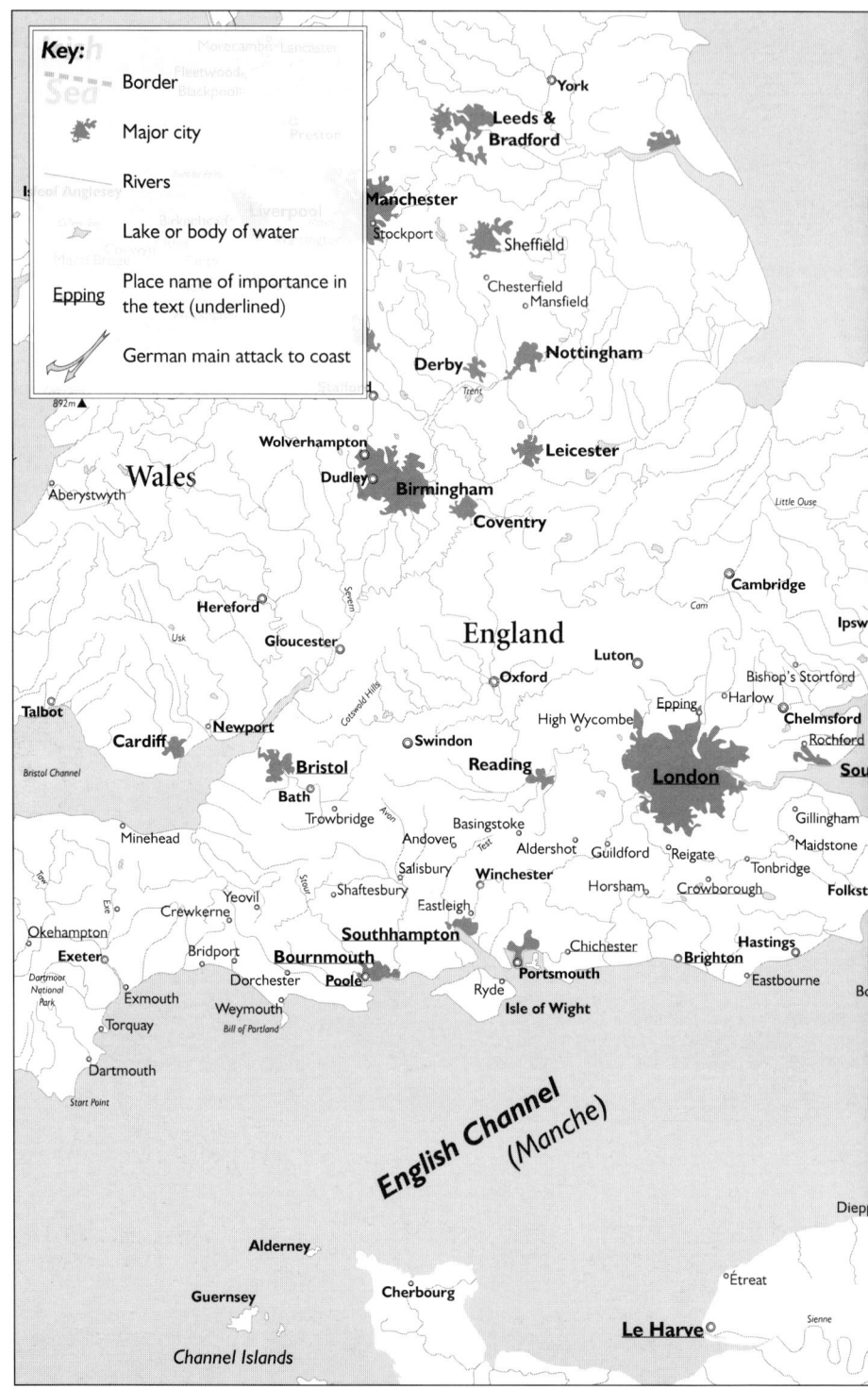

France and Belgium, 1939–1940

hours being whiled away in artistic rearrangements. The inactivity was just too much for some: one Gunner faced 28 days field punishment for contradicting the censorship regulations, and the next day he shot himself in the foot. Major Gregson had perhaps a more interesting time, being posted to the 1st Battalion the Royal Suffolk regiment for two weeks: Lieutenant K.H. Marsden went down with meningitis. February's high point was the shooting of a smoke screen in training at Gondecourt, and anti tank rifle practice carried out at the range at Ablain-St-Nazaire. Even so there was much frustration and some opportunity for mischief: one young officer got incredibly drunk and landed in front of a Court Martial.

At the beginning of March the regiment was moved to Fives near the city of Lille. The other ranks billets were somewhat improved by the change: some were put in a large house by a cemetery, others in flats. It was also near Lille that the 4th Division held a major exercise in which several of 88th Field Regiment's officers acted as umpires. Yet whilst the German forces attacked and swallowed Denmark and Norway, the Western front in France remained pretty well dormant. Though there was little action British strength had nevertheless been gradually increasing all the time, so that by now there were about a third of a million troops on the ground in support of the French allies. The teeth of this strength was three fighting Corps of ten divisions, with General Headquarters at Arras.

The storm finally broke in May 1940. On 10 May Neville Chamberlain resigned to be replaced by Winston Churchill: the same day the German onslaught on the Low Countries began. Gliders and paratroops took out the Belgian fort at Eben Emael: there was widespread bombing, and the Panzers began to flow across the borders. This violation of the neutrality of the Low Countries was the trigger for the 'Dyle Plan', according to the provisions of which the British and French armies would advance to the assistance of Belgium. They were then supposed to form a defensive line with the Dutch and Belgians. If all went well the Dutch army would take the northern flank, and the Belgians would occupy a sector in the northern part of their country, whilst the British held the central part of Belgium east of Brussels. The French would protect their frontier, and the southern part of Belgium.

Within a few hours of the German attack the Belgian government abandoned its neutral stance and called on Allied assistance. The first British forces across the border were the armoured cars of 12th Royal Lancers, which raced into Belgium even before some of the Belgian border guards had been appraised of the situation. Not long after the 88th Field Regiment was involved, for an hour before midnight on Sunday 12 May they set out for Machelen in Belgium in accordance with the intention to halt the enemy at the Dyle river. Here they were to form part of 2nd Corps in the defensive line.

Whilst on reconnaissance around Berchthembosch Stanford saw the first effects of the war on the civilian population, and Belgian troops 'racing about on bicycles endeavouring to locate enemy parachutists'. By the night of 14 May

'B' and 'E' troops of the regiment were established on the outskirts of Louvain, and the nearby roads were choked with refugees and retreating Belgian soldiers. Not for the last time 88th Field Regiment, and the BEF in general, were in an extremely precarious position, for though they could not know it, Bock's Sixth German army was tasked for a breakthrough between Louvain and Namur. Yet this was just part of the story for further south von Kleist's 1st, 2nd, and 10th Panzer Divisions, supported by infantry and dive bombers, were already smashing their way into the French lines at Sedan. With the main German effort aimed here, the Allied forces which had advanced into Belgium had effectively put their heads into a trap.

Just a few hours later at 3 a.m. on the morning of 15 May the regiment received their baptism of fire. At the 'B' Troop position there was heavy enemy shelling which actually bowled over two of the artillery tractors. A panicky report was received that Berchthembosch wood was occupied by German parachutists, and at 4 a.m. shells also dropped around the regimental headquarters. This however was the extent of things until the evening when 351 Battery was allowed to fire its first seven rounds in retaliation, and the Engineers of the 'Light Aid Detachment' were able to recover the wrecked tractors. So far the regiment had suffered no fatalities, but on 16 May this was to change suddenly and tragically. Two Bren gunners mistook members of 'B' Troop for enemy parachutists and opened fire: Gunner Tyrer was killed, and thus it was that the regiment's first death in action was the result of 'friendly fire'. There was however no time to consider the matter as at 6 p.m. the regiment moved back according to its orders, harassed by German aircraft. RAF cover was limited, for though the Germans had also taken losses the British had already had over 200 aircraft destroyed.

That same day French Prime Minister Reynaud was despairing that the battle was all but lost. Drastic measures were clearly imperative. The British plan to avoid being outflanked or trapped, as prearranged with their allies, was to fall back as far as was necessary. The first move would be to the Senne line, which linked Charleroi with Brussels and the Willebroeck Canal; the next to the Dendre line, on the Dendre river and the towns of Mons, Mauberge, and Termonde; and the final shift to the Escaut line, being the river of that name, and the ancient town of Ghent. The Escaut line, though strengthened by the water obstacle, was far from impenetrable. It was 33 miles in length, and generally lacked the benefit of fixed defences.

By 18 May the exhausted 88th gunners were back to Belleghem Bosch, near Mouscron, within a few miles of the Franco-Belgian border. Despite some of the orders being couched in terms of an 'advance' to a position in the rear, and the prevalence of the story that the Germans were simply being lured into a trap it was pretty obvious to most that the British Expeditionary Force was in headlong flight. A retreat precipitated by French collapse further south no doubt, but a rapid retreat nonetheless, and one badly impeded, as the regiment's War Diary points out, by dive bombing and refugees. More than one 88th

Gunner recalled mid May as a confused period of night moves, lack of sleep, and attempts to avoid both refugees and Stukas.

General Gort's orders placed him, and the BEF as a whole, under the French Commander in Chief 'North East Theatre of Operations', but were ambiguous in the sense that if any order 'appeared to imperil the British Field Force' he could 'appeal' to the British Government. For the time being this mattered little save for the necessity of coordinating the army's immediate movements with those of the French, but within two weeks these strictures were to assume a paramount importance. Already, however, many troops on the ground were more than puzzled by the conduct of the campaign; since, in the course of a few days, they had first advanced sixty miles, and then fallen back almost an equal distance.

The 88th Field remained a part of 2nd Corps, 'Corps Troops', and together with four Medium Regiments, a light anti aircraft regiment, and a regiment of the Royal Horse Artillery could be deployed flexibly as the Corps commander wished. So, on 19 May, the regiment was ordered to be superimposed across the 1st Division front with 351 Battery at Nechin, 352 Battery at Leers and the headquarters at Toufflers. Observation posts were positioned on the bank of the river Escaut itself in accordance with the prearranged plan. The troops of 1st Division which the regiment supported were nine battalions of infantry in three brigades and included two battalions of Guards as well as a battalion of the Gordon Highlanders, and the 1st Battalion the Loyal North Lancashire Regiment. The scene was set for a major battle should Lord Gort so desire, but his Corps commanders warned that the position was unlikely to hold for very long, not only due to the fact that the Germans could outflank it given time, but also because of the relative weight of numbers. Perhaps more worrying yet artillery ammunition was in short supply, so much so that the 'Official History' has it that 2nd Corps restricted its normal use to five rounds per gun per day.

On 21 May the Germans struck again. First came shelling followed by ground attack. This assault met with partial success as the Germans succeeded in getting across the Escaut and nosing their way between the 3rd Battalion of the Grenadier Guards, and 2nd Coldstreams. Soon 1st Division was engaged in counter attacks, 88th Field Regiment in particular laying a smoke screen on Mont-St-Aubert to allow the 1st Battalion of the Loyals to go forward. One of the significant bombardments of the campaign was therefore fired by 88th Field over the heads of old Preston friends and rivals.

Yet soon the situation was deteriorating on 1st Divisional front: one of the Guards battalions began to fall back, a circumstance blamed at the time, not on confusion and enemy strength, but a 'pseudo Colonel' who issued a retire order. The Duke of Northumberland, serving as a Lieutenant in the Grenadier Guards was killed; and Lance Corporal Harry Nicholls, also of the Grenadiers, won a VC defending a ridge overlooking the river with his Bren gun. After a distinctly worrying moment the situation was retrieved by the 4th Battalion of the Gordons who came forward to lend weight to the defence, and whose carrier platoon hunted down enemy stragglers. The rest of the infantry were given a chance to regroup, and a fresh counter attack went in at mid day, again with supporting fire from 88th Field.

Although the regiment had come through the day virtually unscathed, and 1st Division front was not in imminent danger of collapse, the pace of the action elsewhere, in more thinly held places, was about to dictate the course of events. Far to the south west German 2nd Panzer Division had broken through to Abbeville, whilst 1st Panzer Division smashed through the line at Albert, badly damaging a battalion of the Royal West Kents and pretty well destroying 7th Battalion of the Royal Sussex. They then carried on to Amiens helping to create a yawning gap which the French could do nothing to fill. The armoured 'scythe cut', or 'Sichelschnitt', was headed directly at the Channel coast. In the face of these concentrated tank thrusts, the essence of 'Blitzkrieg', it was looking increasingly although the BEF was about to be entirely cut off from its French allies. It was also possible that if it did not secure its lines of communication very promptly it would run out of supplies, or even lose its ports of embarkation and disembarkation.

Thus it was that the BEF continued to tumble backwards across France at an ever increasing rate. A spirited thrust south by British tanks at Arras met with momentary success, and gave von Kleist a momentary pause for thought. It also elicited a demand from Hitler to his Generals for both information and counter action: but one small success was as nothing against the tide. On 22 May the regiment was making full speed, reaching Wasque late that night. Observation posts were established at Ham on 23 May, but these never seem to have been used. The next day the whole of the BEF was put on 'half rations' in recognition of the fact that the Germans were effectively behind them, Boulogne and Calais were under threat, and that food supplies were bound to be affected. Belated French counter attacks in the direction of Amiens were making little impact.

Panzer General Heinz Guderian, amongst others, was of the opinion that a quick advance was now of vital importance to end the campaign. Yet at this critical juncture Hitler issued orders that this was not to be a headlong rush against the last defence of the Channel coast, but a considered manoeuvre in which it would be the task of the Luftwaffe first to 'break the resistance of the surrounded forces' before the army finished them off. 'Führer Directive 13', issued on 24 May, thus gave a small breathing space to the beleaguered BEF. It also gave a short respite to those German Generals who felt that the German divisions were in danger of outrunning their stamina and supplies.

Whatever the reasons: whether hesitancy on the part of the Führer himself; a wish to conserve the amour for later fighting; or caution on the part of the commanders in driving too far troops who had already conducted a brilliantly successful lightning campaign, the last push was slow in coming. Nevertheless even Churchill seems to have realised the extreme perilousness of the situation, and the possibility that the conclusion of useful resistance could be at hand. He duly signalled Lord Gort that in the event of communications being cut, and the beaches irrevocably lost, he would be the 'sole judge of when it was impossible to inflict further damage upon the enemy'. The end could indeed be very near.

By Sunday 26 May the situation was critical. Driver George 'Bob' Pemberton, who was driving a 15 cwt cable laying truck, had begun to notice that communication cables were being laid to the battery positions, but there was never time to wind them up again. If this went on much longer they would be totally reliant on dispatch riders and runners. A regimental reconnaissance party reached Neuve Eglise that same day only to run into bombing and straffing: nevertheless the regiment followed up to spend the night here.

That evening the Admiralty sent the now famous message 'Operation Dynamo is to Commence'. It was to be evacuation from Dunkirk. Lord Gort cabled Anthony Eden that even under the most favourable circumstance it was highly likely that, 'a great part of the BEF and its equipment' would be lost. Though the Navy already had a plan for evacuation it was soberly estimated that the defence of Dunkirk could last but 48 hours, and that as a result perhaps only a quarter of the troops would get away. Disaster was staring the British command in the face, though needless to say this was not to be communicated to those fighting on the ground; especially those to be tasked with the defence of the final perimeter.

The next morning the 88th set out via Poperinghe, Proven, and Beveren to Leysele, from whence they spied the burning oil tanks of Dunkirk itself. In peacetime the long sandy beaches of Dunkirk, sloping away very gently into the water, backed by rolling Dunes, had much to recommend them. Yet in war it was otherwise, for seagoing vessels could only dock in the harbours and there was precious little shelter within easy reach of the sea. Moreover the area immediately inland was mainly flat and treeless, and appeared extremely vulnerable to armour. From a tactical point of view the only redeeming feature were the canals and streams which any attacker would have to cross. The defenders could quickly improve their value by destroying the bridges, and opening dykes, so as to inundate the ground.

In many ways 27 May 1940, the day of the departure of the first evacuation vessels, and of Belgium's capitulation, was the worst yet experienced. German attacks were now pushed across the defended canal lines. One significant problem for the regiment was that much of its 'impressed' transport was now on its last legs. Vans and Royal Army Service Corps wagons alike began to break down, and some were simply pushed off the road and into the ditches. Broken dykes may have impeded the enemy, but the boggy ground also precluded any proper 'digging in' by the defence. In the skies overhead the regiment were witness to dog fights during which two Messerschmitt 109 fighters were brought down by RAF hurricanes. It was also on this day that Lieutenant Bennison was wounded, Major Gregson was killed, and 'F' Troop of 352 Battery was overrun, apparently by Germans who managed to outflank them by advancing through a wood.

The circumstances of Major Gregson's death are still disputed, but there is a consensus of opinion that he met his end during a motorcycle reconnaissance which was being conducted in an attempt to locate 'F' Troop and bring it to a position where it could be established in an anti tank role in defence of the Dunkirk perimeter. Accompanying him were another officer, and driver Ayrton. Coming to a crossroads Gregson decided to examine one fork of the road taking Ayrton with him, whilst the other officer turned off in another direction. Gregson had not gone far when he and his companion were ambushed from one side of the road: one bullet scored up Ayrton's arm slightly wounding him, another burst a tyre, but being an experienced motorcyclist he swung his machine around on the spot and roared away. Gregson was slower to turn and apparently not so lucky. A report published in the *Lancashire Daily Post* during the war had it that Gregson was not killed outright, but surrounded 'by Germans who came out of a nearby cottage and marched away'. Members of the regiment who have been interviewed on this point believe that he was not captured, but died immediately in a hail of bullets. In yet another version of events Gregson was running away when shot.

In the meantime 'F' Troop had been caught unawares by the Germans and overrun. Upwards of 20 of them landed up in captivity, and Gunner Foulkes would later die during their imprisonment. Lieutenant Sturton, who was also

Disabled British transport, photographed by an officer of the regiment in the flooded landscape near Dunkirk, May 1940.

Officers and men of the 88th Field Regiment wait for transport in holes on Dunkirk beach. The officer in glasses, foreground right, is Lieutenant Anthony C. Dickson.

amongst those captured, also did not survive the war, being killed during a POW escape attempt from a train.

On 28 May the regiment was still in the thick of it, but was finally pulled back without further mishap to a position extending just in advance of the Bergues-Furnes canal line, with 352 Battery deployed in an anti tank role in the vicinity of Bergues itself, and 351 at Leysele. In front of regimental headquarters all the surplus transport was gathered and burnt by Captain Pote-Hunt. The flooding was still a problem, preventing use of deep trenches or gun pits, and since local water supplies were now contaminated the regiment was forced to rely on its own 'water cart'. The flooded ground also led to other more gruesome problems: Driver Bob Pemberton recalled that he found a dead dispatch rider on the road and was detailed to help bury him. The deeper they dug the more wet mud and the less earth there was: ultimately the unfortunate man was effectively buried in water. Tom Orritt conducted the funeral.

By this time 88th Field were attached directly to General Alexander's depleted 1st Division, which included the Guards Brigade. When enquiry was made whether there was a specific reason for this, the reply came that they were to form a part of the final rearguard, thus helping to allow the rest of the BEF to escape. It was, as one officer put it, 'a nice cheerful thing to tell the chaps'.

Second Lieutenant Cook with 352 Battery just south of Bergues soon got a taste of what this meant in practice. He had the four guns of his troop aimed

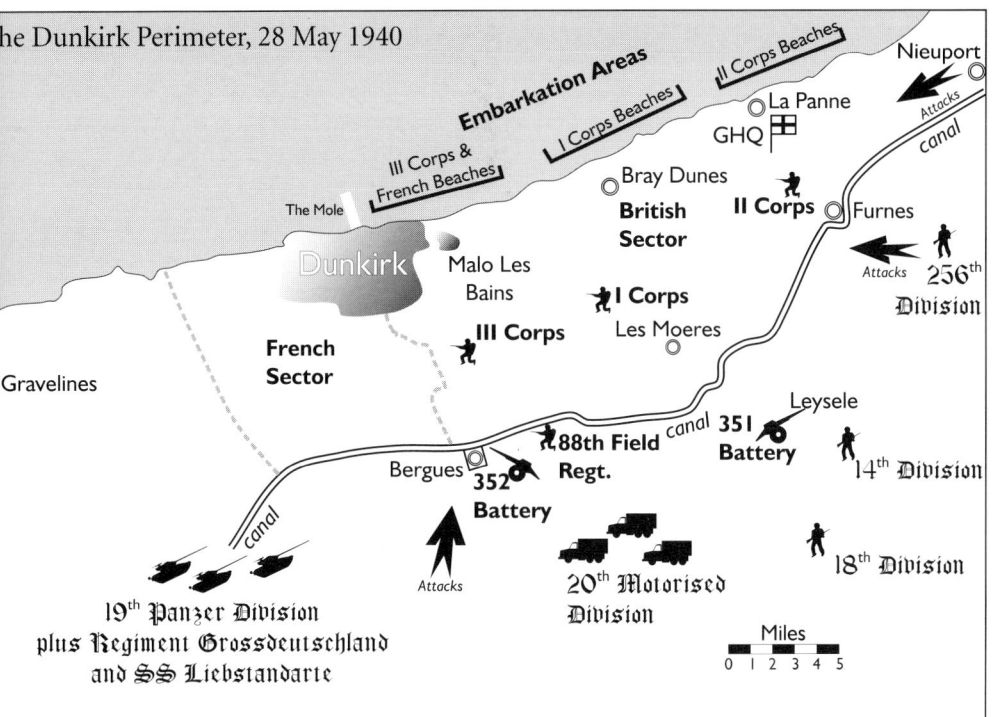

at the nearby railway, with the intention of stopping enemy tanks crossing. Not long afterwards infantry appeared running across the fields. These were at first thought to be friendly, but suddenly they opened up a rapid fire on the gunners. According to one account it was at this point that Gunner Hodgkinson was wounded.

One gun rapidly set to, returning fire on the Germans, whilst the others fell back. When the enemy were so close that the last gun was in danger of capture Cook sent this back as well, personally covering its retirement with a Bren gun. Further back the 25 pounders were again unlimbered and opened a spirited bombardment, until eventually German infantry again threatened to overrun the gun line. Cook dismissed the detachments and destroyed the guns himself so that they would not fall into enemy hands. He was immediately awarded a Military Cross. With grudging admiration he was duly dubbed 'madman' Cook by his brother officers.

That afternoon the remainder of the regiment was pulled back further still so that it was based on Les Moeres, with 351 Battery on the Les Moeres-Krommelhoek road. The whole British position was now basically behind the Bergues and Furnes canal, with only the slenderest six mile deep toehold on the continent of Europe. Gort's headquarters was now at Le Panne: the position was tenuous, but made marginally stronger by the demolition of the canal bridges. There was imminent danger that should 9th Panzer Division, or the German Fourth and Sixth armies launch a determined attack, the BEF would not merely be swept into the sea, but annihilated.

In practical terms this meant the defenders of the perimeter delaying the enemy as long as possible, whilst allowing every unuseful pair of hands to depart for the beaches. As early as 29 May Stanford was selecting men not immediately necessary for the defence, and marching them down to the sea, whilst their colleagues hung on grimly at the gun line. On 30 May Le Panne was under fire. 351 Battery was likewise very heavily engaged, and itself made every use of shells which were apparently no longer rationed. About 1000 rounds were fired on that day alone. The morning of 31 May was quiet and more men were sent down to the beaches in the remaining motor transport, but that afternoon heavy shelling came down, a lot of it in the vicinity of 'C' Troop. Several casualties were sustained, including at least one senior NCO, and Bombardier A.D. Woodworth, who was carried to the rear badly wounded. As a result of the confusion of the next few days a further two years would elapse before it would be officially determined that he had died of wounds.

Meanwhile in the 'C' Troop gun positions things had reached a hazardous juncture, fire had broken out, guns were temporarily out of action, and as Captain Cornish's command post had been hit there was no officer on the spot to give orders. Shelling was also playing havoc with communications, so that more than one man had to risk rifle and shell fire to repair telephone lines. Fortunately Lance Sergeant R.S. Marshall had his wits about him and was able to step into the breach. He took charge, and at great personal risk, extinguished the fire and organised the remaining detachments so as to keep two guns in action. He displayed considerable coolness and initiative, and was duly awarded the Military Medal. Also highly commended, not only for action on this day, but during the preceding two weeks, were Lance Bombardier A. Alabaster who was himself wounded on 31 May; Captain C.D. Cornish, and Lance Corporal C.G. Stringfellow, a signaller of the Royal Corps of Signals attached to 88th Field.

At 0130 on the morning of 1 June the regiment was pulled back for the final time, and the perimeter was now manned by just the last few thousand British and French troops. Ammunition had run short, but it proved possible to replenish the troops from pre established dumps, and keep the guns in action. More enemy fire came down, sometimes with hideous effect, as at Le Panne where some men were physically blown through the metal railings which lined the road and eyewitnesses saw the gutters run with blood. In 88th Field Regiment the bombardment claimed a fatality in the shape of Sergeant Chalker of 'B' Troop. Not far way that morning 1st Battalion of the East Lancashires were having a particularly hard time of it, and were in danger of having their flank turned by Germans who had crossed the canal line. Here disaster was averted by Captain Ervine-Andrews who won a VC defending a barn with a Bren gun.

The 88th Field Regiment kept up fire until dusk, when finally the order

A German photograph of British dead, Dunkirk, 1940.

came to disable the guns and head for the beaches. Between 9.30 and 11 p.m. that evening this was accomplished. The textbook method of destroying the guns was employed in a number of instances, and this involved exploding a shell in the barrel: a spectacular if dangerous procedure. Artillery instruments were smashed and buried, or dismantled and scattered over a wide area.

Everywhere round about this same scene of destruction was being repeated. As a man from another unit recalled: 'New wireless sets ... were placed in rows in the fields, twenty in a row, while a soldier with a pick axe proceeded up and down knocking them to pieces. Trucks were dealt with just as drastically. Radiators and engines were smashed with sledgehammers; tyres slashed and sawn after they had been deflated. Vehicles that were near canals were finally pushed in. Some canals were choked with wrecks, all piled on top of one another'.

The scene on the beach was equally bizarre; with the last of the men struggling back towards the sea to join the long snakes of troops winding across the sands, and knots of soldiers cowering in shell holes. At least two photographs were actually taken on the beach of a party of officers and men of the regiment looking tired, bewildered, and less than adequately protected by shallow scrapes. Yet tolerably good order was retained considering the circumstances, and it seems that the policy of sending back men as soon as they were no longer required had paid off. The regiment was fortunate indeed not to lose heavily in its disarmed and vulnerable state, waiting to be taken off the beaches at this eleventh hour. As the official history of the campaign put it, ' ... it was the

Troops huddle on the deck of *HMS Vanquisher* during loading at Dunkirk.

enemy's bombing that caused the heaviest damage. The scale on which evacuation was proceeding had been reported by their air reconnaissance formations and "the bulk of the German bomber forces were employed to prevent the enemy achieving this and to annihilate him"'.

Bombing and straffing inflicted casualties, and sank many vessels including the famous paddle steamers *Gracie Fields* and *Crested Eagle*, the sloop *HMS Bideford*, the destroyers *HMS Havant* and *HMS Keith*, the boarding vessel *King Orry*, and the passenger ships *Normania* and *Lorina*. Yet there were other significant threats still lurking off the beach. These hazards included torpedo attacks which sank the destroyers *Wakeful* and *Grafton*; collisions and groundings which claimed the drifter *Comfort* and damaged the destroyers *Scimitar*, *Montrose* and *Mackay*; and mines which took the passenger ship *Mona's Queen*.

Serious as these losses were, over seven hundred vessels were involved in Operation Dynamo and the majority got through. These ranged from regular full size naval craft, down to the rag tag of 'little ships'. Though these smaller boats carried relatively few men, they proved especially useful in ferrying men from the beaches to the larger transports. Some of the minor craft pressed or volunteered into use were commercial, others privately owned pleasure vessels, and included amongst their number some truly weird and wonderful boats.

The *Count Dracula* was remarkable in that it had previously seen service as a German Admiral's launch, then been scuttled and since salvaged. The *Endeavour* was a racing yacht which belonged to pioneer aviator Tommy Sopwith. There were also 19 life boats, tugs, motor boats, refuse barges, and a fire brigade tender. Drifters, whalers, and cutters were aplenty. Amongst the river launches was one named *Marchioness*, a vessel destined for disaster on the Thames long after the war was over. Though many of the little ships were given naval crews, others sailed straight to France under the control of their original owners. The result was that several pensioners, a man who was profoundly deaf, and at least one 14 year old boy saw action at Dunkirk.

Though out and out panic was rare, organisation was often stretched to breaking point. Thus it was that some members of the regiment simply joined orderly queues and stepped aboard from jetties without even getting wet feet; others struggled up to their necks in water and found themselves exhausted, half drowned, and entirely amongst strangers.

Captain Denis Houghton reached the front of a queue quite unscathed, and still clutching a large regulation suitcase which he had preserved with great effort and against all ills throughout the campaign. The vessel which he was about to board had precious little room, and none for luxuries. He put down the case, and with a mental curse for wasted efforts, pushed his baggage gently off the mole with his toe and into the water below. Lieutenant E.C. Dickson reached his destroyer a little more dishevelled but in one piece, finding only when he was aboard that his revolver had gone missing. He was still wondering what became of it half a century later. At the time this was but a detail, because soon the ship was making full steam under air attack. The destroyer replied with everything that would fire and regained England in safety.

Gunner Livermore had already heard that the area by the breakwaters had an ill reputation, and viewed the prospect of clambering over planks lashed to semi submerged lorries with distinct misapprehension. He therefore did his best to approach the rescuing ships via the town. Avoiding some wrecked Anti Aircraft guns he managed to make it aboard on one of the last sailings of HMS *Grenade*. It was standing room only in the forward compartment, but nevertheless he was back in Dover by early the next morning. The ship was not so lucky: on a subsequent sailing the *Grenade* had just loaded, and was departing, when hit by bombs and turned into a blazing wreck. She was towed clear of the harbour before sinking.

Driver G. Pemberton made his way back to England in the company of Lance Bombardier G. Haworth courtesy of the splendid old paddle steamer *Medway Queen*, and its crew of Royal Naval Reservists, many of whom hailed from Devon. Reaching the vessel was no easy matter and involved wading chest high, merely to get to its lifeboat which had been launched to serve as a tender. As the water got deeper, and with German mortar fire already dropping on the beach, it occurred to Pemberton that there was little point in being out of pocket as a result of the exercise, so he approached the yelling boatmen pay book extended above his head. The sailors stood on no ceremony and simply plucked him from the breakers by the scruff of the neck. When he eventually reached the paddle steamer he was overcome with tiredness and dropped asleep. It was only later he realised how much the crew of the ship had been through, making no less than seven journeys between Dunkirk and Dover and rescuing some hundreds of soldiers.

Regimental lore of the 88th has it that one gunner was very badly wounded in both legs and reluctantly left by a comrade under the sea wall. He was captured by the Germans who tended his injuries before allowing him to be repatriated; to his own surprise he recovered well enough to rejoin the army and fight in North Africa with a different unit. This man is believed to have been Gunner Bill Whitely of Bamber Bridge. American reports stated that about 700 wounded soldiers were indeed captured by the Germans in the vicinity of Dunkirk.

In addition to those officers and men of the regiment already noted as awarded medals or commended, a further list of personnel was published a few months later as 'Mentioned in Dispatches' for their part in the campaign. These were Major Gregson; Captains Berry and Cornish; both of the Dickson brothers; Regimental Quartermaster Sergeant Beardmore; Battery Sergeant Major Gardner; Sergeant Warburton; Lance Bombardier Pinder; Gunner Milham and Driver Walker. The regiment had acquitted itself as well, if not better than most: but in truth it had been an experience that few would care to repeat. Practical experience had been gained the hard way.

3

The Defence of the United Kingdom 1940–1941

According to the official history a total of 224,000 British officers and men came back to the UK from Dunkirk in May and early June: another 144,000 were later evacuated from the ports further west. About 27,000 military personnel had been brought out prior to the commencement of the main withdrawal, making a grand total of well over a third of a million British soldiers plus their Allies. Only about 10,000 men had become casualties around Dunkirk. This was doubtless a miraculous achievement in the face of disaster; yet there was no way that 'Operation Dynamo' could be portrayed as a victory. Most importantly the army had lost the vast majority of its heavy equipment. The deficiency would take many months to rectify. In the case of 88th Field Regiment the most pressing problem would be guns. Production of 25 pounder field pieces had been barely one a month in the early part of 1939 – rising to about 35 per month in the summer of 1940. Yet each division needed 70 such guns, and there were at least 12 divisions either short of artillery or totally devoid. The queue for precious equipment was a long one.

Thus it was that the 88th suffered the temporary indignity of acting as infantry. Moreover the perilous military situation, and the perceived danger of German invasion would mean that the regiment would spend the remainder of 1940 in a constant state of flux and alert, with many rapid redeployments and changes of role. Over the period of the next year they would process from place to place all the way along the south coast from Devon in the west, to Essex in the east.

Though many of these minor movements must have appeared inexplicable, even pointless, at the time, the early redeployments were broadly dictated by the 'Ironside' plan. Given the paucity of hardware and the unpredictability of the time and place of the German invasion General Ironside had decided that the country be divided up internally by 'stop lines' of pillboxes, whilst the meagre supplies of tanks and anti tank guns were kept in hand as a flexible reserve. Much of the infantry and many of the ill-equipped field artillery regiments would be devoted to form the 'outer crust' of the defence. The plan was that they would literally fight the enemy on the beaches and landing grounds; beating off any small raids, and buying time for the mobile reserve to come into action against the main invasion.

Since the regiment had come back as different groups, most of them without transport, it would be a while before they could be reassembled. In this respect

The officers of Regimental Headquarters, pictured at Poole, 1940.
Back row, left to right: Lieutenant 'Doc' Dickson RAMC; Captain D.A.S. Houghton; Lieutenant R. Bradley; Lieutenant A.C. Dickson.
Front row: Major Geoffrey M. St Leger; Lt Col. Henry M. Standford (Commanding Officer, 1939–1940); and Major Charles Findlay.

'C' Troop outside the Queen's Head, Bradwell, Essex, February 1941.

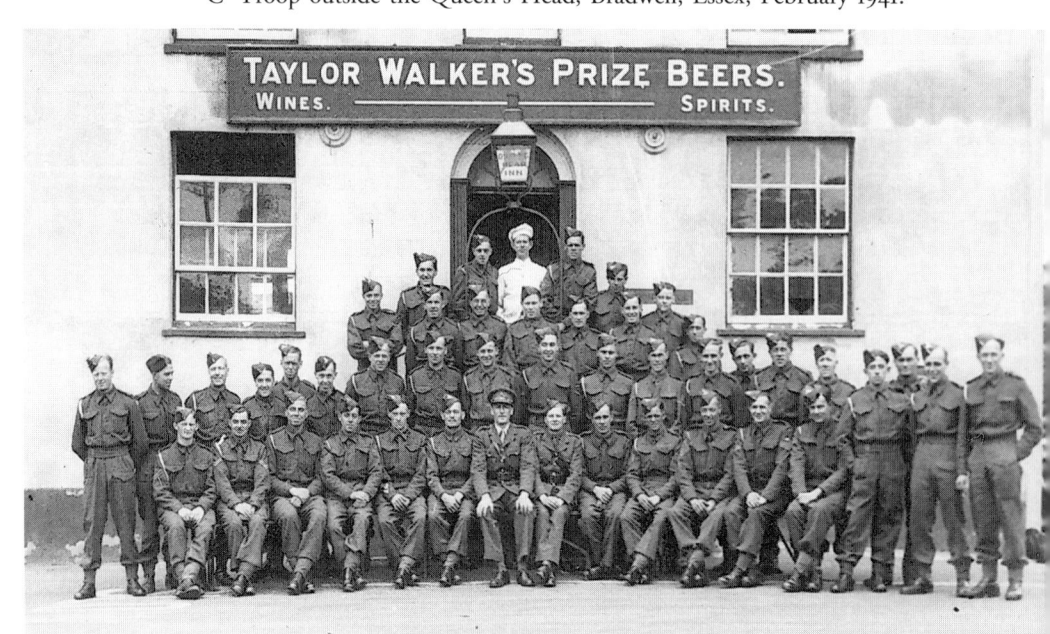

The Defence of the United Kingdom 1940–1941

Drivers pose with one of the regiment's motorcycles, May 1941. Tom Orritt, now promoted to Bombardier, is at the handlebars. Jim Pemberton is standing, left.

the experience of Driver Bob Pemberton was by no means exceptional. He found himself packed on the first available train, which happened to be bound for Stoke. Arriving with a mixed group of men he was encamped briefly at Alton Towers where surviving rifles and other small arms were handed in and new uniforms were issued. Conversely Gunner Livermore's route took him to Andover, and from here to some sort of tank depot. There was then a brief sojourn at a camp on Salisbury Plain before he returned to the unit.

Within a couple of days it had been decided to reform the regiment at the Royal Artillery Practice Camp at Okehampton in Devon, and it was here that the men began to trickle in from 6 June. Within a few days virtually all were present – and it was apparent that despite the debacle losses had been mercifully light. For though there were a number captured or wounded, mainly from the ill fated 'F' Troop, only seven personnel had actually died.

At Okehampton the other ranks were delighted to discover that cider was still plentifully available in what had, until now, been a backwater of the war. They were less pleased to find out that their new armament was a rifle and fifty rounds of ammunition. Though handsome compared to the provision for the Local Defence Volunteers, it was a sad come down from artillery, and not meditated to inspire confidence.

On 14 June 1940 the main body of the 88th entrained for Poole on the Dorset coast; still led by Lieutenant Colonel Stanford with Major St Leger commanding 351 Battery, and Major Findlay in charge of 352. Regimental Quartermaster Sergeant Buswell now received his commission thereby becoming

Lieutenant Quartermaster Buswell. The 'acting infantrymen' had only been in Poole for two weeks however before they moved again: but this time it was only a matter of a few miles into, and just beyond, Bournemouth. The regimental headquarters was now at the picturesque little town of Boscombe, whilst 351 Battery centred on Westbourne and 352 on Stourcliffe. The regiment was to be responsible for just over ten miles of coast, and trenches were dug along the cliffs, and manned even by night. One member of 352 Battery recalled spending 15 days out of 17 on such duty.

On 9 July Stanford was promoted to inspector of gunnery at Larkhill, and so sadly took his leave of the regiment whilst command devolved upon Major St Leger, who received the temporary rank of Lieutenant Colonel. At about the same time Captain Cornish was made acting Major; Lieutenant Dickson acting Captain; and Sergeant Lawer received an OBE. Just three days after Stanford's departure the regiment was mobile again. This move was another relatively short one, to Eastmoors camp near Ringwood in Hampshire. This was followed by another rapid, and rather longer transfer to Tunbridge Wells, arriving on 15 July.

The regimental headquarters was now reestablished at Lye Green House, whilst 351 Battery took up position at Crowborough, and 352 at Groombridge. The regiment thus occupied a pleasant patch of about five miles of the Kent and East Sussex borders. Yet more digging of new defensive positions ensued, enlivened slightly for those of a sporting disposition by the discovery that some of the regiment shared their pitch on Hornung's stud farm with the aged but still famous race horse 'Papyrus'.

On 20 July the regiment began a welcome rehabilitation to the ranks of the artillery when the first antiquated, but still useful, 75 mm guns began to arrive. These weapons have been variously described as either 'French' or 'American'; and probably had a little of both in their ancestry. The French model 1897, 75 mm, field gun was judged very advanced at the time of its introduction, and was standard issue to the French army during World War I. It was also adopted by the Americans, and in several slightly different forms was reexported to Britain in its hour of need. In British service these old wooden wheeled guns were known as 'Ordnance, Quick Firer, 75 mm'. Despite various drawbacks associated with age the weapon was still capable of pretty rapid fire and a range of about 12,500 yards with a 15 lb shell. Within a week the regiment had 16 of these field pieces on hand. Not enough by any means, but sufficient to make the 88th count as gunners again.

This welcome but partial re-equipment by no means heralded a return to stability. As if to underline the transience the 88th now welcomed and said farewell to its shortest lived commanding officer. According to the regimental War Diaries Lieutenant Colonel R. Hilton was appointed on 30 July; but just four days later was given command of another force. The doubtless bemused Major St Leger reassumed his temporary position. There was no time to ponder the vagaries of promotions or War Office procedure however, because the

A new 25-pdr field gun with 'A' subsection at Larkhill, 1941. The group includes Gunners Lockyer; Moore; Turner; Groves; and Whitley. Gun teams lived, worked and fought together.

Members of 'A' subsection clean their new 25-pdr with the aid of cloths and canvas buckets, Larkhill, 1941.

regiment was itself on the move again. On 4 August the regimental headquarters was set up at Buckingham House, Shoreham; with 351 Battery west of Brighton and 352 in the Rottingdean area. The 88th thus straddled Brighton covering the coast. Shortly afterwards a couple of 4.5 inch howitzers were added to the establishment; the first of at least four which were used by the unit that summer. It was in the Brighton area that the regiment took up some of its most unusual battery positions. At various times 'D' Troop mounted pieces in the grounds of Roedean girl's school; in a barn; and on the racecourse: a signal exchange was put in the golf club.

August remained a very tense period with invasion still generally presumed to be imminent. Some members of the 88th recall being in a Brighton cinema when, in mid programme, the film was stopped and everyone was bundled outside and told to return to their units. On doing so they discovered that this was just one of several rumours and false alarms which served to keep nerves on edge that summer. Some were enjoying their war more than others however: Captain Denis Houghton, for example, turned photographing crashed enemy aircraft into a virtual sport, charging about the countryside with his camera. Others made the best of the summer weather, limited supplies of beer, and the friendly locals. In a few places, beach and river defences permitting, swimming was even possible.

The somewhat ambiguous command situation was cleared up for the time being by the appointment of Lieutenant Colonel H.S. Macdonald from 63rd Anti Tank Regiment. The regiment now enjoyed the almost unheard of luxury of more than a whole month in the same place, under the same commanding officer. By October, and with the commencement of rough autumn weather, it was becoming increasingly apparent that the war was entering a new phase. The threat of 'Operation Sea Lion', as the German invasion of Britain was code named, was receding week by week. Moreover aerial onslaught had by no means cleared the RAF from the skies. General Sir Alan Brooke, who had replaced General Ironside in charge of home defence, was beginning to develop a new strategy, aided by the speeding up of production. More troops were now to be retrained and rearmed, and where possible pulled back from the coast to create more aggressive formations.

At the end of October the regiment made the journey back westward to the Chichester area, with the headquarters first at North Mundham, later on the Northlands Estate. Yet despite the slightly more hopeful outlook there was no let up in aerial activity; and in their new positions the 88th were witness to more than their fair share of action. On 7 November there were air battles overhead; bombs fell near 'Tamarisk' observation post and Walberton House, and incendiaries were dropped on 'B' Troop area. A Spitfire came down near 'C' Troop; and the pilot who survived his ordeal pretty well unscathed was entertained in 'C' Troop mess. The following day a Hurricane made a forced landing nearby, and again the pilot was taken into the mess. After a slightly quieter interlude bombing raids at the end of November blocked the roads at

Selsey and Pagham. Later a German fighter came down on Stocker's Lane; and a few days subsequently two German air crew were reported at large in the area, though these were later captured.

It was also at Chichester, on 1 December 1940, that the regiment underwent a major reorganisation in accordance with new establishments. Instead of two batteries the regiment was arranged in three, each of two troops. The existing batteries were already sometimes referred to as 'P' and 'Q', thus it was that the new creation, commanded by Major Kelly, was initially dubbed 'R Battery'. Dispositions were now so organised that two batteries were kept in defensive positions, allowing the third to undertake training in reserve. On 16 January 1941 'R' was given the new designation '464 Battery'.

Ten days later there was another scare and flurry of activity due to heavy gunfire off Selsey – reputedly the result of an incursion by enemy surface craft. On 19 February the regiment finally left Sussex, moving north and east to Essex. Here the headquarters was established at Winterborn Lodge, Wickford. The batteries were separated in support of the infantry so that 351 were with 13th Battalion of the Sherwood Forresters at Southend; 352 was further north, in the Dengie sector with 7th Battalion the King's Own Yorkshire Light Infantry, and 464 near Rochford with 9th Duke of Wellington's Regiment. The object of these dispositions was not only to protect the Thames estuary and east coast, but to cover the airfields at Bradwell and Rochford. The headquarters was moved to Downham Grange on 23 February, and in mid March came a weeks training at West Down Camp, Salisbury Plain.

March and early April 1941 also saw a significant shake up in terms of personnel with the arrival of about 70 reinforcements. Medically unfit men were now weeded out and exchanged for men in better shape picked from defence regiments. One victim of this cull was Gunner Livermore whose 'height

Officers at Larkhill, summer 1941. Major C.D. Cornish (*right*) is wearing the Service Dress cap; the other officer is in fighting order, with steel helmet, 1937 Pattern web equipment, binocular case and gas mask.

to weight' ratio was deemed undesirable. Assigned elsewhere he applied to be posted back to the 88th, but was refused. Despite this exercise the regiment undoubtedly retained a distinctive Lancashire character with many men from Preston, Lancaster, Blackpool, Manchester, and other parts of the county, but there was, nevertheless, an increasingly cosmopolitan element. A later audit shows a few Scots, Irish, and Welsh in the ranks, as well as some from London and the south of England: but there were also some from much further afield.

Gunner F.W. Sargeant may have come from the most geographically distant part of the United Kingdom, having been born in Liskeard, Cornwall, but there was at least a minority whose origins were overseas elsewhere in the Empire. Bombardier E. Alldis and Gunners J.I. Johnstone; R.W. Bowell; and E.C. Smith had all been born in India; Gunner C. Simpson in South Africa. Gunner J.C. Ives hailed from Edmonton Canada. Amongst the officers were some even more exotic pedigrees with Captain R. Pote-Hunt born in Shanghai; Second Lieutenant J.B. White in Hong Kong; and Second Lieutenant A.A. Huxtable, who joined the unit in April 1941 born in Kuala Lumpur. In terms of sheer distance from Stanley Street Preston of his place of birth Lieutenant D.P. Friend must surely have taken the prize, having first seen light of day in Auckland New Zealand.

This important period also saw other practical steps taken towards fitness for action. On 28 April a large party of the regiment attended the 'Sector Gas Compound' for instruction. Whether by accident or design a very stiff dose of one particular gas was administered, reducing them all 'to a very poor state for half an hour'.

According to the War Diary 18 May 1941 was a 'Red Letter Day', as it was then that the first of the brand new 25 pounder field guns was received. The enthusiasm of the writers of the War Diary may be readily understood when it is realised how much superior the latest model 25 pounder was to the 75 mm. The new guns were not only capable of an extra thousand yards range with a heavier shell, but could also be used against armour. An interesting feature inspired by the 4.1 inch howitzer, and indeed shared with some existing guns, was the box trail carriage, incorporating a circular firing platform The platform travelled secured to the underside of the trail, but on reaching a battery position could be quickly set on the ground and married up with the pneumatic tyres of the carriage. The weapon was now relatively easy to traverse through 360 degrees; no mean advantage when in prolonged use, or when several different targets had to be engaged. As one expert has since observed, the 25 pounder of 1941 was 'both a highly effective light howitzer and a good anti tank gun', with a good range, though the shell was a little lighter than that fired by the equivalent American and German equipments.

Less than a month after the arrival of the new ordnance the regiment was joined by its last commanding officer, Lieutenant Colonel S.C. D'Aubuz, whilst Lieutenant Colonel Macdonald was posted back to the depot. It was perhaps surprising that at the age of 42 D'Aubuz was just about the oldest man in the regiment, just a fraction older than Quartermaster Buswell. He was also more than twice the age of the youngest. Neither was D'Aubuz a man without experience for he already had a very long career in the Royal Artillery behind him. He was a graduate of the Staff College whose first commission in the Royal Regiment of Artillery had come in the latter part of the Great War, and he had achieved the rank of Major in 1938. His last appointment, prior to taking up command of the 88th had been as senior staff officer at the headquarters of Western Command. Some of those who were acquainted with him were impressed by his modest, even bookish nature. Not long after the appointment of D'Aubuz the regiment also received a new Regimental Sergeant Major in the shape of E.J. Busby.

These new arrivals were followed by a flurry of activity which was not perhaps entirely coincidental. All three batteries took part in a fire and movement exercise at Larkhill from 10 to 12 July, and ten days later the regiment handed over its old positions to 142 Field Regiment and moved off closer to London and the Epping area. Here the headquarters was located at Thornwood Camp, whilst 351 Battery took up position at Harwood Hall near Romford; 352 went to Hill Hall, Theydon Mount, whilst 464 Battery obtained arguably the most scenic posting at Moor Place, Much Hadham. These somewhat scattered stations were chosen so as to support 223 Infantry Brigade in protection of the local airfields.

Whilst the general fitness of the regiment had obviously improved during the summer of 1941, with influxes of both men and guns there were still difficulties to contend with. Rather alarmingly one inspection suggested that though the guns were now in excellent shape, about three quarters of the vehicles were unfit for overseas service. Several officers, including lieutenants A.R. Wynter-Bee, and G. le Gosselin were hospitalised around this time with various illnesses; and one night at the end of June Battery Sergeant Major Orr was killed. This unfortunate night time motorcycle accident served graphically to underline the dangers of driving in the blackout. Orr was one of six non commissioned officers and men who were killed or died whilst the regiment was defending home shores in 1940 and 1941. Lieutenant A.H. Raven was also injured in a road accident, but fortunately made a good recovery.

The first inkling that the long period of watching, defending, and training was coming to an end came in a preparatory order received in early August 1941, which demanded readiness for overseas service. This was followed by the ominously named exercise 'Duck', and range practices. It is also interesting to relate that although many were ignorant of the regiment's likely theatre of operations at least the commanding officer and the adjutant must have had an idea as early as 12 August. On that day the War Diary records that the scale of equipment for the regiment was to be 'as for Malaya'. The possibility that action really was imminent was further reinforced by a bout of anti tank practice at Foulness ranges, and a recalibration of the guns at Larkhill at the end of August.

Right: Officers of 464 Battery on board the *Empress of Canada*, October 1941. *Back row*: Lt J. Fitzgerald; Lt G.E. Shield; Capt. A. Bannister; Lt A.R. Wynter-Bee; Lt A.H. Raven; unidentified. *Front row*: Capt. E.C. Dickson; Major D.A.S. Houghton; Major J.E. Kelly; Capt. D.C. Taylor; Lt L.E. Barton.

Left: Drivers of Regimental HQ on board the *Empress of Canada*. Driver J. Pemberton is front row, left, next but one to E. Bamber. Bombardier T. Orritt is prominent in the second row from the front, fourth from the left.

'F' Troop, 88th Field Regiment, on board the *Empress of Canada*, *en route* to the Far East, 1941. The officers in the centre of the front row are: Lt Court; Captain Taylor; and Lt Fitzgerald.

4

The Malayan Campaign, 1941–1942

The 88th now travelled by rail to Gourock in Scotland, and the train was unloaded on the dock right next to an imposing 21,517 ton three funnel liner. This troop transport was the *Empress of Canada*. The *Empress* had been built by the Fairfield Shipbuilding and Engineering Company on the Clyde in 1922; and had done lengthy service on the Canadian trans Pacific service between Vancouver and Yokohama, before being requisitioned for service. She was eventually destined to be sunk by a torpedo off Freetown West Africa in 1943 with the loss of 392 lives. As the gunners of the 88th toiled with stores and helped load them onto the ship they became uneasily aware that the vessel was effectively surrounded by the 'Red caps' or Military Police. Perhaps they were there simply to keep the public and prying eyes out, but to Jim Pemberton at least it seemed that they were about in order to prevent young soldiers like himself from thinking better of it and making for home.

The *Empress of Canada* sailed out into the cold and rough North Atlantic on 30 September 1941 as part of a large convoy. Some of the officers now opened the packets of maps that they had been given expecting to find confirmation of their destination: they were puzzled to find charts of the Isle of Wight. This inspired no great confidence in the venture, whatever it was, but forebodings were pushed aside by the kaleidoscope of exotic foreign places and experiences which the voyage was providing.

First port of call was Freetown West Africa on 14 October, where the vessel was refuelled and a concert was held on shore. On the afternoon of 19 October the *Empress* departed Freetown, probably already under scrutiny of at least one U-Boat, for a submarine was detected the next day. Most of the men were below decks when the naval escorts began to steam too and fro at full speed depth charging the waters. This time the ship escaped but it was a terrifying introduction, and by no means a good omen.

Cape Town was reached on 30 October, and again there were some brief shore visits allowed, before the voyage was resumed on the morning of 4 November. A few days later variety was provided by exchanges of escorts: at one point the mighty *HMS Repulse* came alongside, band playing. On 14 November the *Revenge* took over from the *Repulse*, and three days later was herself supplanted by the *Glasgow*. All of which provided interesting subject matter for the brush and paints of Lance Bombardier Bettany. Columbo warranted only a one day stop, on 23 November, and Singapore was finally reached five days later.

Quite why the 88th had come to the Far East when Britain was not actually

'E' Troop, 464 Battery aboard ship. Most of the officers and NCOs are seated in the second row: Sergeant W.E. Hardacre; Sergeant J. Singleton; B.S.M. F. Muir; Lt A.H. Raven; Captain E.C. Dickson (Troop Commander); Lt A.R. Wynter-Bee; Sergeant Swinburne; Sergeant J.A. Marsh; Sergeant A. Lodge. Also identified in the third row are Gunner M.A. Hammond (*far left*), Bombardier E.W. Parry stands immediately behind the Troop Commander. The last six men in this row are: Bombardiers R. Ayrton; N. Edwards and R.B. Walsh; Gunners F. Race and Wilkinson. Sixth from left in the front row is R.J. Hardacre, brother of W.E. Hardacre.

at war in this part of the globe was doubtless a mystery to many. Yet there were already dangerous signs, and with hindsight there was disaster waiting to happen. In 1941 Malaya was useful to the British war effort for several reasons: perhaps the two most important of which were the fact that she supplied over half the rubber, and more than a third of the tin, produced in the world. Both were vital war materials, especially necessary for the making of vehicles and aircraft. Singapore, an island linked by a causeway to the southern tip of the Malay peninsula, was seen as the strategic key to the whole area, for it housed a major naval base and was defended by coastal artillery. Propaganda of the time portrayed it as an impregnable 'fortress'. Churchill, writing in 1939 as First Lord of the Admiralty, had stated that it would be a 'mad enterprise' for the Japanese to attack: but in truth Singapore was not quite as powerful as its image would suggest. The site for the new base had been selected in 1922, but construction had been slow and erratic, due to both changes of government, and the signing of the London Naval Treaty in 1930. Not long afterwards Japan had withdrawn from the treaty, and began an intensive Naval building programme, the result of which was a review of British policy in the Far East.

Defence planning in the mid 1930s had stated minimum times that Singapore could be expected to hold out in the face of attack, and set targets for the arrival of relieving forces from elsewhere. In 1937 the time it was intended to hold out was 70 days; this was raised to 90 days in 1938, and finally, in 1939, the resistance period was set at 180 days. Such predictions were not entirely realistic, and even complacent, for they were not backed with commensurate increases in defence forces. Indeed it was also the case that Imperial Japan, the prime candidate to be an aggressor in the area, was not only growing in stature, but had crept nearer to Malaya with the expansion of her Chinese empire. By 1941 she would move closer still by gains in French Indo-China.

At the time there was neither the means, nor the will, to respond decisively to this potential threat. As yet Britain was not at war with Japan, and there was more than enough to do combating Nazi Germany. It was also true that Roosevelt had given Churchill reason to suppose that should Malaya be attacked, this might provide the political lever to bring the United States into the war on the British side. Putting too much effort into the defence of Malaya might therefore be a double loss, for even if it could be massively strengthened this might mean not only a weakening of British forces in Europe and the Middle East, but America standing on the sidelines indefinitely. In short Malaya was just not seen as a priority, and was given the minimum provision. As late as the spring of 1941 Churchill was telling the Chiefs of the Defence staff that it was unnecessary to maintain Far East forces even at their present level, and that Hong Kong in particular should be garrisoned by no more than a token force on the grounds that it would be impossible to hold.

Even so some consideration had been given to the modernisation of Britain's defensive response. General William Dobbie who had been General Officer Commanding in the late 1930s had demanded that defensive lines be built on the north side of Singapore Island, and in southern Malaya, but he had been starved of funds for this far sighted project and his successors had abandoned it. Even so it had been appreciated that to mount a practicable defence Malaya would now require aircraft. Given the relatively small size of Singapore island, and the possibility that an aggressor might approach from the north, airfields were duly built in northern Malaya. The aeroplanes to base on these fields were harder to come by in war time, but a total of 246 were scraped together, of which 158 were really deemed fit for front line service: but even these were not of the most modern types. Japanese air forces available for this theatre would be approximately double this strength. It was perhaps a measure of the stress placed upon the role of air power in the Far East that Britain's new Commander in Chief for the area was Air Chief Marshal Sir Robert Brooke Popham, appointed in October 1940. As late as September 1941 Popham would remain sanguine about the Japanese threat, estimating that if a Japanese attack came at all it would not be for several months, probably not until the spring of 1942.

The commander of the ground forces was now General A.E. Percival, appointed 'General Officer Commanding, Malaya', in May 1941. His troops available for the defence of Singapore and Malaya initially numbered a fairly respectable 89,000, but for the most part these were not battle hardened veterans: of this total nearly 17,000 were locally recruited Indian, Malay, and Chinese volunteers. Another 37,000 were Indian state troops from the subcontinent; 15,000 were Australians; and just 22,000 were British. The largest single group therefore were the Indians, and even these were not of a single language or religion. The majority of the troops were organised into three divisions: 9th and 11th Indian, and 8th Australian, with other forces allotted to static coastal, anti aircraft, and airfield defence.

None of these international contingents were the very best that their mother countries could provide, as there was an understandable tendency to send the best trained and equipped to active theatres of war such as the Middle East. This was especially noticeable in the case of the Indian units, many of which had been 'milked' of their best officers and NCOs. There were no British tanks in Malaya whatsoever. Last minute reinforcement as the campaign progressed would bring in 18th British Division, and other smaller units totalling perhaps another 50,000 men. The ultimate number of troops finally in theatre would therefore number about 130,000.

The key to British strength in the region had to be whatever naval forces were kept in the base at Singapore. A strong naval force would not only be able to do battle with enemy squadrons and cut supply routes, but frustrate any combined operations plans an enemy might be hatching. The main problem with these suppositions was that in mid 1941 there were no large modern vessels maintained for the defence of Malaya and Singapore: nothing indeed which could have prevented the Japanese navy from dominating the Gulf of Siam or the South China Sea if it chose to put a serious effort into doing so. Pre-war planning had been conducted on the basis that Britain could dominate her own home waters, and that in the Mediterranean the power of France would balance out any potential of Italy. In the event of course the French fleet had been neutralised, and more British vessels had been needed in the Mediterranean. The result was that there was no 'spare' British fleet of substance to base in the Far East. On the eve of war with Japan Churchill would seek to rectify this omission by the dispatch of a fast battle squadron, 'Force Z'. The three most powerful ships of this flotilla were intended to be the battleship *Prince of Wales*, the battle cruiser *Repulse*, which the 88th had already seen at close quarters during their voyage, and the aircraft carrier *Indomitable*. Tragically the *Indomitable* ran aground in the Bahamas; but the others carried on, hoping to be at least a deterrent.

The Japanese force tasked with the attack on Malaya was Lieutenant General T. Yamashita's 25th Army. The original order of battle of this formation

The *Perseus* and *HMS Glasgow*, sketched in watercolours by Desmond Bettany in convoy to the Far East, November 1941.

included as its major components the Imperial Guards Division; 5th, 18th and 56th Infantry Divisions, and 3rd Air Division. In the event 56th Division would be left behind as a strategic reserve, and subsequently deployed against Burma. Even without 56th Division Yamashita's Army had a paper strength of 125,000 men, two thirds of which were front line combat troops. Though some units were undoubtedly under strength, and not all units saw action, it is improbable that the actual total available was less than 100,000, and for the most part these were soldiers who had already seen action against China. They also had the positive advantage of being of the same nationality and speaking the same language. Yamashita also had 180 light and medium tanks.

It can be readily appreciated therefore that, although it might not have appeared so at the time, the overall balance of power between the British and their Allies and Japanese forces in the Malayan theatre was a relatively fine one. The British eventually had an advantage of better than four to three in terms of sheer troop numbers, and they should have been significantly aided by the fact that they were defending a prepared position. On the other hand the British generally had little conception of the Japanese strengths: the armour, and the experience and homogeneity of her infantry. Perhaps they should have had, since in March 1941 a fairly detailed memorandum on the Japanese Army had been issued which accurately detailed these matters. At sea the position was no clearer in terms of advantage: much would depend on whether 'Force Z' could reach the right place at the right time together with suitable air cover, and perhaps catch the Japanese in their transports. If it did not the Japanese naval 'Southern Force' might enjoy superiority at sea. In the air the Japanese had a clear two to one advantage, and if they could achieve mastery of the skies, then their aircraft could help to tilt the balance on land and sea.

There were also hidden problems in the British command, some the fault of local commanders, others which should have been foreseen at home, and some which could be put down to the thorough preparation of the enemy. Perhaps the biggest fault of all was underestimation of the Japanese. Critically, though some thought had been given to a planned defence, land, sea, and air objectives were scarcely coordinated. The air force were intended to overfly potential invaders from the northern airfields. The army, insufficiently strong to defend properly the most advanced of these airfields, put the coast defence of the seaward side of Singapore Island, and the eastern coast of Malaya as high priorities. In the event of war, the navy, who initially were only in token presence, would be expected to interfere with attempted landings wherever they might be.

At lower levels there were other problems. One of these was a lack of training in jungle warfare which would put the British at a significant disadvantage in the coming battle. Another of almost equal weight was the effort that the Japanese had put into intelligence gathering: Japanese agents had been extremely active in Malaya prior to the war, and there was a 6,000 strong Japanese community to harbour them, or camouflage their activities. Not all espionage work required much guile however, and it was something of a standing joke that the Japanese golf club in Singapore overlooked a fair stretch of the defensive line. Although British counter espionage was hardly at a peak of activity there were numerous arrests. As early as 1934 a Japanese businessman had been arrested trying to buy plans of airfields, and a group of five suspects were deported in 1938.

During 1940 there were more arrests for spying, and for spreading propaganda amongst Indian troops. The Japanese were well aware of the existence of Indian independence movements, overt, and covert, and lost no opportunity to stir up trouble to cause embarrassment to the British, or weaken the morale of the Indian Battalions. The picture was further muddied by the belief that the Germans and the Italians had significant intelligence presences in Malaya. Perhaps worst of all it appears that a British officer working for Air Liaison was also a spy, and from his privileged position was able to pass back details of air defence plans and readiness almost before they were available to friendly forces. At the outbreak of war there were many arrests of suspects during operations 'Collar' and 'Trousers' but by then it was far too late.

In the event of attack from the north there were two potential plans for the land defence, one a simple retirement, southward in the direction of Singapore, the second far more daring. This second plan, which came to prominence in late 1941, was 'Matador'. It was thought most likely that the Japanese would have to attack neutral Thailand before they attempted anything against Malaya, and 'Matador' was intended to throw a significant spoke into any such plan.

The launch of 'Matador' would be left to the discretion of the local commander, who, if he believed that the Japanese were about to land forces on the east coast of Thailand or Malaya, was authorised to attack into Thailand with a major thrust to Songkhla on the coast and a lesser move over the mountains halting any landing force coming from Patani. A major plank of the blocking force plan was to be a column on the Kroh road, known in army speak as 'Krohcol'. The real weakness of the whole scheme was the heavy responsibility it laid at the feet of the local commander, in this case air force chief Brooke-Popham. He would have to decide whether a specific convoy did indeed constitute a real threat of landing, and then push his troops into a neutral country. It might just have worked, and its audacity might have been just the thing to give the Japanese pause for thought. On the other hand it was ill calculated to gain American sympathy.

Into this uncertain situation stepped 88th Field Regiment, disembarking from the *Empress of Canada* at Singapore on 28 November 1941. Together with other artillery units arriving at the same time General Percival described them as 'consisting of excellent material but ... lacking in experience'. He immediately allotted them to the Indian III Corps, which consisted of the 9th and 11th Indian Divisions commanded by General Heath. The majority of the 88th now boarded a train for Mantin camp which lay 210 miles to the north: here they would come under General A.E. Barstow's 9th Indian Division, whose Headquarters lay at Kuala Lumpur. A party of 40 men stayed behind for the longer job of unloading stores and guns; and these would rejoin the main body by road, setting out on 6 December for a two stage hop to Mantin.

Despite the novelty of the Far East many of the young Gunners of the regiment were less than excited about the corner of the world in which they now found themselves. As Driver Jim Pemberton wrote back to his mother explaining:

> The camp is situated in the centre of a rubber plantation miles from anywhere. It's OK only there's nothing but rubber trees to look at. Don't expect many letters from here because I'm not going to have anything to write about. The weather is not so good, one minute the sun is shining and the next it is pouring with rain, it's so hot all the time and there's not a breath of wind, everywhere is damp and clammy. The mosquitoes and flys are a bit of a pest, they are always flying around and taking lumps out of me. It's a hard job getting any sleep at nights there's all sorts of noises going on all night. There's plenty of company in this hut too, what with large spiders, centipedes and rats running over everything ... Money does not go so far, I only draw $5 dollars per week. A dollar is worth 2s 4d and it goes about as far as is in England.

Pemberton was right on most scores, except that of having nothing to write about.

On the night of 7 December the road party appeared, tired, and with some stores broken during transit. Almost at the same moment the Japanese struck, with a landing on the southeast coast of Thailand and the northeast coast of Malaya, just as the 'Matador' planners had predicted. What the planners had not been able to take into account was that Japanese air forces would also attack Pearl Harbour, and sink a sizable portion of the American Pacific Fleet. Soon the 'Matador' plan lay in ruins: Brooke-Popham was unable to determine the intentions of the Japanese landing forces in time, and shrank back from throwing his forces into Thailand. Percival's divisions were prepared to execute the offensive plan, but events had overtaken them and they would now have to be redeployed for defence.

Time was at a premium, for the Japanese timetable was advancing at cracking pace. The first troops had landed from their transports at about 1 a.m.; Singapore was bombed two and a half hours later, and while Hudson bombers had been able to inflict losses on the invaders at Khota Baru, landings at Singora and Patani were opposed only by token Thai resistance. Early the next morning the British airfields in northern Malaya felt the full weight of Japanese air power. Many planes which had been scrambled during the night were caught on the ground and destroyed.

That same morning 88th Field Regiment received orders from 9th Indian Division to proceed by train north to Kelantan State to support the opposition to the Japanese invasion. Owing to incomplete readiness and lack of stores, as well as the fact that the breakdown lorry and stores vehicles would have to be dismantled to go on the train, it was decided that part of the Regimental Headquarters with the Commanding Officer, and the Signals Officer would entrain first, forming an advanced 'Z' Group. They would be followed shortly by the rest of the Headquarters and 464 Battery under Major J.E. Kelly, made up to full strength by drawing on the other batteries.

Lieutenant Colonel D'Aubuz and his 'Z' Group arrived at Kuala Krai in Kelantan at mid day on 9 December. The first news was that

Lt Col. S.C. D'Aubuz, Commanding Officer, 88th Field Regiment, as caricatured by Desmond Bettany. The headgear is the distinctive red over blue Royal Artillery coloured Field service cap.

the Japanese had broken through and were within eight kilometres of the station. Despite this alarming intelligence D'Aubuz decided to drive north in the direction of Khota Bharu, and near here made contact with his brigade. Having got his orders from the Brigadier the next thing to do was to carry out a reconnaissance, and plan a position for the guns. Even before this was achieved new orders came through cancelling the order for the regiment to move to Kelantan, and telling him to report to the Corps Headquarters near Kuala Lumpur. He now had to turn round and retrace his steps to the station, and reload his vehicles onto a train. This was more easily said than done because some of the station staff had bolted on hearing that the Japanese were upon them. Even so he was on a train for Kuala Lipis by midnight: fortunately 464 Battery had also got the news of the change of plan and were detrained at Jerantut.

The blackest day of the campaign so far came on 10 December 1941. Admiral Tom Phillips, anxious to play a constructive role with his powerful naval battle squadron, had left Singapore a couple of days previously and steamed northward. His objective was to interfere with the Japanese invasion and supply convoys, and perhaps inflict such damage as to alter the balance in the land campaign. Having no aircraft carrier he was dependent on land based planes for reconnaissance and air cover, yet as the battle on land saw the abandonment of the northern air fields, and aircraft losses mount, the cover evaporated. Realising that he had probably been discovered, and that the risks were increasing, he had turned south again without having inflicted any losses on the Japanese. Soon after 11 a.m. on 10 December his 'Force Z' was hit by an air strike of 85 Japanese bombers and torpedo bombers, *Prince of Wales* and *Repulse* were both sunk: Phillips himself was drowned. The loss of two capital ships sent a shock wave around the world; but the local effects were perhaps even more important. The Japanese Southern Force now had mastery of the seas in this theatre of war. With both the Air Force and the Navy crippled, the British and Empire land forces would have to depend largely on their own resources to win or loose the campaign.

The same day that Admiral Phillips' force was hit the Commanding Officer of the 88th received yet more new orders as to the disposition of his scattered regiment. They were not encouraging. His 464 Battery which had already travelled up and down the country to no effect was now to be detached and would serve on the east coast with 22nd Infantry Brigade at Kuantan: the other two batteries would make for Sungei Patanei camp near the west coast. These movements were accomplished after darkness fell on the night of 12 December, and 'B' Troop of 351 Battery was now promptly detached to form local defence for Butterworth aerodrome. Again Percival's dispositions were overtaken by the pace of the Japanese assault, for even as these deployments were being completed the enemy broke through at Jitra, just north of Alor Star. The Indian 11th Division was badly mauled, and 15th Brigade in particular took heavy losses.

Thus it was that no sooner had the two remaining batteries of the 88th settled into the wire perimetered camp under the rubber trees at Sungei Patani that fresh orders came through. They were to leave again, this time to set up a defensive position nearby at Gurun in the hope of stemming the Japanese assault on the road and rail route, under the steep jungle covered Kedah Peak. As Lieutenant Colonel D'Aubuz put it,

> Trouble arose early in that, at about 0030 hours, the first of an uncoordinated rabble of Indian drivers started to arrive at both entrances to the camp, and, disregarding traffic policemen effectively blocked both exits and prevented the regiment from marching. It took three quarters of an hour of many threats, including the use of the revolver, to clear a passage to let the regiment through. By 0615 hours, the last vehicle had however left the main road, and had found cover under the rubber of the Guar Champedak estate.

Battle at Gurun and Kampar

The Gurun position, as it was now established by General Murra-Lyon's battered 11th Indian Division, was on a two brigade front. On the left of the railway line which bisected the battlefield lay Brigadier Lay's 6th Brigade with two battalions of Punjabis and 2nd Battalion the East Surrey regiment, many of whom had their backs to the mountain. On their right, in thick rubber and jungle was 28th Brigade, with three battalions of Gurkhas. The reserve, placed to the rear, was the remains of 15th Brigade. The left appeared tolerably secure, anchored as it was on the mountain, but if the Japanese were prepared to penetrate the jungle there was little else that would stop them turning the right. The battery positions of 88th Field Regiment were less than ideal as they were supposed to fire in support of 6th Brigade, but owing to the flooded terrain, mountains, and tall trees, had to do so from young rubber plantations in rear of 28th Brigade sector. The barrels of their 25 pounders were thus pointed across, rather than down the field. Some of the Forward Observation officers for the guns were located up on the mountain where they had an excellent view over the flooded paddies to the north, and others well forward near Chempedak railway station.

The Japanese approach march on Gurun was by no means an easy matter, as was described by Colonel Tsuji who ran into 25 pdr gun fire driving up the road on 13 December. 'We stopped and jumped out … After taking cover in the ditch by the roadside for some time, we again returned to the car. There, amid the flashes from bursting shells which dazzled us and the noise of explosions which shook the ground, I suddenly felt as though I had been stabbed in the buttocks with burning chop sticks. Blood poured down my thigh and began to seep through my trousers … ' The wound was slight, but a good example of how discomforting harassing artillery fire could be.

That same evening Lieutenant Colonel D'Aubuz attended a conference of the Commander Royal Artillery about five miles south at the Harvard Estate Bungalow. It was over by midnight, and he had his orders, but it took three hours to drive back to his batteries, a circumstance put down to the 'indifferent driving' of the Indian troops in the division. He may have had a point: 3rd Indian Cavalry for example was supplied with 16 new armoured cars during

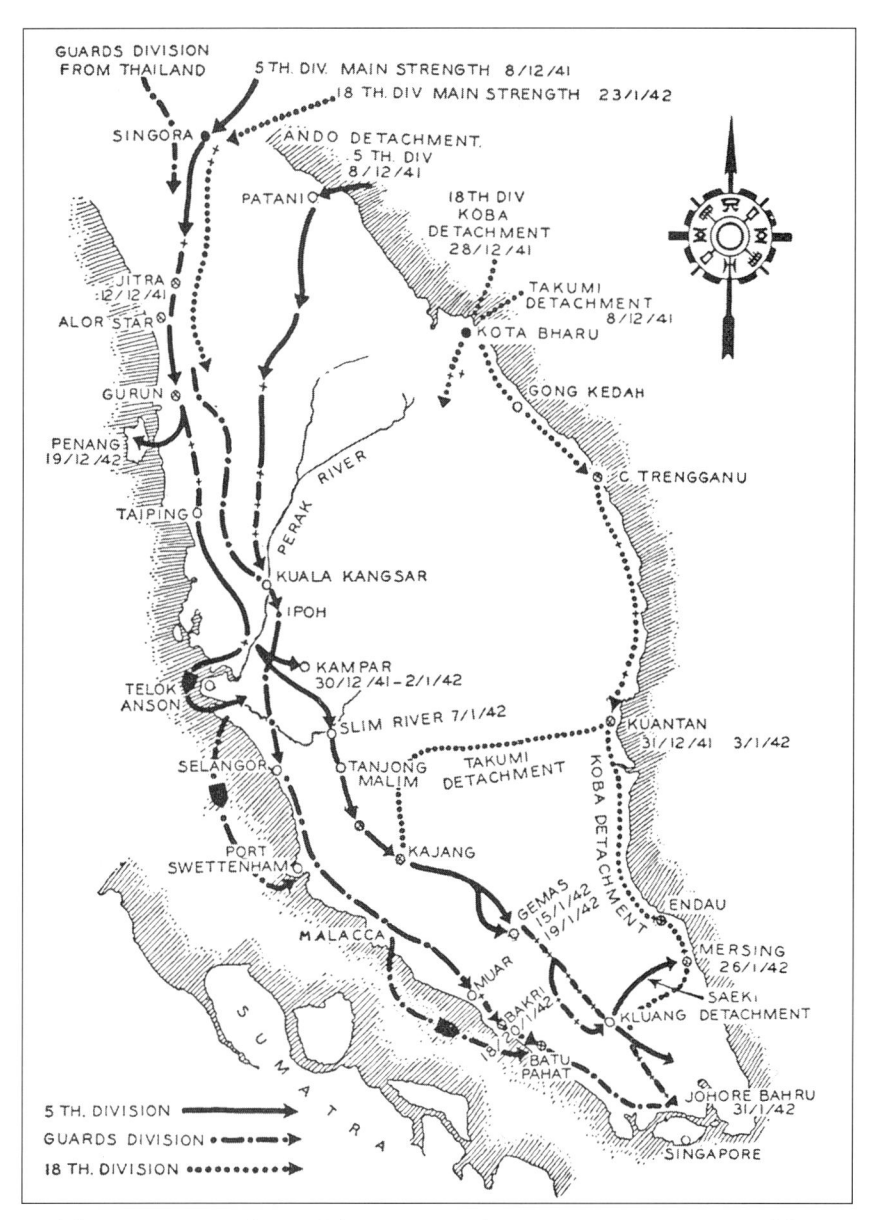

The Japanese attack on Malaya, 8 December 1941 to 31 January 1942. The assault began with landings at Patani and Kota Bharu on the north-east coast and a drive from Thailand. The locations of the 351 and 352 Battery actions at Gurun and Kampar are to be seen near the west coast.

December, 13 were 'rendered unserviceable' not by the enemy, but by awful roads and poor driving.

One thing that D'Aubuz seems to have gleaned from the conference was an awareness of the Japanese armour, for at dawn 'D' troop of 352 Battery were moved to Gurun, with the intention that they should be able to fire down the road in an anti tank and close support role. It proved to be a correct move, for about 2 p.m. the Japanese columns appeared and engaged the British position all along the front, harassing the defenders with light mortar fire. The attackers made some headway against the Punjabis, but were pushed back by a local counter attack led by Brigadier Lay in person. Late in the afternoon enemy infantry began to filter around the Gurkhas on the right and off into the jungle. Three tanks now appeared near the cross roads followed by a dozen lorry loads of troops. This provided an 'admirable target' and the observers up on Kedah Peak called down everything that the 88th could shoot: the lead tank was smashed and set on fire and the column halted. Night fell with the Japanese having made limited gains.

During the night Brigadier Lay planned a surprise counter attack, which was to be supported by every available gun. This however never materialised because the Japanese got in first attacking Gurun from the north between 3 and 4 a.m. with infantry and two tanks. By 6.30 the East Surreys were left clinging to Gurun whilst the Punjabis were being forced to back away off to the west. With the situation looking critical the Commanding Officer of the 88th, the Adjutant Captain A.C. Dickson, and the Survey Officer Captain R. Bradley joined the Headquarters of 6th Brigade near Gurun. At about 7 a.m. in the midst of their conversation a wounded officer burst in and told them that the Japanese, who had now succeeded in outflanking 28th Brigade, were in the trees nearby. The next moment the wooden building was riddled with machine gun fire and they were charged by Japanese infantry with fixed bayonets.

In the wild meleé the British officers scattered. The Commanding Officer made it to nearby 'D' Troop where he prepared them for all round defence over 'open sights' and was shortly joined by Brigadier Lay. Captain Bradley got to Regimental Headquarters, and here prepared the batteries to move. The Adjutant, his orderly Gunner Graves, and the Chief Clerk Sergeant Gardner failed to escape. One of the last to see them was the Colonel's batman, Bombardier Parry, who had shouted for the officers to get clear whilst he engaged the enemy with his Tommy gun. According to his version of events Captain A.C. Dickson was slow to emerge from the building, and was last seen 'on the verandah with his revolver drawn'. He and the two others were later posted missing presumed killed. Captain A.C. Dickson's death in the incident was later confirmed. As General Percival would later relate these were but some of the casualties sustained, since 6th Indian Brigade also lost its Brigade Major; a Staff Captain; Signalling officer and 'many others'.

The problem now was how to extricate as much as possible from a quickly collapsing position so whilst 'D' Troop held off the enemy as best it could, killing a good number of the enemy on the road, and receiving mortar fire and bullets in return, preparations were made to pull out. In order to do this the Gurkhas of 28th Brigade were now pulled back in the direction of Gurun to attack and relieve the pressure, whilst 351 Battery would redeploy and prepare to fire in support.

It was a reasonable plan, and worked in part, for whilst the Gurkhas ran into stiff opposition and a Japanese counter attack 'D' Troop was able to extricate itself and retire. General Murray-Lyon now intervened personally and directed the whole of 351 Battery back to Sungei Patani. Having heard this Lieutenant Colonel D'Aubuz, already one of the best travelled officers in the division, now set off on a motor cycle to rejoin his 'D' Troop. He promptly ran into a group of Japanese and was fortunate to escape for a second time that day. Remarkably the whole regiment now succeeded in getting clean away, reaching Sungei Patani soon after 2 p.m., and then being redirected to Bukit Me a further nine miles south. The *Official History* has it that the Japanese inability to follow up their success immediately was at least in part due to the losses inflicted on them by artillery fire. Considering how thoroughly the Japanese had succeeded in infiltrating the Gurun position and how closely 'D' Troop had been entangled with the enemy, losses to the 88th had been remarkably light. Apart from the three men mentioned only a handful of others were unaccounted for.

Amongst these others, missing, presumed dead or captured, were the two Forward Observer officers on Kedah Peak Lieutenant R.E.J. Carter and Second Lieutenant P. Lane, and their attendant signallers. In fact Lane had realised by about 5 a.m. that things had gone seriously awry when he found an officer of the Punjabis behind his observation post who told him that the Japanese had broken through down the main road. He had returned to his position and tried to contact 352 Battery, but without success. He was still there at 6 a.m. when a runner came up from Lieutenant Carter to tell him that he was retiring. The incentive to do likewise was reinforced by incoming shells, some of which appeared to be coming from behind, and which were taken to mean that friendly guns were trying to engage nearby Japanese.

Lane then began to follow the retiring Punjabis down the mountain, keeping his small party inside the jungle and out of view as far as possible. As he did so the men that he was following disappeared from sight, and it proved difficult to relocate them and catch up. Even so they were down the mountain by 11 a.m. and a fair sized body of men then gathered together to prepare and eat a sack of rice which had been bought from a local Chinese. The party was then sorted out into two groups Carter, Lane, and two officers of the Leicester Regiment leading 13 men of the 88th, Signals, and Leicesters, and the Punjabis under their own officers. Carter and Lane's party then set off with the intention of retiring until they met up with friendly forces. It poured with rain as they plodded through the jungle until late afternoon when they found a hamlet and were given coffee by villagers who later provided a guide who led them

Right: A 25-pdr gun and crew in action in Malaya. A Quad gun tractor is just visible in the background. Watercolour by Desmond Bettany.

Left: Air attack on the Kuantan Ferry as 464 Battery make their crossing. Desmond Bettany.

Right: The crew of a Quad tractor attempt to shift Major Kelly's upturned vehicle at Buloh Kasap. By Desmond Bettany.

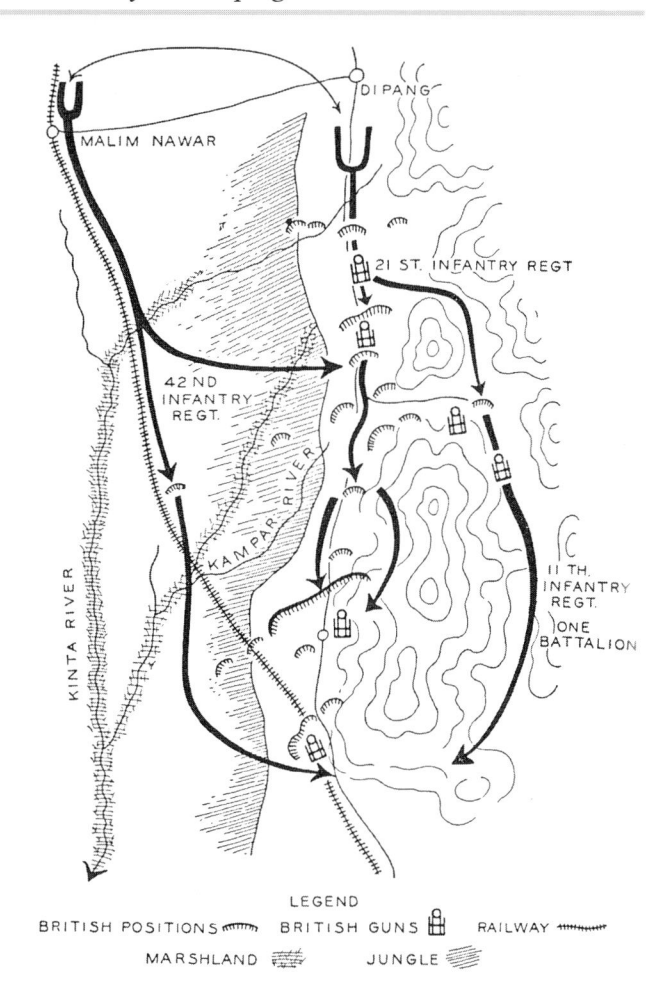

A Japanese plan of the battle at Kampar, 29 December 1941 to 2 January 1942. Note the positions of 88th Field Regiment indicated blocking the main road between the high ground and the jungle.

on until the evening. Learning that the Japanese were not far away they continued with the aid of a second guide, until they finally halted and tried to sleep, assaulted by mosquitoes, about 11 p.m.

The next morning the trek continued, cheered somewhat by the fact that local people again provided coffee, cakes, and food, and ferried them across the mouth of one river. Their next obstacle would be the river Muda, and whilst clothes were being dried out a cyclist was sent ahead to reconnoitre. He returned with the news that the bridge was intact but was to be blown shortly: spurred by this news they set off at a gruelling pace, only to find that the bridge had been cut by the time they arrived. Lane tried to swim the river with a rope but was swept back by the current: then they tried to build a raft, which promptly sank. Eventually they decided to follow the river down to the sea, which was by now only a couple of miles away.

Here they managed, by a mixture of bribery and threats to encourage the native fishermen to ferry them across to Penang Island. On the way across they ran into a violent tropical storm which had everyone bailing to avoid sinking, but fortunately they made it, only to find that the Island had already been abandoned by friendly forces and European civilians. Having rested and eaten there was nothing for it but to head back to the mainland, and carry on south, in the belief that British forces would be doing likewise. This they did the next day, narrowly missing a strike by 27 Japanese bombers which hit the Georgetown waterfront just after they had sailed on a requisitioned Sampan. They rejoined their unit soon afterward. They had been away for almost five days.

Despite the minor successes and narrow escapes which the 88th had pulled from the jaws of defeat there was no disguising the fact that the battle at Gurun had been a complete Japanese victory based on determination and superior tactics. The battle carried with it several lessons for those who had a mind to see them, not least concerning the detail of Japanese methods. American military intelligence would later observe that, the 'Japanese tactical doctrine insists vigorously on the inherent superiority of the offence': the preferred method of this offence, as was amply demonstrated at Gurun, was envelopment 'accompanied by a determined frontal pressure'. Similarly the Japanese were not afraid to launch off into the jungle in the hope of turning a flank. As Japanese instructions regarding the jungles had put it,

> Such places are the haunts of dangerous animals, poisonous snakes, and harmful insects, and since this is extremely difficult terrain for the passage of troops, it will be necessary to form special operations units for the task. This type of terrain is regarded by weak spirited Westerners as impenetrable, and for this reason – in order to out manoeuvre them – we must from time to time force our way through it. With proper preparation and determination it can be done.

Nor did the Japanese have scruple about throwing forward costly frontal attacks if it was felt they could catch their opponents off guard by so doing. Though the 88th had sustained losses it had come out of Gurun in better shape than most. For as General Percival would later confirm the battle had been a moral and material defeat: indeed a scarcely averted catastrophe. He blamed the 'chaos and failure' mainly on lack of communication between divisional headquarters and the forward troops. Since there had been no time to lay out a totally independent field telephone system there was much reliance on the civilian network, and much of this was destroyed along with the rail links. The Indian 11th Division, already tired before the action, was pretty well wrecked after it. Percival would later admit to 'crippling losses in men, guns, ammunition, small arms, equipment, transport and supplies'. The battered 11th was now collected back between the river Muda and Bukit Mertajam, as Percival put it, 'tired out, dirty, dispirited and with their few remaining weapons clogged with mud and rust'.

Despite the setbacks a high level conference in Singapore, chaired by Duff

Cooper, Resident Minister for Far Eastern Affairs, would now endorse a plan by General Percival to hold the Japanese as far north in Malaya as possible. To attempt to do this would clearly need more resources, including aircraft, tanks, and a fresh division of infantry, none of which were available immediately, but orders were issued for their dispatch. Percival imagined that all being well these fresh troops and weapons would arrive in mid January. To allow time for their deployment for the protection of central Malaya it would be necessary to hold the enemy north of the Kuala Kubu road junction until about the middle of January. Such an expectation was undoubtedly optimistic considering the course of the campaign so far, but there was still space on the ground which could realistically be sold little by little to gain time.

Just before Christmas Lieutenant General Sir Henry Pownall took over command in the Far East from Air Chief Marshal Brooke-Popham. Confusingly this arrangement was not to outlast even the festive season: between Christmas and New Year 'ABDA' command would be created in the Far East embracing American, British, Dutch and Australian forces. It would be under the overall command of General Wavell, and Pownall would then act as his Chief of Staff. It is difficult to escape the conclusion that such rapid changes did little to help those fighting on the ground, being more of a signal that international will existed to do something about the Japanese menace rather than an ability for imminent action. After all the Anglo American policy was 'Germany First' and other matters were going to have to wait in the short term.

For the time being the army in Malaya, including the Lancashire gunners on the West Coast, was in full retreat. Picking up 'B' Troop, 351 Battery, which had been detached at Butterworth, 88th Field Regiment continued south with the remains of 11th Indian Division. The next chance they were likely to have of stemming the Japanese advance would be on the Krian River, the main crossing points of which were at Nibong Tebal and Selama. By 17 December the regiment had retired behind the river, and had been placed under Colonel Selby who was now the Commanding Officer of 28th Brigade. One section of 'D' Troop, 352 Battery, under Second Lieutenant S.W. Robinson was detached and sent through confusion and flood water to join two battalions covering the crossing at Selama. Even before he got there however he received notice from the officer in charge at Selama that he had plenty of guns and was to turn round and go back to 352 Battery.

In the meantime the bridges had been blown, and on 18 December Japanese cycle troops had begun to appear at various possible crossing places. The guns were now allowed to shoot 'registration' fire, so as to zero their pieces on target areas on, and north of, the river. One shell crashed down on a half demolished bridge and surprised the Forward Observation officer by exploding the remaining charges there. On 20 December further orders arrived directing Colonel Selby to hold the enemy north of the line Selama to Bagan Serai, thus covering an attempted regrouping of the rest of the division around Ipoh. Given the few men at his disposal Selby decided not to try and hold the full length of the Krian river line but to retire his left behind the canal at Bagan Serai. A crucial element of this defence line would be 88th Field Regiment, with 351 Battery covering the approaches to Bagan Serai and 352 Battery in the Kamunting area near the Krian road.

Sadly no sooner had these dispositions been made than the predictable news arrived that the Japanese had crossed high up stream, above Selama and were threatening the right flank. Worse a Japanese column on the Grik road was making even better progress, and there was some possibility that the 28th Brigade would be cut off altogether. There was nothing for it but to continue the retrograde movement. The 88th were ordered back to Chemor behind the Perak river, which they reached successfully, but the confusion on the road was dreadful with traffic control being negligible: 352 Battery had the worst of it with the force from Selama crossing in front of them. Two of the regiment's vehicles, a gun tractor and a stores lorry, broke down and had to be abandoned. At Sungei Siput contact was made with 12th Infantry brigade and the Blackpool gunners of 137 Field Regiment, but as usual there was more bad news. The Japanese had been reported rafting down the Perak river, and there was again every chance they would get behind the British.

Now the 88th were ordered back to Ipoh, and 'A' Troop under Captain R.G. Swainson was detached to cover a crossing. Most of the regiment were fortunate however in that they got to spend a night, the first of the campaign, in proper buildings with electricity and running water. Any sense of rest or recuperation was short lived. On the morning of 23 December Ipoh railway station was dive bombed by Japanese planes. Here a fatigue party, which was led by Captain J.A. Berry and included Lieutenant D.P. Friend and the Quartermaster Lieutenant W.J. Buswell, was loading stores on to lorries when it was badly hit by a low level attack. An ammunition train was set alight and three men from the regiment, Sergeant Stephens, and Gunners Bennett and Ingram were killed. According to one account of the carnage a lorry was blown onto its side and flung burning against the wall of Ipoh Post Office. One British soldier was trapped badly injured under the wreckage, amidst a sea of flame. As there was no way to extract the victim an NCO of the 88th was forced reluctantly to accede to his pleading to be 'finished off' with a pistol shot.

Air activity by the enemy would continue virtually uninterrupted all through Christmas Eve, and much of Christmas Day, making road movement pretty well impossible. Parit and Blanja bridge in particular formed a focus for enemy attacks, with machine gun straffing as well as bombing. Air superiority was clearly beginning to tell as the Japanese began to use the captured air fields of northern Malaya, and Air Vice Marshal Pulford took the decision to conserve at least a few of the remaining planes for the defence of the naval base at Singapore itself.

The Japanese also used aircraft to send peculiar Christmas greetings to the

Indian troops in the form of leaflets which purported to come from the 'Free India Council' and read,

> The cruel English without tanks and planes are keeping the Indians here for sacrifice. You may have heard that their whole fleet has been sunk. Think and save yourselves. For your protection a large army has joined us. Escape to us.

As a result of the situation the regiment was again prepared to move, and 'A' Troop was withdrawn from its forward position and replaced by 'B' Troop who were placed just west of Pusing. No registration fire was possible, so Captain Bradley the Survey Officer made prediction according to astronomical methods. As the enemy arrived at Blanja crossing 'B' Troop landed a bombardment slap on target, despite the extreme range. No further fire was attempted the next day due to British patrols being out well ahead of the gun lines. During 27 December Colonel, now Brigadier, Selby's force received orders to withdraw to the Kampar area. Preparations were being made here for defence, and at last it appeared there was an opportunity to stand and fight Even so, those who had to do the fighting were nowhere near the peak of efficiency, as one eye witness put it,

> The troops were very tired. Constant enemy air attacks prevented them from obtaining any sleep by day. By night they had either to move, obtaining such sleep as was possible in crowded lorries, or had to work on preparing yet another defensive position. The resultant physical strain of day and night fighting, of nightly moves or work, and the consequent lack of sleep was cumulative and finally reached the limit of endurance. Officers and men moved like automata ...

Weak as the defending forces now were the Kampar position did offer certain advantages as a potential strong point. Indeed General Percival would later offer the opinion that it was probably the strongest position which the British would succeed in occupying throughout the campaign. In the centre was the dominating feature of the massive Bujang Melaka mountain, around the right hand side of which passed a jungle road through the villages of Sahum and Kinjang. It was decided that this could effectively be blocked by 28th Infantry brigade supported by some howitzers. On the other side of the hill, that nearest to the coast, lay Kampar, the railway line, the main north road, and more open country which had been extensively cleared by tin mining. On this side of the mountain would be the main defence, with the advantage of relatively good artillery observation, and fields of fire for the infantry which frequently extended a thousand yards to the front. This was a rare luxury indeed in a country dominated by rubber plantations and forest.

Here, to the west of the 4000 foot mountain, would be placed 88th Field Regiment, with two Troops of 351 battery west of the railway, and two Troops of 352 battery just north of Kampar. These would cover the men of the 'British

Battalion' to their front on a feature known as Thompsons Ridge. The grandly named 'British Battalion' was in fact an amalgam of units, the Leicesters and East Surrey's, lumped together to make an ad hoc group of battalion strength under Lieutenant Colonel Morrison. In the rear were three Punjabi Battalions supported by a battery from another regiment. The defence would be commanded by Brigadier A.C.M. Paris, who had succeeded to the command of 11th Indian Division on Christmas Eve.

This time there would be a little more opportunity to prepare, provided by 12th Brigade which was fighting a delaying action out in front. With them was Second Lieutenant Rowland of the 88th, acting as liaison officer to make sure that the regiment knew what was happening, and when to open fire. In the main Kampar positions the gunners now prepared slit trenches, camouflaged their guns against detection from the air, and laid up an extra 200 rounds per gun in addition to the normal supply. All superfluous vehicles were sent to the rear. Time was taken to place Forward Observers, and survey certain of the positions likely to be taken by the enemy.

About 4 p.m. on 29 December Second Lieutenant Rowland reappeared at Regimental Headquarters with the news that the enemy were approaching fast and that the Argyll and Sutherland Highlanders were fighting a rear guard action at Dipang bridge. Not long after the bridge was blown and the Argylls began to receive shelling and mortaring. In response 352 Battery began fire designed to harass the Japanese as they came on, 900 rounds being fired during the night. The next day both batteries were in action, firing between them 1100 rounds. A total of 2000 shells undoubtedly did some damage to the advancing Japanese, and the regiment's sole loss in return was Gunner Gardner, wounded whilst at one of the hazardous Forward Observation posts which were now under heavy small arms and rifle fire, and had to be withdrawn not long after.

On New Year's Eve the battle hotted up in earnest, with the Japanese bringing up their own artillery to return fire and bombing the rear areas. Two bombs crashed down near 'D' Troop, but fortunately missed their target. In response 278 Battery, which had been the unit supporting the Punjabis, was moved up and added its voice to the British barrage. Its guns were immediately to the rear of the Brigade Headquarters and its shattering deliveries made it 'far from popular' with the staff. As was expected Japanese infantry of the 'Ando' regiment now began to work their way forward, and made efforts to envelope the position of the British Battalion from the right, and 352 Battery was engaged on 'S.O.S' shoots in response to the battalion's requests for close support.

From the other side of the lines Colonel Masanobu Tsuji gave testimony to the heat of the action:

> Leaving our car concealed in the rubber trees, we made our way along the main road to the front line, which was roughly 300 metres from the enemy. On arrival

there we were caught in a violent barrage and it was impossible to advance or retire. Closely scrutinising the enemy line, it appeared to me that our left wing (British right) was an important sector. The enemy presently counter attacked with a bayonet charge, and hand to hand fighting ensued; one could say that it was impossible to distinguish between attacker and defender.

During the night 'D' Troop was withdrawn to the rear of Kampar to prevent it being encircled by the Japanese manoeuvre, but it was ready for action again at first light on the New Year's day 1942. That day the Japanese launched their main attack, which as usual contained a mixture of envelopment and frontal assault. Their 42nd Infantry Regiment tried an encircling move around the British right whilst their 21st Infantry attacked astride the road against the British main position. These attempts would be supported by tanks and three artillery batteries. Meanwhile about 20 miles west, between the British and the coast, a battalion of the Imperial Guards made its way south in a wider sweep.

The 11th Infantry Regiment, which had long since embarked on boats, also made its way south along the coast, attempting to land behind the British and cut off their retreat. In retrospect the exploits of this unit were indeed remarkable, making maximum use of the new found mastery of the sea. According to Japanese sources forty of the small vessels used in the West coast operations had actually been involved in the initial landings in the East. They had then been taken overland by road and rail to the Alor Star river, relaunched, and added to the boats which had been captured at Penang. Eventually the Japanese were able to ferry about one and a half battalions of infantry with attached guns and engineers thus menacing the main British lines of communication.

This time however the 88th were determined that the Japanese were not going to have everything their own way, and the regiment may claim that they, along with the 'British Battalion', were primarily responsible for administering a 'bloody nose' to the Japanese in the midst of what was otherwise a disastrous campaign. The first attack came down the road at 7 am, but was held on, and against, Thompsons Ridge. In the early afternoon pressure was increased with eight or more Japanese tanks appearing, and lending support to their infantry. These were immediately spotted by the regiment's Forward Observers, who directed both batteries to open fire, and so deluged them that they promptly withdrew. Next 352 Battery and 278 offered help to the 'British Battalion', answering 'S.O.S' calls and firing close support. It was a close run thing, and during the battle 'C' Troop's Observation Post commanded by Captain R. Pote-Hunt was almost overrun when a nearby machine gun position was taken by the Japanese. Driver/Mechanic Walker who happened to be returning with the rations to the post at that moment, bumped into the Japanese infantry. Without hesitating he drove them back again single handedly with his tommy gun. He was immediately awarded the Military Medal.

In another Observation Post Second Lieutenant Rowland was controlling the fire of 352 Battery, despite heavy and accurate mortar fire which wounded two of the men in the position. Apparently indifferent to the danger he continued to direct the battery until the enemy attack was stopped within 50 yards of his position. For this he was decorated with the Military Cross. Back with the batteries things were scarcely less pleasant, for the Japanese were using aircraft to direct their own artillery, and a good deal of fire was falling on the roads and railway station. One particular battery of 105 mm howitzers appeared to be firing random shoots over the British positions when a salvo landed on 351 Battery Headquarters severely wounding Lieutenant R. Trethewy, who later died. As General Percival's somewhat laconic summary of these dramatic events would put it,

> The enemy tried to outflank us and he tried to infiltrate between our posts. Defended localities were isolated but held their ground. Observation posts were lost but recaptured by counter attack.

The next threat came from deep in the west and south with the landing of the Japanese 11th Infantry but Brigadier Paris had received reliable intelligence concerning this surprise move and troops were dispatched to halt this attempted encirclement near Telok Anson, supported by the Blackpool gunners of 137 Field Regiment. Amongst the other redeployments ordered to deal with the new Japanese movements was a shifting of 352 Battery further south to Temoh to cover possible avenues of counter attack. In limbering its guns and driving down the road it had to pass through an area being shelled by Japanese 75 mm guns. An unlucky shell landed by a gun tractor, and one of the men, believed to be Gunner Bartlett, was killed. Nevertheless his colleagues managed to rescue their field piece and successfully made their escape.

At 5 a.m. the next morning the Japanese came on again with a vengeance, fighting their way onto and around the mountainous right flank of the 'British Battalion' on Thompsons Ridge. Since 352 Battery had been withdrawn 278 and 351 Batteries had plenty of hot work, sometimes firing at a range of only 300 yards from the enemy. The Observation Posts either side of the north road were in the thick of the action, and there was hand to hand fighting which involved not only the infantry's machine gun posts but gunners with small arms. At one point the eight Japanese tanks which had previously made an appearance showed themselves again but were promptly shelled and again made themselves scarce. Even so the pressure on the 'British Battalion' was such that an extra company of Jats had to be brought up to bolster the position. The remarkable performance of the 88th was specifically noted by General Percival who observed that they worked in 'complete harmony' with and 'no less gallantry' than the infantry.

By the evening of 2 January the Kampar position had been held for three days, and the gunners had fired off several thousand rounds. In view of the ever increasing danger of encirclement it would however have been folly to remain longer, and Brigadier Paris, who had already been in touch with his Corps Commander General Heath and Lieutenant General Percival on the matter, ordered the evacuation of the Kampar position. By now 88th Field Regiment knew the drill only too well, and except for the usual traffic jams on the roads, had made a smooth exit by 9 p.m.: only a little ahead of the enemy who even then were pushing fresh attacks down between the road and the railway line. So it was that the enemy eventually took the Kampar position, 'with great difficulty', 'heavy casualties', and a significant blow to morale, as was admitted by Colonel Tsuji.

It had been satisfying that the Regiment had discharged its duty so well, but this minor success made very little difference to the shape of the campaign as a whole. The army still lacked air cover, and was still being pushed pell mell down the Malayan peninsula. The new position to which 88th Field Regiment was directed lay a further 40 miles to the south on the Slim River. By dawn 351 and 352 Batteries were gathered with 278 Battery under cover in a coconut estate, near one of the Gurkha Battalions. Lieutenant Colonel D'Aubuz went to get his orders from 11th Division's advanced headquarters, which, when he arrived, he discovered had been badly bombed. Lieutenant E.W. Sowerby of the 88th was detached to help replace casualties in the Divisional Headquarters, and the rest of the regiment was then sent on towards Kuala Lumpur. Riding ahead on a motor cycle was the irrepressible Second Lieutenant P.W. Lane, and it was he who first discovered the unexpected news that the regiment's next duty would be in coast defence.

Kuantan, Gemas, and Yong Peng

At this juncture Major Kelly's 464 Battery were to rejoin the rest of the regiment from their station on the East Coast, and whilst they had been much less heavily engaged than their colleagues, their last three weeks had not been entirely uneventful. Having arrived at Kuantan on 10 December they had been put under the command of Lieutenant Colonel Jephson of 5th Field Regiment. 'E' and 'F' Troops had then occupied various defensive positions intended to cover the threat of attack from the sea. During the first fortnight 'E' Troop withdrew west of the Kuantan Ferry, with one section supporting the 5/11 Sikhs, and the other covering the aerodrome. 'F' Troop had originally been situated on the edge of the golf course, but was later moved to a less vulnerable post outside the town.

It was only on Christmas Eve that a potential threat from the north was perceived, and whilst other units of 22nd Brigade were redeployed further in land Lance Sergeant M. English of 464 Battery set up a new Observation Post on Bukit Pengorok, a peak about three and a half miles east of Balok. On 27 December transport had appeared moving along the beach north of Balok. The observers promptly called down fire, damaging two enemy vehicles and dispersing the rest. The next day 'F' Troop engaged and silenced mortars which were firing on Lance Sergeant English's post, and also fired concentrations on likely spots where the Japanese were believed to be mustering. Enemy aircraft appeared overhead and machine gunned the rear areas.

On 29 December 'F' Troop was again subject to enemy air attack. A total of 18 bombs fell near the Bukit Pengorok Observation Post, without causing serious damage. The only losses were one vehicle with a damaged radiator, and a 3 Ton ammunition lorry which was blown into a river. Orders were now received that the battery was to pull back.

The next morning saw sinister developments: Indian troops who swam the Sungei Balok back to friendly lines reported that the enemy were advancing inland, and that the Bukit Pengorok post had been captured. Thus it was that the whole of 464 Battery now fell back across the damaged Kuantan ferry and established itself on the far side of the river. On the morning of New Years eve both troops were again in action against the advancing Japanese, but at 13.00 received fresh orders to retire to the west. This they duly did, harassed by enemy aircraft. The only really cheering factors were that 464 was now on its way back to the rest of the regiment: and that the overrunning of Bukit Pengorok was not in fact the end of Lance Sergeant English. Like other forward observers of the regiment who had so recently found themselves in perilous situations, he too managed to rejoin at a later date.

Remarkably Lieutenant Colonel D'Aubuz was now to be made responsible for the artillery cover for a 55 mile stretch of the west coast of Malaya, from Kuala Selangor in the north to Kuala Linggi in the south. For this task he would have the whole of 88th Field Regiment 351, 352, and 464 Batteries; their old friends 278 Battery; 73 Battery with eight 4.5 inch howitzers; and a Malay volunteer battery with four old 18 pounders. D'Aubuz's group would be responsible to Brigadier R.G. Moir, who also had an ad hoc body of infantry units under command. This was not a particularly inviting prospect, for though an impressive amount of artillery was involved it meant an average density of less than one gun per mile. It also suggested that there was no longer any realistic prospect of naval cover for these shores, and that the threat of new Japanese landings was taken seriously.

These planned dispositions made sense in view of the threat from the sea, but arguably weakened the forces facing the main thrust from the north to an unacceptable degree. A few days later the Japanese would catch up with the enervated 12th and 28th Brigades on the Slim River, and with the aid of their tank force administer a crushing defeat, which in the words of the *Official History*, so damaged 11th Indian Division that for some time to come it 'ceased to be an effective fighting force'. Amongst those caught up in the disaster were the 88th's old friends and colleagues, Blackpool's 137 Field Regiment, who were surprised in the Cluny estate by enemy tanks, and raked at close range with gun and machine gun fire. In the meantime the Japanese Imperial Guards' epic march down the coast, through fifty miles of flooded paddy and swap, on tracks which did not qualify to be marked as roads on the map, was ready to make nonsense of any plan which placed seaward defence as the top priority.

As early as the afternoon of 4 January the regiment had intelligence that everything was far from well with the new scheme. A plaintive phone call from the store keeper in the fishing village of Karang, on the spit of land separating Selangor Swamp from the sea, asked what was to be done about the crowd of Japanese soldiers which were now outside his door. As a result a scratch force of Jats and others, backed by 'C' Troop, 352 Battery, were sent to delay the enemy, believed to be advancing in a body about 400 strong, on the bridges north of Batang Berjuntai. Major Ford, leading the 88th detachment, met the local commander on one of the bridges, and here was hatched a plan for a local counterattack to a position just north of the crossings. The gunners fired 40 rounds in support of the operation over the easterly bridge, which effectively answered the enemy machine gun fire. Observing and directing the 25 pounders was not however easy, since 'C' Troop had insufficient telephone cable left to reach its observers. The link was therefore made mainly by the civilian telephone system with the first 400 yards from observer to the first telephone covered by a runner, and the last 500 yards from the second telephone to the guns by a dispatch rider.

By 7 January the bridge positions were under such pressure that Brigadier Moorhead decided on a fresh operation with the object of driving the Japanese further back from these strategically useful objectives. This time the barrage to support the infantry was fired by 352 Battery, and 22 Mountain Regiment. The shells were landed with good accuracy at ranges over five miles with the help of an astro fix made by the Regiment's survey officer the previous night. Nevertheless the defeat on Slim river made further efforts here futile, and the guns were now ordered to consolidate on Batang Bajunti, and from hence move on to Kuala Lumpur. During these moves 352 Battery was to form a rear guard for other units, which entailed dangerous daylight movements. In moving along the main north south road 'C' Troop was caught by enemy dive bombers and mercilessly attacked. There were eight casualties, and two tractors, a trailer, a car and two trucks were all wrecked. Sergeant Jones, though himself wounded, showed great gallantry in rescuing one of his gun detachment from a burning tractor whilst under attack.

Meanwhile 351 Battery had been attempting to continue the coast defence role which the Commanding Officer had been set. On 9 January they sighted two junks off the coast near Morib, which the naval liaison officer could not verify as friendly. A warning shot was fired, but since the vessels made no response the battery opened fire in earnest and sank them. Reports were later heard that a small body of the enemy had landed in the small creeks immediately north of Kapar. Use was made of a short lull that day to fill some of the gaps which combat and transfers had made in the ranks of the officers of the 88th. Captain Court was appointed Adjutant, whilst Lieutenant Parker from the reinforcements came to replace Lieutenant Sowerby at Regimental Headquarters. Lieutenant Carter was put in command of 'C' Troop, and Lieutenant Friend now replaced Lieutenant Carter in 351 Battery.

As the evacuation of Kuala Lumpur was now nearing completion, and 11th Indian Division was now no longer in any state even to delay the Japanese, a fresh retirement was now ordered. This time the intention was to remove 11th Indian Division from the front line, and instead block the enemy east of Gemas with 'Westforce'. This 'Westforce' was to be a combined group of 9th Indian Division and an Australian Brigade under the Australian General Gordon Bennett. Furthermore General Percival now expected that all elements of the fresh but untried British 18th Division would arrive by the end of January, and they could take up and defend the position in Johore, southern Malaya, previously covered by the Australians. Perhaps over optimistically, he even considered that there might be scope for offensive action.

General Wavell, the Supreme Commander for the theatre, stopped in Singapore on his way to Java, and met not only Percival but Generals Bennett and Heath (commanding III Corps 9th and 11th Indian Divisions). He agreed the general strategy, putting the emphasis on delaying the enemy, and freeing the Australians to fight. He viewed the matter, so he said, 'as a time problem between the rate of Japanese advance and the arrival of reinforcements'.

These decisions meant some complex manoeuvrings for the troops on the ground, not least 88th Field Regiment. The main task of the regiment for the next few days would be in support of the rearguards as they went back to, and later beyond, Tampin. Once this was accomplished they would join up with the Australians. This was a nerve wracking operation which involved staying one step ahead of the Japanese and the right side of any bridges to be demolished, all the time hiding from enemy aircraft. In one instance as 352 Battery tried to leave Seremban, the bridge which they were to have used exploded, its demolition charges having been struck by lightning. There was nothing for it but to jury rig the bridge using local materials, and creep across before the position was threatened. Nevertheless, and despite one miss order which took a column several miles out of position, the movements were eventually completed so that the regiment, along with other batteries, was deployed in support of the Gemas position on 14 January. Two batteries, 352 and 464, were put in the rear of the Australians at Batu Anam on the main road east of Gemas, whilst 351 Battery at Segamat was to fire in support of 22 Indian Brigade on the side road which led to Jamentah.

The lead Australian company was positioned in thick jungle, near a bridge which had been prepared for demolition, with the artillery trained on the vital spot. At 4 p.m. on 15 January the Japanese advance guard ran slap into the ambush which the Australians had prepared. The ambush party waited until cyclists of the Japanese Mukaide Detachment had crossed the bridge, then blew it up and opened fire. Lieutenant Colonel D'Aubuz later estimated the enemy losses at 700 men and nine tanks. The Japanese were heartily surprised by this 'obstinate resistance'. Colonel Tsuji's account makes mention of the 8th Australian Division fighting with 'a bravery we had not seen before', and concentrated shell fire which now blew men about the battlefield.

However the next day the Japanese put in strong attacks and the Australians withdrew under covering fire of 352 Battery which fired 450 rounds on Gemas and nearby bridges. The operation continued until 17 January, by which point the Japanese had managed to bring up their own mortars and 75 and 105 mm guns with which they returned fire. Air reconnaissance reported huge columns of Japanese lorries moving forward, but there were few bomber or fighter aircraft to take proper advantage of the situation.

On 18 January there was news of a Japanese thrust down the coast, near the mouth of, and south of, the Muar river. The Imperial Guards Division was continuing its old tactic of advancing down the coast, whilst ship borne detachments attempted to land ahead. As a result a battalion of infantry and some guns had to be detached from the main position to be ready to help out 45th Indian Brigade which was covering the river and coast.

In view of the uncertainty of the situation Lieutenant Colonel D'Aubuz and Captain E.C. Dickson went out ahead of the regiment to the north west, to reconnoitre potential positions from which their batteries might be able to put down harassing fire on the enemy. They saw neither friendly nor enemy troops, but having returned enemy mortar fire broke out immediately. That evening heavy attacks were delivered down the main road: 352 Battery answered numerous calls for supporting fire which were directed by Major Ford. Despite the extreme precariousness of the situation, and the surrounding of various companies of 1st Battalion the Indian Frontier Force the line was held.

The next day the gun lines were pulled back to 1000 yards in front of Buloh Kasap, and despite the fact that both the British and Australian gunners had separate commands, and some scrambling for the best battery positions, the retirement was worked out amicably. The pressure continued: 464 Battery had to fire a heavy programme in answer to enemy fire, and later 'E' Troop had to be withdrawn a further mile. 'F' Troop followed on a little later, by which time there were fires burning fiercely in Segamat. Unfortunately Major Kelly's armoured car, which was acting as a mobile observation post, turned over, and he was killed. Finally that evening news came that the Japanese threat down the coast was serious and the whole force fell back on Labis. Here a new position was set up on the road, flanked by dense jungle, and it was hoped that the Japanese could be surprised here, as they had been at Gemas.

The head of the enemy column was sighted at 2 p.m. on 21 January, nosing its way cautiously down the road. Two hours later it had advanced about a quarter of a mile beyond the lead troops of the ambush, so that about two platoons were now in the jaws of the trap. For whatever reason the ambush was now sprung slightly prematurely; D'Aubuz had it that the operation was betrayed by a sneeze from one of the Indian soldiers as he lay in wait. Whatever the reason ten minutes of mayhem now broke out, to which the 88th added considerably, deluging the road with high explosive. Japanese losses were far fewer than at Gemas but nevertheless the lead units were slaughtered, and 351 and 352 Batteries continued harassing fire for some time afterwards. This gave adequate time for 464 Battery, which had already set off further down the road, to begin the preparation of yet another potential position. This was done under command of 8th Brigade, the actual direction of the battery being by Denis Houghton, who was now acting Major after the loss of Major Kelly.

Yet whilst the British were becoming accustomed to the Japanese tactics, and answer them with swift movement and ambush, the Japanese were getting used to the idea that a new ambush was likely to lay ahead. This time, as soon as first contact was made, just after 11 a.m. on 22 January on the road to Yong Peng, the Japanese reaction was to send out immediately strong flanking forces into the jungle. Their object was to get round behind the ambush and take the British themselves by surprise. The action between Labis and Yong Peng therefore quickly dissolved into a general engagement, with the two troops of 464 Battery reinforced by 'A' Troop, 351 Battery, firing many shoots in response to 'S.O.S' calls from the infantry, and 'counter preparation' onto the main north road. By 2 p.m. the situation was quite serious, and it appeared quite possible that 'E' Troop might be outflanked or overrun. It was therefore withdrawn behind 'F' Troop.

It would have been expedient to withdraw the whole 8th Brigade group including 88th Field Regiment at this point, but it was decided to hold on longer as there was news that an Australian force had been cut off on the Maur to Yong Peng road, and there was every danger of it being annihilated. Brigadier Lay was therefore ordered to hang on as far forward as possible, at least until 3 a.m. the next day, in order to keep an escape route open. This was done, but even so only 900 men of the combined Australian and Indian force which had been holding Maur would escape what one survivor called the 'pitiable inferno'. Another major Empire formation had virtually ceased to be: as the *Official History* put it 45th Indian Brigade now existed 'in name only'. Maddened by the casualties which the Indians and Australians had inflicted on them the Japanese slaughtered many of the remnants in an orgy of death at Parit Sulong.

By first light on 23 January the three batteries of the 88th which had been closely engaged had successfully extricated themselves to good natural positions around Yong Peng itself. Here they continued to fire, still under orders to help to deny the Japanese uninterrupted access to the town and crossroads. Now the Japanese were having difficulty pushing down the jungle road and out of the defile which had been blocked by demolitions, and accordingly called up straffing planes and three batteries of their own, but were unable to spot the British guns which were well hidden and firing at intervals. By evening however things were again critical with the Japanese forces converging on Yong Peng from two directions.

Whilst the Preston and Lancaster gunners of the 88th pointed north, helping to stall the enemy 21st Brigade which was closing from the direction of Labis, the Blackpool gunners of 137th Field Regiment pointed south at the Imperial Guard formations which had been dealing with Batu Pahat and Maur. By this time however the 137th were badly weakened having lost the best part of two batteries on the Slim River and in other actions. As Gunner Leo Rawlings of Blackpool recalled;

> Yong Peng, where Captain Alan Grime, 137th Field Regiment, R.A., bravely distinguished himself in action, was probably the last main stand by Allied troops of any account before the withdrawal to Johore and finally Singapore. My own unit, C Troop of 350 Battery 137th Regiment, held a gun position for four days. Partly hidden by banana trees, our command post in a small planter's house, we fired an almost continuous barrage on a variety of targets. Heavy supplies of ammo were piled high behind the guns and the intention was, we were told, to make a big stand here at last ... At dawn on the fourth day heavy attacks on dive bombers blasted us out of our position.

It was with some relief then that the order to retire was finally received, and the Batteries limbered up to fall back during the night. Those of the 88th went to a rubber estate between Rengham and Simpang Rengham.

Though the British public had been told very little up to this point, and the official story for those doing the fighting was that there was every prospect of relief or reinforcement, towards the end of the third week of January Percival and Wavell were well aware that they were staring defeat in the face. The 'Westforce' and 'Eastforce' plans were seen to be failing already, and although the Australians had made a hopeful start, this had been quickly reversed, and they were being pushed back every bit as hard and fast as those who went before them. Wavell cabled Percival instructing him that,

> You must think out problem of how to withdraw from the mainland should withdrawal become necessary and how to prolong resistance on the island ... Will it be any use holding troops on southern beaches if attack is coming from the north. Let me have your plans as soon as possible. Your preparations must of course be kept entirely secret. Battle is to be fought out in Johore till reinforcements arrive and troops must not be allowed to look over [their] shoulders. Under cover of selecting positions for garrison of island to prevent infiltration of small parties you can work out scheme for large force and undertake some preparation such as obstacles or clearances but make it clear to everyone that battle is to be fought out in Johore without thought of retreat ...

Percival duly dispatched a secret and personal letter to Generals Heath and Bennet, and the Singapore Fortress commander Major General Simmons. In it he outlined the plan to hold a line Batu Pahat-Kluang-Mersing across southern Johore. If this proved impossible all roads were to be used to a last bridgehead on the mainland at Johore Bahru, covering the crossing to Singapore Island.

Whilst Wavell chivvied Percival, Wavell himself was being given instructions in no uncertain terms by the Prime Minister Amongst the latter's communications at this time was a cable which read:

I want to make it absolutely clear that I expect every inch of ground to be defended, every scrap of material or defences to be blown to pieces to prevent capture by the enemy, and no question of surrender to be entertained until after protracted fighting among the ruins of Singapore city.

Whether Churchill's instructions and Wavell's advice were simply well intentioned, if ill conceived, attempts at morale stiffening, or whether they were belated indicators of a realisation of the likely public opinions in the event of defeat, is difficult to judge. What is clear is that without a swift injection of sea and air power they were no more than rhetoric.

At this point Percival must have already been wondering whether there was any serious prospect of holding out, and indeed what level of hopeless sacrifice he could be justified in asking his troops to entertain. Serious mistakes had been made at army level, and cynical, if logical, political calculations and omissions had also occurred, but whether opening Singapore to sack and slaughter after a Japanese storm would in any way assuage the inevitable recrimination was improbable. Before him he had examples such as the 1937 'Rape of Nanking' in which the Japanese, forced to attack a town, had massacred their prisoners. Surrender was ignominious, but perhaps it might be preferable to wholesale murder. It was probably with some difficulty that thoughts like this were put out of his mind whilst the campaign went on.

The 88th which had just been in action for three consecutive days, in three different places, under three different brigadiers, had been hoping that the end of the action around Yong Peng would mean a brief respite. Whatever rest there was was brief indeed, for within seven hours of halting orders had come through for them to move north west to Kluang where they would support a counter attack by 22nd Infantry Brigade. Matters were somewhat complicated by the fact that 5th Field Regiment was already in the locality; and the commanding officers of the two regiments therefore agreed to leave the communication cables laid by 5th Field Regiment in place, their cable being made up from an equivalent amount that the 88th's signallers had on their drums.

By late afternoon on 24 January however the counter attack preparations had already been overtaken by the Japanese advance. At 6 p.m. they were approaching the Kluang aerodrome, and one group was feeling its way around the east of the position in an attempted encirclement. The action therefore deteriorated into a confused defensive fight: 352 Battery which came into action just south of the airfield was almost overrun and had to pull back promptly, and 5th Field Regiment had to remain in order to achieve sufficient firepower to stabilise the position. The defence then managed to organise itself into two defended perimeters, the 'Infantry Perimeter' of Kluang itself which also enclosed 352 Battery, and the 'Artillery Perimeter' three miles further south. This contained all the remaining guns arranged around the outside with the vulnerable transport inside. Remarkably the Japanese did not launch any further attack that night, and it remains open to question whether this was the first sign of serious fatigue on the part of the enemy, or whether the exhausted 22 Brigade had itself been panicked onto the defence, being in ignorance of the true strength and intentions of the enemy.

In any case most of the 88th were given the breathing space to deploy back on Rengham, leaving 352 Battery only under the charge of 5th Field Regiment. At Rengham there was some shelling and bombing by enemy aircraft, until on the evening of 26 January orders were received for 464 Battery to go back to the 9th Division headquarters at Sedenack, whilst 351 Battery remained forward to act as support to 22nd Infantry Brigade. It was now all too clear that an evacuation to Singapore Island was in prospect, and that whilst 351 and 352 Batteries were to take part in the delaying actions, 464 was to go ahead and find suitable positions for the regiment in their allotted part of the island defence.

On 27 January 351 Battery was shooting in support along the railway line near Rengham, with Second Lieutenant J.B. Green acting as a Forward Observer with the infantry: at one point the targets were as close as 1,500 yards before the guns received orders to pull back. Since it was daylight, and the enemy maintained total air superiority, it was necessary to move the vehicles at 15 minute intervals thus minimising the straffing risk. That night 351 and 352 Batteries rendezvoused with their Commanding Officer, and withdrew along the causeway onto Singapore Island. Before dawn they were in hidden positions near Kim Chuan village, not far from Paya Lebar.

Thus it was that the vast majority of the regiment were ensconced in relative safety: however, as was so often the case, things were not so easy for the forward observation posts. Captain Berry was lucky to extricate himself and rejoin the regiment almost immediately, but not all were so fortunate. Lieutenant Green and Gunner Winterbotham succeeded in falling back on 22nd Infantry Brigade after the fight on 27 January, but whilst attempting to bypass Layang were caught up in a bloody close quarter battle. The Gawali infantry were worsted by the pursuing Japanese, and a large group including Green and Winterbotham were forced off into the jungle. Their party, which included 20 stretcher cases, now had to hack its way through the undergrowth with painful slowness. On 29 January this sorry column emerged from the jungle into a plantation of pineapples, which they devoured, but on reaching Sedenak they discovered that 8th Brigade had already withdrawn. The enemy had managed to infiltrate between the 22nd and the 8th Infantry Brigades.

The result was that the fugitives picked their way through Japanese lines at night. For a further two days they pressed on through the rubber trees, with sinking morale and failing stamina. They skirted Kulai and avoided Senai, which was already occupied by the enemy, but were forced to dump much of their heavy equipment and subsist on handfuls of raw rice. They succeeded in leaving their wounded with friendly troops, but on 2 February ran into a fierce skirmish with a body of about 50 Japanese. Many of the Sikh troops bolted, but Green stuck with the loyal Gawalis, and the largest remaining body, and was guided as far as Febroso, only to discover not only that the Japanese were again between him and Singapore, but that the Causeway had already been blown.

Brigadier Paynter then called a council of war with the remaining officers of his shattered command. The decision they reached was that the Brigadier, his Staff and the survivors of the Gawalis should surrender. Seven attached officers, including Green-plus the plucky Gunner Winterbotham, were free to carry on. These last eight set off into the pouring rain, but were forced to take cover before they had gone a mile, due to the appearance of an enemy cyclist.

Carrying on warily into the thick rubber, they were again surprised, this time by a group of Japanese, and froze. Though they avoided detection, Winterbotham became separated from the rest of the party. The officers now managed to find guides and were taken via Plenting, down to a spot on the coast about three miles from Johore Bahru, narrowly avoiding a large body of the enemy. That night Green succeeded in attracting the attention of friendly forces by signalling across the Straits with a light. A naval launch appeared shortly afterwards, rescued them, and ferried them to the British side.

Winterbotham, now thrown entirely onto his own resources, also made his way to the shore. He walked into the water, but his first attempt to cross was abortive, and he was fortunate to regain land. He managed to swim the Straits at a second attempt. Completely exhausted he spent some time in hospital but was later able to rejoin the regiment.

The Defence of Singapore Island, 1942

Unaware of the minor details of the drama which was still unfolding on the mainland, the main body of the 88th now established battery positions on Singapore Island. From their new stations the guns of the 88th could fire across the Johore Strait, and cover the movements of the rest of the army as it negotiated the bottle necks on the main road and at Johore Bahru. The task was considerably hampered by the Japanese infiltration between 22nd and 8th Infantry Brigades, which caused considerable havoc. It was later learned that the enemy had succeeded in ambushing and killing General Barstow, and that a major portion of 22nd Infantry Brigade had been cut off.

On 29 January the covering batteries on the Singapore side were reinforced and reorganised under the Australian Major Kerr, and 351 and 352 Batteries of the 88th were joined by an Australian regiment, and 350 Battery of 137 Field Regiment. The total artillery available here was thus six batteries, or more than 40 guns, and over the next 24 hours 300 rounds were dumped for each piece. Despite problems integrating the efforts of the Australian and British commands, and the sweeping away of the submarine communication cable which linked the mainland and the island, a potent umbrella was placed over three remaining retreating infantry battalions.

On the morning of the last day of January the last Allied fighting troops left mainland Malaya, and as Lieutenant Green had discovered, at 8.30 a.m. the causeway was blown. The last bastion in this corner of the globe was now Singapore Island, a portion of land about the same size and shape as the Isle of Wight, but the Straits around it were neither as wide or deep as the Solent. Singapore's defenders, who now totalled about 130,000, were of two major types; the exhausted, like the 88th who had just retreated the length of Malaya; and the fresh but inexperienced like 18th Division who had literally arrived within the last few days.

Had this really been the Isle of Wight the defenders would doubtless have had benefit of modern if not numerous aircraft overhead, and considerable naval power; they would also have had a civilian population behind them totally committed to allied victory. As it was they had none of these things, and no real prospect of relief. Air defence in particular was now practically non existent, and relied for the most part on a few Hurricanes which had been shipped in packed in crates. Facing them across the Strait was a fewer number of Japanese troops; 5th, 18th and Imperial Guards Divisions, who did have considerable air and sea support. What was perhaps not so well appreciated by Percival and his advisors was that the Japanese themselves were near the end of their tether. The enemy supply lines were now almost impossibly long, and whilst victorious advance tends to be less exhausting than retreat, it is only a matter of degree.

Percival's defensive plan put the emphasis on the perimeters. He split the island into four parts, north and west areas facing the Straits with the bulk of his troops, and the southern and reserve areas which were relatively lightly held. The Western Area was held by 8th Australian Division; Northern Area contained the new 18th Division, and parts of the old and battered 11th Indian Division. The 88th Field Regiment was to be attached to 18th Division in this Northern Area. The remnant of the hapless 9th Indian Division, shattered both physically and morally, was disbanded. The dockyard, which had all along been one of the primary reasons for retaining Singapore, was now overlooked by the Japanese on the opposite shore: all skilled personnel were withdrawn, and many evacuated entirely. This, and the 'denial scheme' which involved demolitions and destruction of war materials to prevent capture, did little to help bolster the resolution of the defenders. Japanese air raids and shelling continued throughout the short time remaining for the preparation of the defence.

Over the next few days 88th Field Regiment's guns were in action, firing on numerous occasions either in response to the Japanese, or undertaking 'harassing programmes' on likely Creek mouths and route junctions on the mainland. Ammunition was now being rationed since Percival's defence plan was based on the premise that they would have to hold out months rather than weeks. In retrospect this was almost certainly an error, for when the time came there were still 140,000 25 pounder shells left to fall into enemy hands on Singapore Island.

On 8 February the enemy bombarded the Australian Western Area, drawing on a total of 168 guns, and that night threw across the narrow Straits a mass of small craft which headed for the north west of the island. These contained the first waves of 5th and 18th Infantry Divisions, and their immediate objective was Tengah airfield. Australian machine guns took a heavy toll, and a number of boats were sunk, but the Japanese soon gained a good foothold. As was reported to the 88th's Regimental Headquarters this first push contained only 'about 2,000 men', but even if so few it was rapidly and energetically reinforced. Later the same evening the Imperial Guards Division launched its attack just west of the causeway; they fared less well, but after a hard fight which involved three Australian battalions as well as the Chinese recruits of 'Dalforce', General Nishimura's Guardsmen obtained a secure bridgehead.

Relatively little had yet happened on the 88th's brigade front, but almost immediately units were drawn off from 18th Division's Northern Area to reinforce the hard pressed West. These battalions were formed into the ad hoc 'Tomforce' so called after its commander Lieutenant Colonel Thomas. The 88th Field Regiment was called upon to put down a heavy programme of 'harassing fire' from its existing locations. It was quite apparent to D'Aubuz however that the situation in the west was 'far from favourable'.

General Wavell who paid his last visit to Singapore on 10 February, and came close to being killed for his pains, had also come to much the same conclusion. When he had regained the relative safety of Java he cabled the Prime Minister,

> Battle for Singapore is not going well. Japanese with their usual infiltration tactics are getting on much more rapidly than they should in the west of Island. I ordered Percival to stage counter attack with all troops possible on that front. Morale of some troops is not good and none is as high as I should like to see ... The chief troubles are lack of sufficient training in some of reinforcing troops and an inferiority complex which bold and skilful Japanese tactics and their command of the air have caused. Everything possible is being done to produce more offensive spirit and optimistic outlook. But I cannot pretend that these efforts have been entirely successful up to date. I have given the most categorical orders that there is to be no thought of surrender and that all troops are to continue fighting to the end ...

With such exhortations Wavell, who had made a better showing in North Africa, had made his excuses and left. He had been dealt a very poor hand when he had so recently taken up the command, and can have had few illusions about the efficacy of eleventh hour counter attacks.

On 11 February a brigade of 18th British Division duly began a counter attack to re-establish control of Bukit Timah and the area of the race course where the Japanese were already breaking through with tanks. To assist 352 Battery accompanied them, now under Major P. Halford Thompson. Meanwhile Lieutenant Colonel D'Aubuz was left with the rest of the regiment, and

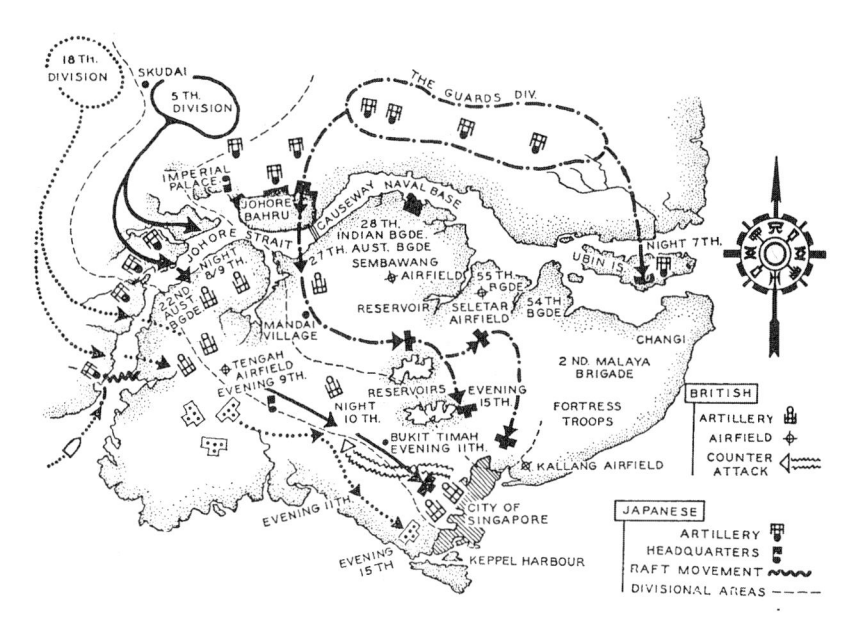

Japanese plan of the final advance and the fall of Singapore, 8–15 February 1942.

just two companies of the Cambridgeshire Regiment and a few Indian State troops in his immediate locality. The position now appeared so dire that it seemed likely that he could be attacked at any time and from any direction. The headquarter positions were therefore surrounded with barbed wire and prepared for all round defence. The next day the news was no clearer but orders were received that the remainder of the regiment was to proceed to the front, and to rendezvous at the junction of the Braddell and Thomson roads. This they duly did, and 464 Battery was deployed in close country south of the Braddell Road whilst 351 was positioned on the Serangoon Road near the St Michael's wireless station.

By now Percival had pretty much abandoned the thought of further counter attacks, and reverted instead to trying to hold the main built up area of Singapore itself. Orders to this effect, to be acted on 'in case of necessity', were already in the hands of his senior commanders, and now they carried them out. One of the final expedients was putting rifles in the hands of the clerks and storemen of Singapore, and calling this last ditch force 'X Battalion'. Such desperate measures made little impression. To 88th Field Regiment's front the lines at last appeared to dissolve: according to D'Aubuz two notable exceptions here were 5th Battalion the Suffolk Regiment, and a detachment of Anti Tank gunners who had acquired rifles, and stood their ground.

On the night of 13 February the 88th was moved one last time, to stand with 352 Battery in the Balestier Road area pointed north, and 464 Battery near Singapore 'Jalan Besar' Stadium with a line of fire to the north west. At this point 'F' Troop of 464 was positioned just north of the New World Exhibition buildings, but it was 'E' Troop which attracted enemy fire, and Gunner Collins was killed. Though 'E' Troop shifted as a result, the enemy guns found them again, leading to speculation that enemy agents were reporting their positions. It was equally possible however that Japanese forward observers had now wormed their way close, as there was now sporadic small arms fire from nearby buildings. This made any movement in the open extremely hazardous.

Even at this late stage there were deeds of heroism. Lance Bombardier W. Haslam of 464 Battery, already noted for his 'devotion to duty', was hit in the chest by a shell splinter on the evening of 14 February. Rather than keep out of the way he had his wound dressed and carried on. The next morning he was ferrying ammunition from a dump under enemy bombing.

Behind the regiment in the centre of Singapore a bizarre *Gotterdamerung* was being enacted. The Royal Engineers, the Public Works department, and a motley collection of volunteers were busy destroying thousands if not millions of pounds worth of stores, rubber, and other materials which the bombers had somehow missed. Down the drains went a million and a half bottles of spirits, and 60,000 gallons of the potent Chinese 'Samsu': doubtless this helped to some degree to cut down the mayhem to be wrought by looters or drunken Japanese. Some civilians fled, some tried to prevent the 'denial' operation, some deserters skulked or hid. In front of the regiment things were no saner: during the hours of darkness the Japanese patrolled and set off fire crackers goading the less experienced into replying with fusillades of rifle fire. Air raids and intermittent shelling completed the demonic picture.

On 15 February Lance Bombardier Geoffrey Haworth's war came to an unexpected, abrupt, and abominable end. He had been wounded a few weeks previously by a mortar bomb which had blown him from one of the regiment's few remaining motorcycles, and been left with multiple fractures of the leg. He had finally been taken to Singapore's Alexandra Military hospital, and here was put in traction. Early that day it became apparent that small arms fire was getting closer; eventually the reports were so loud it became clear that the firers were literally next door. Moments later Japanese troops burst into the building, threw open the ward where Haworth was lying with his leg suspended and treated the occupants to a long burst of automatic fire. Lying helpless he had only time to notice that the bullets were whizzing over him at chest height, and to hope that the firer did not alter his aim.

Next Japanese ran in with fixed bayonets and commenced shooting and skewering staff and patients alike. In the midst of the havoc the occupant of the next bed turned to Haworth and offered him a razor blade, inquiring whether he wished to end it all there. Haworth had only time to decline before his bed was up ended and he was thrown out on the floor, broken limb and all. He would lie there amongst the dead and the detritus for a couple of days before being found by medical officer T. Smiley who had himself been bayonetted. He survived and was captured, but many were not. One crowd of staff and patients was herded into an adjoining building before being massacred. Gunner J.H. Whitley of the 88th disappeared and was believed killed. The Alexandra hospital incident was one of the most infamous atrocities that would be perpetrated during the campaign.

On the same day the Suffolks were withdrawn onto the line of the Thomson road, and the 88th now found themselves facing the Japanese Imperial Guard in the very front line. Though they were shelled it was curious that they were not actually closely attacked. At about 2 p.m. the reason for this deliverance became clear; Regimental Headquarters was informed that an armistice was to come into effect at 4 p.m. Not long after another call was received telling the gunners to destroy their guns and stay where they were. With a sense of sadness they complied.

Artillery units in the British army have no 'colours' to embody their regimental spirit, instead they have the guns, which are treated as though they were the flags of the regiment. There was no 'Hara Kiri' as might be expected from the Japanese, but the destruction of the guns was the closest equivalent in the British code of behaviour. At 4.30 General Percival met General Yamashita at the Ford building; at first he played for time and looked for statements of fair treatment for the civilian population. Finally he agreed that all hostilities should cease, and that the surrender should take place at 10 p.m. Nippon time. The British soldier's reactions ran the gamut from disbelief, anger, and shame, to relief, apprehension, and a sense of betrayal, which would remain for half a century: and is likely to last as long as any survivors remain alive.

Why many felt this sense of betrayal is easy to fathom. Some believed, perhaps correctly, that the defence of 'Fortress' Singapore had been something of a sham all along. Whilst Britain's main efforts had gone into the war in Europe, just enough to appear convincing was left in the Far East. That this was the case, and had to be the case, was dissembled from the soldiery as much as from the public and the enemy. In truth 'Matador', Brooke-Popham, and the generals had not served them well. The R.A.F had not had the machines it needed, and the navy, though fearless, had effectively been wiped out in one day.

When it came to it there could be no new Dunkirk, no victory from the jaws of defeat, and no escape. Someone had to stay and pay the price, a price more terrible than any, to be fair, had yet imagined. Perhaps even worse the fall of Singapore came to be painted as the British army's worst defeat, and some of those on the receiving end would feel tarred, by implication, with the brush of incompetence and ineptitude. Some of the most cynical surmised that the real role of the 'green' 18th Division, to which the 88th had landed up being attached, was a political ruse to make sure that some 'white faces' landed up in captivity, thereby freeing the British Government of the charge of negligence, or leaving their colonial subjects to fight a war on their behalf.

As Lance Bombardier Lord summed it up; those who were left behind in Singapore certainly got a 'raw deal'.

> People sometimes tell me Singapore was a disgrace, but I would sooner be at Dunkirk 100 times than the last days at Singapore. Without any planes to protect us, the Japs in control of the water, shells coming in from all sides, not to mention 1,000,000 women and children in the centre of the ring … was the end a surprise? … As in France the Preston lads were first in and last out.

Lance Bombardier Haworth was of the opinion that the loss of Malaya had been a matter of both attitude, and Japanese personal equipment and training. On the British side there had seemed to be a misplaced confidence that all was well, and a lack of ruthlessness in execution. Not only were the penalties against looting severe, but there was a story flying round about avoiding damage to the rubber trees. The Japanese on the other hand appeared not only fanatically determined but able to exist on minimal supplies: a little rice and a few bullets appeared to be all that their fighting men really needed. Their infantry equipment may not have been sophisticated but it was lightweight, and he was impressed by their rubber soled canvas 'tabi', or boots with separate toes, ideal for tree climbing. Their Arisaka rifles were again not of the most modern type, but firing a slightly smaller cartridge than the British, but were perfectly capable of the few hundred yards range beyond which visibility was in any case likely to render fire ineffective.

Lieutenant Colonel D'Aubuz clearly felt that no stigma applied to the 88th, and one must agree that at the very least they had proved themselves well above the average in the Malayan campaign. It is worth quoting their commanding officer's comments in full on this point, for in effect it was the regiment's epitaph, at least as far as the fighting unit was concerned.

> The Regiment, apart from the East Coast operations, had fought a delaying action over 400 miles of country which has well been described as a 'Gunner's Nightmare', and had taken part in 14 separate engagements on the mainland, including two which could be dignified by the name of 'battles'. It was probably unique in being the only regiment to bring all its guns back to the Island.
>
> Its losses in personnel were: Killed and died of wounds, 2 officers and 13 other ranks. Wounded, 26 other ranks. Missing, 1 officer and 10 other ranks. Its losses in material were not severe, consisting chiefly of vehicles shelled or bombed, and motor cycles, which had crashed and had to be abandoned. Only two three ton lorries were abandoned owing to being ditched and failing to be released before the arrival of the enemy. The equipment, though not altogether suitable for forest fighting, stood up well to what was required of it, except the 'No 11' wireless sets which were a disappointment throughout the operations. For fighting in this type of country, it became clear that the scale of equipment for transport allowed was over-generous and could well be cut down. It can be said with truth that the regiment did its job, and on several occasions earned the commendation of the infantry command to which it was affiliated. All ranks behaved well under novel and difficult conditions,

and in particular, the work of the Signallers and Line Maintenance Men is deserving of notice. In the absence of facilities for observation, normal in this type of country, the work of the survey section was invaluable, and without them the regiment could hardly have done its task. Finally the administration of the regiment was most efficiently undertaken by Major P.D. Weir, Second in Command, and the Commanding Officer at no time had need to worry on that score. In spite of continual withdrawals and disappointments, the morale of all ranks remained good to the end.

Yet there were a good number of the 88th who refused to admit that this was the end, and viewed captivity under the Japanese with a distinct sense of foreboding. One complete troop picked up their small arms, and led by their Troop Commander made straight for the docks. Major Houghton followed them and told them that it was the commanding officer's wish they should all stick together: moreover there appeared to be no reasonable prospect that they would actually be able to get away. His orders were complied with. In retrospect this was probably the right thing to do, for of about 40 vessels that did leave Singapore at this time the majority were sunk. Many men died in this way, and one particular party of shipwrecked nurses were massacred on the beach.

Despite the terrible risks there were at least three members of the regiment who managed, through various circumstances, to slip away and escape. Gunner N.N.R. Gardner was wounded just prior to the surrender, and unbeknownst to his comrades, successfully evacuated. Captain A. Bannister was listed as missing in action, but subsequently made his escape. The third was Lance Bombardier Lord, and it was Lord's hair raising adventure which has been best documented.

According to Lord's own written account he had been present with Regimental Headquarters, when, at about 4 pm, the front had fallen deathly silent and a white flag had been nailed to a pole. He was directed by the Regimental Sergeant Major to help build a bonfire of things which were not to fall into enemy hands, whilst Captain Court took charge of burning the papers. During these proceedings Lord, who had already been wounded twice during the Malaya campaign, once by enemy mortar fire and once by a misdirected Gurkha bullet, could think of nothing but escape, and confided his intention to 'Doc' Dickson. The Medical Officer noticed that Lord was still suffering from a bad foot and damaged toe, and so offered him his own gym shoes to improve his mobility. The unit had already surrendered, so surely now anyone who could get away was escaping, not deserting. Lord then canvassed his comrades as to whether any were prepared to hazard passing through Japanese lines, but found only two who were willing to take the huge risks, Bombardier Stevenson of Preston, and a Gunner from Blackpool with whom he was unfamiliar.

Finding that the direct route to the coast was already firmly shut Lord and his friends simply set off down the main road. Pretty soon they came across an abandoned car which had belonged to an Indian unit, and before long they were bouncing along attempting to dodge the bomb craters. Either side of them were scenes of terrible devastation, men hanging around waiting to be captured, and a litter of equipment and air raid debris. Nearing the beach they were informed by a Corporal that the route was blocked by a burning ammunition dump: Lord decided to risk it and drove through the flames as he put it 'like a Hollywood stunt actor' with the other two clinging to the running boards. Now they could see thousands of army lorries, and more troops milling aimlessly. Civilians were helping themselves to stores from the transport. They parked the car and put the keys put down a drain.

The three now scoured the Quayside for a likely looking vessel, and settled on a sampan. It was wedged hard against the beach and the tide was receding so it took a 'herculean' effort to shift it, but eventually they succeeded in casting off, despite being shot at. Having got this far however Lord's companions now had doubts as to their ability to handle the ship at sea, and they could also make out worrying looking Japanese observation balloons over the city. So they put back to the beach, where they were promptly misinformed that the fighting was continuing. They therefore rejoined a unit on beach defence, and had gone off to sleep that night before being awoken and told the truth of the matter. Lord now set off again, the others having lost stomach for the venture. He promptly fell in with another disparate bunch of eight stragglers from units as diverse as the Malay Volunteers and the Norfolk regiment.

This desperate crew managed to secure two small boats, some water, and a sandbag full of provisions. A few miles out Lord's boat came across a Chinese junk which had already been commandeered by another party, but they refused to let the men in the smaller boat board. Lord's party therefore clung on to the junk's dinghy and were pulled along by it for some distance before the dispute was dramatically resolved by a burst of machine gun fire from the shore which holed the small boat. At this Lord's little party were grudgingly allowed onto the junk. About a week later, with hands festering as a result of falling into barbed wire, and Malaria symptoms, he made it to Sumatra.

5

Changi Jail

The Japanese were almost as bewildered by their victory as the British public were by the loss of Singapore. They had estimated that the campaign could be concluded successfully in 100 days: but they had managed it in 70. Yet by the end their own reserves of materials and stamina had been close to exhaustion, and although it is dubious whether continued resistance would have done anything more than waste civilian lives, the Japanese were taken by surprise by the rapidity of the final fall. They were now left with a huge 'bag' of prisoners, a half wrecked town, and a sea of semi smashed naval and military equipment. Each side had lost about 10,000 men in action, but 130,000 British and Empire troops had been captured. Shortly after the fall the debris of Singapore was surveyed by Lieutenant Colonel Masataka Numaguchi of the Army Technical Headquarters, and Major Katsuji Akiyama of the Army Heavy Artillery School. Their report made interesting reading.

On the south coast of the Island they found a well developed defensive line with wire entanglements, pill boxes, log barriers, remote controlled mine fields, and anti submarine netting. No less than 52 artillery pieces had been mounted for permanent coast defence, the majority pointing south, a few east and west, and almost nothing to the north. Of all these weapons only three had survived demolition, or were modern enough not to be scrapped by their captors. One gun still had a huge 15 inch shell in its breech. Despite last-minute efforts, relatively little had covered the north of Singapore Island, except what had been put there by the army's Field Regiments and Anti Tank Regiments. Even so it was a myth that the big guns had played no part at all in the defence, some had been turned to bear, and several hundred rounds had been fired from 15 inch, 9.2 inch, and 6 inch guns. The two Japanese officers found that almost 400 smaller pieces had been taken. Most of these were damaged, but only a quarter of them completely beyond repair or 'cannibalisation' to make complete guns.

Of the 150 25 pounder field guns the majority were damaged, but they reckoned that half might yet be made to serve. Whilst many of the captured pieces were of obsolete types they found the 25 pounder a 'recent type' of 'great fire power', worthy of every attempt to try to restore and repair. For these guns they put forward two plans: either they should be returned to Japan to give to any forces which might have to meet the Soviets, or they should be reconditioned locally and used to defend the new conquests in South East Asia. Clearly the Japanese had grown to respect the 88th's armament.

The prisoners were more of a problem than the hardware. Indeed to the

Japanese way of thinking the whole issue was inexplicable; for according to the 'Senjikun' or combatant's code published by the Army Minister in January 1941 no Japanese soldier was to survive 'the dishonour of capture'. The instruction was given weight by the fact that some prisoners repatriated by Russia in 1939 had been given pistols and made to commit suicide on their return. Though the Japanese government had signed the Geneva convention, it had never ratified it, and at least some of the troops on the ground had never even heard of it. They were not therefore expecting to have to deal with prisoners: however the Japanese soon reduced the scale of the problem by recruiting a good number of the Indian troops into their own puppet 'Indian National Army', and releasing others 'on oath', but there was no such option for those of European extraction.

On 16 February 1942 the Japanese issued an order for the concentration of allied prisoners at Changi on the eastern extremity of Singapore Island. For the 88th this would mean a gruelling 14 mile march in the heat, with inadequate water, carrying equipment. The new prisoner compound was not one building, but a complex. The original 'Changi Jail' was a building designed for 600 inmates, constructed in 1936. Soon after the fall of Singapore this was occupied by European civilians, some of whom had left pathetic messages scratched into its walls. Nearby were a number of other buildings, many of which had been used by British and Empire forces before the war. These included Selarang, Roberts, Kitchener, and India Barracks, the Sime Road Camp, and various workshops, batteries, and stores. There was also tented accommodation in the so-called 'Java Lines' which were located north of India Barracks.

Initially, until the camp system was established, British senior officers would administer the complex under General Percival. For the first few weeks the Japanese were little in evidence. Although this arrangement may have had some advantages in that it created some sort of buffer between the captives and the captors it was not without its problems and its critics. For one thing it made the position of the British senior officers an invidious one, too much collaboration and they were likely to be seen as Quislings by their subordinates, too little and they would be the butt of Japanese hostility. It was also possible that the men would see them, rather than the Japanese, as the authors of their misfortunes. Major Denis Houghton of the 88th viewed the departure of the 'Top Brass' to Karenko Formosa, in August 1942 with some relief; for with them went at least some of the continual saluting.

Lance Bombardiers Haworth and Bettany of the 88th landed up in the old Changi jail after sometime in outlying barracks. Their particular 'cell' was not really a cell at all but a ward of the prison hospital which had been cleared to make a general dormitory. They thought that as a ward it was likely to have accommodated one to two dozen bedded patients. As the Japanese had it arranged there were no beds, but 120 men dossing down direct on the hard floors. One blanket apiece was issued, but they were so filthy that they preferred not to use them if it could be avoided. Even at Changi itself many men were not housed within the structure of the old prison, but in adjoining hutments. Some of these were constructed by the prisoners themselves, under the direction of Royal Engineers. The largest of the huts were not far short of 100 metres in length.

Although the early days at Changi were nothing like as terrible as what would follow, there were immediate indicators that this was no ordinary captivity. Contrary to the practice in Europe officers and men were not separated but kept together, almost until the end of the war. Very soon many men from the 88th were involved in work to clear up Singapore town, demolish dangerous buildings, bury the dead, clear drains. Later they would labour on the improvement of the Changi airfield. For these and other projects large groups of men were taken from Changi to smaller outlying work camps.

In March 1942 the bulk of the regiment spent a week under canvas on a detail at Farrer Park. In April about 400 of the 88th were taken to Towner Road camp where they were lodged in native type huts on swampy ground behind wire. Many worked on vehicles, breaking up those for which there was no further use. D'Aubuz and this party remained at Towner for about six months. Much later a smaller number of men from the 88th were also employed at the Adam Road camp, near which new defence works were being prepared.

In June 1942 the Japanese decided to erect a war memorial and Shinto temple on Singapore Island at Bukit Timah, close by the Ford motor factory. The organisation of the operations was described in the memoirs of Lieutenant Toshiyuki Nekemoto, a liaison officer for the Engineer Corps. He was allotted a mixed 'regiment' of 2,500 prisoners, 2,000 British and 500 Australian.

> We located our camps and the five PoW camps near the race track in Bukit Timah. People living in the area selected for the camp sites had to move out. The PoW camps had only one line of barbed wire around them with one entrance. We could only spare four Japanese soldiers to guard this entrance, not from the PoWs but from outsiders. Each PoW camp was controlled by its own PoW camp commander and its own military regulations. A selected number of PoWs worked every day except Sunday. Our company commander sent in to me the number of PoWs needed for the next day. I sent this order to each PoW camp. The PoWs started working at seven, rested two hours in the afternoon, then worked again from two until five. Every day, each PoW group was led by its own officer to march back and forth between the job site and camp. Two short Japanese soldiers followed behind them. Even in the marching the British were full of pride. They didn't want to be seen by the local people as losers. They marched very orderly with their proud officer leading with his short commanding rod in his hand ...

> Besides the PoWs we had about 200 local people working as labourers or stone masons on the construction of the stone stairs for the temple and the monument. Our regiment had four companies with a total of 1,500 men. One company worked on the monument with the Australian camp while another company

Victory Hill, Singapore, overlooking the causeway, showing the Japanese memorial as seen from the Alexander car park. By Desmond Bettany.

worked on the temple using two British camps. Two companies worked on the roads with the remaining two British camps so all of the PoW camps were directly under the control of our companies …

Appeal to the Japanese authorities brought to the captives two dubious 'privileges' which were apparently secured with the cooperation of the engineer Colonel Yasuji Tamura. The first of these was the organisation of some search parties who would seek out allied as well as Japanese dead for burial or cremation. The second was that the British would have permission to build a small memorial of their own. The contrast between the Japanese temple and the British monument was very striking: whilst the prisoners were allowed to construct for themselves a 15 foot high wooden cross the 'Shonan Jinjya' temple was a substantial edifice atop a flight of stone steps, the access road to which crossed a bright red painted ornamental wooden bridge. The name 'Shonan' meant 'shining south' and corresponded with the Japanese renaming of the whole Island 'Shonan-To'.

Work on the airfield commenced in May 1943 and continued for a total of about 18 months, and here Lieutenant Colonel D'Aubuz was active in the organisation of the work parties, attempting to minimise as far as was possible the hardships of his men. On this project technology would pose a ticklish question of honour, as Lieutenant Toshiyuki recalled:

> At Singapore airport, the construction work had been done by the British before the fall using much modern earth moving equipment. The 5th Division Headquarters told us to see this equipment and try to make use of it in our project. I had read about the usage of this heavy equipment in my school days and saw

it in operation during my travels in the United States. At that time Japan was still not acquainted with usage of this heavy equipment as well as the United States was. They still stuck to the use of manpower. So when we saw this heavy equipment we knew we had no operators, only British operators. I suggested the use of PoW operators but the headquarters did not allow this because, if we let the PoWs operate it, the Japanese military would lose their face ... The Headquarters were afraid of what local people would think when the loser could operate heavy equipment and the winner could not.

Nevertheless work went ahead, and though the labourers were pleased to be briefly out of the confines of Changi they had no intention of aiding the Japanese war effort any more than was strictly necessary to avoid trouble. Pretty quickly it was realised that many of the guards were inefficient at the job of parading and counting their charges, and that the more time was wasted in checking and counting the less labouring would be done. Counting was done by numbering the captives into groups of ten, and adding the leftovers to arrive at a final count. This could be sabotaged by a man covertly shuffling from one group to another, but it was a dangerous game since puzzlement and later infuriation could lead to violence.

Sabotage of actual work was more dangerous still, but it could be done, if only by picking the least efficient ways to carry out tasks. One ploy which Gunner Eric Bamber remembers being used involved the use of the large crabs which abounded by the shore near the construction. Towards the end of a shift numbers of these would be secreted in holes in the newly levelled ground: the next day they would be found to have emerged leaving pot holes in the surface which men would have to be detailed to fill thereby wasting time. Proximity to the sea also gave some opportunity to scavenge for edible marine life.

One of the least pleasant tasks associated with the airport was land reclamation along the shore. Like so many tasks this was carried out by pure muscle power rather than machine. First the trunks of coconut palms were felled and trimmed, then the hefty balks of timber were carried to the site. Here they were up ended, and a group of prisoners using a huge wooden pile driver banged them into the ground to hold together the new areas of infill. The Japanese were particularly keen that this work should be finished without delay, and were not inclined to let trifling matters like the incoming tide or depth of water interfere with the work. Their one concession was to put one prisoner up a pole to act as 'shark watcher' whilst his comrades toiled, sometimes waist deep in the sea. The watcher had a difficult job, since if he failed to notice the sharks an attack might result: if he erred on the side of caution and sounded the alert he had to hope that the shark would then manifest itself obviously. If the Japanese suspected there was no shark, or purposeful delay, the watcher would get a beating.

At Towner road the British prisoners were actually carried to work in Japanese transport, packed up to 70 in a single lorry, and here surreptitious attempts were made either to put vehicles out of action immediately, or to sabotage them in such a way as to shorten their working lives. Either way it was dangerous, and the trick was to make it look like natural failure, or distance oneself from the result. One other form of transport which became increasingly common in and around Changi were the so called 'Changi Chariots'. These varied slightly in size and design but were basically chassis of cars and lorries with all superfluous parts removed. When fully loaded they required teams of about 20 men to pull, and were used not only on work details but to carry the prisoners' own kit when they had to transfer from camp to camp. This happened several times within Singapore Island, perhaps the greatest upheaval coming in May 1944, when most of the regiment were moved within the confines of Changi Jail itself and the hospital was relocated to Kranji near the Naval base. This required enormous labour, 40 trailers a day being shifted for a month in order to construct new huts or re erect old huts under the supervision of the Royal Engineers.

Surprisingly Lieutenant Toshiyuki suggests that in the early days there was limited fraternisation between some of the guards and prisoners; Denis Houghton even acquired a group photograph of the British and Japanese liaison officers posing together. Yet if there was any common ground, or 'convenient' comradeship on the British side, the experience was fleeting at best, because very quickly basic problems were all too obvious. The root of many of these issues was not simply a question of individual ill treatment, but an institutionalised neglect which apparently refused to recognise that the men in captivity were human beings with a right to the essentials of life. Undoubtedly the 'Senjinkun' or Combatants Code, under the provisions of which 'honour' was more highly valued than humanity, was one of the causes of problems.

Yet there were also some who felt that the prisoners were there as an exemplar for the demonstration of Japanese superiority. As a report submitted by General Itagaki Seishiro to Tojo in Tokyo put it:

> We will use them as a material for an intellectual propaganda exercise aimed at stamping out the respect and admiration for Europeans and Americans still secretly harboured ... as well as to bring about recognition of the power of the Empire.

Brutality by the Japanese was a commonplace, but even where a guard may have had a sneaking sympathy for the prisoners the cultural gulf between the citizens of a Western democracy with a long colonial history and the people of the semi feudal hierarchy of Imperial Japan was huge.

Escape from Changi must have appeared remote if not impossible. There was no friendly country within a thousand miles of Singapore, water blocked most avenues of escape, and ships were hardly likely to be sailing to Allied ports. Whilst some men had a basic proficiency in French or German, very few spoke oriental languages. Tall Europeans stood some chance of passing themselves off as Frenchmen but there was almost no possibility of being

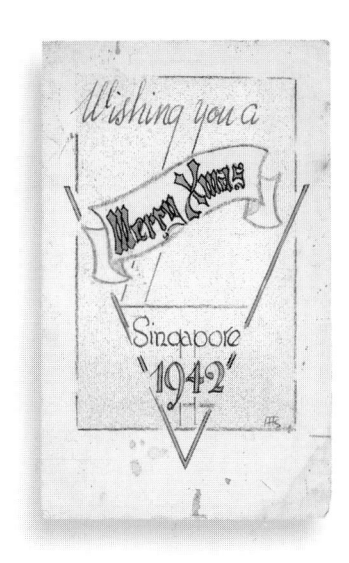

Above: Christmas card given by the other ranks of 464 Battery to Lt P. Lane, Singapore, 1942. Note the 'V' for Victory sign scarcely concealed in the design.

Above: Transport to work from Towner Road, 1942, as depicted by Desmond Bettany.

Above: The 'Changi Chariot', made from stripped-down vehicles and pulled by manpower.

Left: The conditions at Towner Road camp, 1942. Both by Desmond Bettany.

mistaken for a Malay or Thai. The Japanese were therefore not so paranoid about escape as their German counterparts, but even so those authorised to be outside the wire of the camps were strictly controlled, and detailed regulations were promulgated in March 1942.

The measures then enforced included arm bands bearing Japanese characters to identify orderlies and hospital patients, and a special flag for larger organised parties. Legitimate reasons for these larger parties to be allowed out included not only work details but gardening, firewood collecting, water carrying, burial, and sometimes, usually at mid day on Tuesday, bathing parties. At some of the camps in the Changi area the local British commanders demonstrated their small measure of autonomy by placing their own unarmed guards on the inside of the wire, which were checked and inspected by their own officers. Despite security and the apparent hopelessness of escape there were attempts. One of the most daring took place in May 1942 and involved two men who rowed a small boat about 200 miles before recapture.

These escape attempts were one reason that the Japanese commander Major General Shempei Fukuei had a document prepared and presented to all prisoners for signature which stated that 'I the undersigned hereby solemnly swear on my honour that I will not, under any circumstances, attempt to escape'. Since General Percival and other high ranking officers had now been deported to Formosa, the senior remaining British officer was Colonel E.B. Holmes of the Manchester Regiment. He pointed out that prisoners of war were not allowed to give their parole, and all ranks refused to sign. The Japanese reaction to this refusal came on 2 September 1942. Their plan was to cram many of the British and Australian prisoners together under close guard at Selarang Barracks until their intransigence was overcome. As one report put it:

> The conditions at Selarang were such as to cause grave alarm to the medical authorities. Seven barrack blocks in an area of ten acres were allowed for the accommodation of 17,322 prisoners of war. The barracks square had to be used for the digging of latrines and the burying of the dead. Water was extremely scarce, there being only one tap and one leaking point. On the first day no water was available for ablutions, and only minimum requirements for cooking. The medical authorities estimated that under these conditions dysentery and other infectious diseases would have caused, after three or four weeks, some 50% casualties, with a probable mortality of up to 20%. Attempts were made by Officers Commanding to induce the Japanese to allow signature of a certificate including the words 'under duress'. This was refused.

As if further incentive was needed, an example was made of those who had previously attempted escape. The same day the mass of prisoners was herded together, four men were taken to Selarang beach, and here, witnessed by British officers who had been assembled for the purpose, a firing squad was formed of four Indian Sikhs. The shooting was horribly bungled: none of the men died outright and had to be finished off with further shots whilst lying on the ground. One of the victims was dressed only in pyjamas.

With 17,000 men cheek by jowl in the confined space of Selarang the result can have been little better than the infamous 'Black Hole of Calcutta'. For three days the 'Selarang incident' was stalemate, but the Japanese upped the discomfort further by reducing the already slender water supply, and threatening to force the inmates of the Roberts hospital inside the enclosure. With the sick rate rising there was no alternative to capitulate and sign the hated document. Colonel Holmes considered it his duty to order the men to sign to save their lives, and accepted that any repercussions that would follow were equally his responsibility. The prisoners were then moved back to their original accommodation.

Despite the signing of the document it was widely thought that Selarang had been something of a moral victory; and that in any case a statement given under such severe duress could not be binding. The whole exercise had an element of farce and futility about it, and a number of men underlined this very succinctly by signing the declaration forms with a false name. A number of the Australians had the same idea with the result that 'Ned Kelly' made many promises not to escape. The names were never checked, and the statements were never put to any meaningful purpose.

The 'Asiatic Diet'

Lack of food, and even more importantly lack of a diet which included all the necessary vitamins and minerals soon became a serious problem. Colonel Holmes recorded 45 deaths in Changi in August 1942; and although the majority of these were from dysentery, the incidence of beriberi and other diet related conditions was rising. The Japanese authorities appeared to regard feeding their captives as a favour rather than a necessity, and even when rations were regular they were not calculated to keep men fit for heavy labour. The standard Changi fare was supposed to be 400 grams (or about 12 oz) of rice per day, but has been described more precisely by more than one survivor of the regiment as 'minute quantities' of 'maggoty or weeviled rice', relieved only by a 'very little vegetable and leaves'.

A surviving weekly menu for January 1944 gives some idea of the paucity and boredom of the Changi diet, and the ingenuity of the descriptions applied to it. Breakfast then consisted of a pint of 'pap', one teaspoon of sugar, and a pint of tea, which on the face of it was not too bad, until one considered that 'pap' was rice porridge and that the tea had no milk. Afternoon 'Tiffin' as it was quaintly known was a pint of 'hash' with a little palm oil and more plain tea. The 'hash' was of course more rice but supposedly had a little fish and vegetable added. Wednesdays and Sundays were relieved by a tiny rissole and a 'green water' soup. 'Dinner' was the main meal of the day and again was usually a little more rice disguised in some other fashion, tea, and perhaps 'stew'. The stew was the only other dish which would appear with any frequency.

This was a mish mash of vegetables depending on what was available, and might include various green leaves, sweet potatoes or roots. A form of vegetable pasty was also not unknown. Wednesdays and Sundays were again the gourmet days as then there might be a little fruit, presented perhaps as 'Banana cup', 'Changi Slab', or even 'Sweet Yam Jam Effort'.

By early 1945 things were even more difficult. 'Scales of issue' drawn up by British clerks on 10 February showed three possible levels of nourishment for those on 'heavy duty', 'light duty', and 'no duty' respectively. Those on heavy duty were supposed to be entitled to 495 grams of rice, 50 grams of meat (or fish); those on light duties 330 grams of rice and 40 grams of meat; and those without duties 250 grams of rice and 40 grams of meat. All were to have 300 grams of vegetables, plus minute quantities of tea, salt, pepper and oil. Wood for fuel was strictly limited to 600 grams per man per day. Whilst survival on this meagre fare appeared quite possible it was noted that 'with the exception of rice all rations are subject to discrepancies as a result of loss in weight in delivery by the Imperial Japanese Army'. Just a month later on 10 March 1945 rice issues were further reduced so that even on heavy duty a man received just 270 grams, those on light duty 225 grams, and those without duties a tiny 180 grams. A marginal increase in the amount of vegetable by no means offset this starvation diet.

Bread was pretty well absent, and Toshiyuki has it that early on he asked his Headquarters Supply Office for wheat flour, but none was forthcoming. He therefore instigated bread making from rice flour; an achievement of which he was very proud, but the taste of which was unlikely to have been pleasant. Driver Tucker Smith of Lancaster who ran 464 Battery bakery worked on a similar project, perhaps with greater success since he was able, at least early on, to mix rice flour with a little wheat flour, and had managed to produce home made yeast. If anything nutrition at the Towner Road camp was worse than at Changi itself, and it was fortunate that some Red Cross parcels were actually distributed here at an early date. Also extremely useful were the efforts of Gunner Harry Walker who acted as head cook, and in the words of one report 'proved as efficient with a ladle as he had been with a Tommy gun'. Anyway that was the official story; his mates believed that his success was due to his skill and slight of hand in rifling Japanese dustbins. On one occasion he came up with some chicken legs which had been discarded and succeeded in cleaning them up enough to create a meal which several of the men considered the best they had had in captivity. One of the main specialities of Towner was fish, since when the camp flooded small fish and eels were sometimes washed up the drains.

The cooking and serving of food was not helped by the work routines that the Japanese forced on the prisoners. Sometimes they worked literally by the availability of light, getting up before dawn and marching to arrive on site at first light. On other occasions, particularly when there was a brilliant full moon, prisoners would work late into the night. Either way it was usual for hundreds of hungry men to return to their camp simultaneously and the cooks had to be ready. Very often queues would form, not minutes long, but sometimes hours, a winding snake of hundreds of yards. The 'canteen' system with its regulated scales of prices for 'extras' did help, but very often the comprehensive price list belied the fact that most of the things were not available.

By fair means or foul the prisoners efforts to help themselves certainly proved the most effective Major Denis Houghton remembered that gardening became something of an obsession, as a source, albeit a slender one, of fresh food. The projects started small, and perhaps the most modest of all was the sprouting of bean seeds in office drawers, but by the end of the war the British prisoners of Changi had over 100 acres of land under cultivation, and up to 90 tons of produce were being farmed monthly, which as one captive put it, 'literally saved our lives'.

Captain E.C. Dickson found himself looking after gardens in 'Chinese Valley' under the instruction of some experienced Dutch personnel. The crops included sweet potatoes, soya beans and lentils, and the difficulties of cultivation were partly mitigated by the relative lack of seasons in this latitude. Peanuts were good nutritionally, and seemed productive for the efforts expended. Pineapples were a popular thing to produce, but especially vulnerable to theft. Perhaps the oddest fruit grown was the loofah, a relative of the gourd, tough when old and dried, but perfectly edible when young and fresh.

Weird but apparently nourishing recipes abounded, including such delicacies as coconut rock cake, banana skin pie, rice roly poly, and wheat fritters. Eventually the prisoners even kept some livestock. Captain Dickson was put in charge of the chickens in October 1944, but this was a less successful venture than the fruit and vegetables. Unfortunately his arrival amongst the poultry was just before an outbreak of illness amongst the animals, which was soon Christened the 'poultry black death'.

The prisoner's view of the food situation was not improved by the fact that it was soon realised that parcels were soon being sent for their use, but were not being handed over. One rumour which circulated was that some of the cigarettes in the packages bore a 'V' for Victory symbol, and that this had given the Japanese a feeble excuse to withhold them.

As time went on the food situation generally worsened. This is perhaps best illustrated by the prices charged at the Changi canteen as the war progressed. In 1941, before the Japanese took over, sugar could be had for 5 cents a pound, as could peanuts; coconuts were a paltry 2 cents apiece, whilst a cheroot cost just a single cent. By 1944 sugar had reached $11, peanuts $5.50, whilst a coconut was $2.50 and a cheroot was 25 cents. By early 1945 there were few who could afford anything very much, even when it was available. The sugar was now $40, or an 800 times increase on the original price; peanuts were not quite so valuable at $16, but nevertheless had attained the status of a form of currency in their own right. Coconuts were perhaps the most affordable at $4, whilst a cheroot changed hands at $1.40. Oil and beans were purchased with the 'camp messing fund' to which all contributed according to their rank, but it still did not add up to sufficient calories to maintain the human frame, and games requiring physical effort gradually ceased with the need to preserve energy.

Men's weight began to plummet, and by late in the war losses of as much as 10 lb per month were being recorded. As starvation bit even harder prices for the few available extras soared to their final peak. At the end of the war sugar was $65; a pineapple fetched $10; and a single biscuit $1. Clothing and domestic items were almost as hard to come by and were similarly expensive, and for those who had anything to trade could be useful for barter, despite Japanese injunctions against parting with kit. A decent pair of shorts could count for as much as $250; a toothbrush $50; and even a packet of razor blades $5. Perhaps the most audacious commercial venture was the manufacture of a batch of 'medicine' made of chalk, some of which was successfully sold to the more gullible of the guards.

The men's well being, and ultimate survival, was not only linked to the availability of canteen extras, but to their ability to pay for them. In theory prisoners were paid from the latter part of 1942, but the money came via the Japanese, and bore little relation to the prevailing prices. Other ranks were virtually penniless. Even the officers, who were entitled to sums which sounded reasonable, had next to nothing. The pay book of Lieutenant P.S. Lane provides a concrete example of how things worked in practice.

Lane's pay was $85 per month throughout his captivity. Initially a full $60 was deducted by the Japanese for board and lodging: a concept which would have been laughable were it not so tragic. From the remainder further sums were taken by the British administrators. In October 1942 there was a $2 contribution to the 'camp messing fund' of the other ranks, leaving Lane $23. In November he had only $17 because additional sums were given to help support the hospital. Even so at this time it was enough to provide a little extra food. From September 1943 the Japanese reduced the amount taken from his pay, but more was given to the 'camp messing fund' with the result that his disposable income remained about the same. Yet there was now less to buy, and prices had risen sharply. By 1945, when Lane was regularly receiving $24 a month, his pay could be completely spent on two or three pieces of fruit: if they were available.

One of the main missions of the British senior officers at Changi became to plead, argue, or demand supplies of food for their men. They would have to offer concessions, dictate, or cringe, to their captors as occasion demanded, yet at the same time attempt to maintain the morale and discipline of the men under their command. It was no easy task, but it had to be done for survival. The results of these ongoing negotiations were typed up in the form of 'Bulletins'. Bulletin number 12, of 22 November 1944 for example contained both good news and bad. Sufficient materials had been supplied for the making of home made soap within the camp, and it also appeared that the British representatives had won the issue of some soya beans. Another success was that the military prisoners were allowed to pass a little extra of their 'savings' to the civilian internees, and also to send toys that they had made in camp as Christmas gifts. On the other hand prices in the camp canteen were soaring, and supplies of paper for conversion to toilet paper were cut off.

A vital lifeline in the last year of the war at Changi would be the few Red Cross parcels which did actually get through. Some from America arrived in February 1944; and 8577 men shared 1360 boxes between them. Usually seven men shared a parcel, and got a few ounces of meat, a packet of cigarettes, a little soup powder, and perhaps most importantly some vitamin C tablets. A smaller number of parcels arrived from Canada just before Easter 1945, and were distributed on Easter Sunday. There were so few that each parcel had to do 22 men. This meant that each person got less than an ounce of jam and butter, one biscuit, a spoon of sugar, half an ounce of pressed meat, and a share in a bar of soap. A few more arrived in April and May, but it was observed that some were spirited away by the Japanese. The May issue was larger but it was obvious that it had been hanging around for some time as some provisions had deteriorated.

Many prisoners had been involved in the initial unloading details outside the camps and one member of the 88th made a secret count of the numbers of lorries and parcels delivered, and kept a note of the places they had come from. He estimated that the total number of individual parcels over a given period was 43,000, and stated that they had come from not only Canada and the US, but South Africa. In addition to the things the Japanese actually passed on he noted medical supplies, boots, razors, socks and shirts. Obviously huge quantities of supplies intended for the prisoners were either being used by the Japanese, or stored elsewhere and not handed out. The prisoners' indignation was supposed to be forestalled by a parade held on 24 May 1945 at which they were informed that the 'issue of Red Cross Supplies is an act of grace by the Imperial Japanese Army', and was all the more remarkable since the *Awa Maru* which was the supply ship which had carried them into Singapore, was sunk on its way out.

Although Red Cross parcels did make rare appearances the contact of those inside Changi with the Red Cross itself was near zero. The organisation made many applications to visit but most were turned down. One excuse was that much of Japan's 'Co prosperity sphere' was now a war zone and that such inspections could not take place in a war zone. On the occasions on which Red Cross representatives were allowed into camps, the Japanese chose which they were let into. Even here the visits were strictly stage managed, visitors could not turn up unannounced, they could not walk round unescorted, and prisoners could not talk freely to them. In some instances the Japanese made sure that on the day of the visit prisoners received new clothes, or that more food was on show than the prisoners were usually allowed. There were even instances where Red Cross personnel were themselves arrested on trumped up charges of being enemy agents.

Under such circumstances many men became accomplished thieves and liars in their battle for daily survival. Where such deeds were perpetrated against comrades feuds and contempt were the unfortunate result, but in instances where the Japanese were fooled without general retaliation individuals could become minor heroes. This was perhaps deservedly so, since pilfered goods entering the camp economy by their hands would do something to aid the general nutrition of the prisoners, as well as maintain their spirits. Such men risked dire punishment, up to and including the possibility of death. Food naturally became the major target of the thieves, black marketeers, and those who attempted to bribe guards. On certain occasions there were men who managed to get out of camp, not to try to escape, but to trade food from the locals and then smuggle themselves back in. Gunner Eric Bamber's chance came on a work detail, when the lure of extra tinned food became irresistible. Having stolen a can however there was nowhere to secrete it, and he landed up having to go on parade with a tinned steak and kidney pudding balanced on his head under his forage cap.

The most extraordinary and desperate food theft of all was mounted by Lance Bombardier Geoffrey Haworth and three colleagues. The plot commenced with careful study of the guard system which discovered who was on duty, and when. The conspirators noted that the guards walking between the inner and outer wire were 'Indian National Army', former British Indian Army troops who had turned coat and were fighting for the Japanese. It was apparent that at one specific time these troops received a rice ration, and that for a while at least they walked the perimeter with their rice bag hanging at the waist. This was too tempting a prospect, offering to strike back against those who had betrayed them, at the same time as filling their empty stomachs.

The four therefore picked a dark and wet night, at a spot where the guard would be likely to avoid overhanging bamboo and brush against the inner wire. Here they laid their ambush, one man reaching through the wire low down to grab at the guard's legs, another smashing down with an iron bar. The plan worked like clockwork, the unfortunate being knocked senseless and dragged inside the wire. Having ascertained that the man was dead, his rice was deftly removed and the body, together with the guard's rifle disappeared down the camp latrines. The Japanese launched a major search, more concerned about the weapon than the Indian soldier, but nothing was ever found.

Various efforts thus eased the food situation a little, but nevertheless disease and malnutrition began to bite as the prisoner's bodily reserves of vitamins and minerals ebbed away. According to notes made by the 88th's Medical Officer M.C. 'Doc' Dickson the malaises caused by vitamin deficiency manifested in a distinctive pattern, with a particular peak being reached by the summer of 1942. Some were slight with minor skin irritations and pains in the feet, but in some instances full blown beriberi or spastic paralysis was the result.

These circumstances led to the keeping of a regimental 'Strength Chart' on which every man was entered as a statistic according to his fitness, graded from 'A' to 'Z'. On the one undated chart which survives only a single officer and 17 men were accounted as at the peak of health.

As real medicines and food became scarcer and scarcer the medical personnel had to become every bit as inventive as the camp artists and handymen. One of their attempts to deal with vitamin deficiency was the prescription of 'grass extract'. This glutinous green liquid was made by crushing coarse grass in an oil drum with chains, and contained, so it was hoped, some of the nutriments the men so badly lacked. Another possible potion was 'rice polishings' the leftovers of rice husks, liberally mixed with weevils, which hugely unappetising though it appeared, did contain valuable vitamins. According to 'Doc' Dickson the administration of rice polishings was something of an art. Ideally good quality polishings were eaten raw so as to preserve the best vitamin content, but if they were of poor quality they could be boiled for five minutes, then allowed to stand all day and stirred from time to time, and then boiled again. Marmite was more effective, but the tiny quantities available were hoarded as long as possible.

Derris root, which grew particularly well in the Changi area, was found to be a useful treatment for scabies. Its application was, if anything, less pleasant than the grass extract or rice polishings. First the patient was thoroughly scrubbed with a brush and soap as available, often until bleeding, then the derris root was applied with a softer brush The ointment stayed on all day, and the treatment had to be repeated three or four times. Somewhat more acceptable was the making and drinking of soya milk, which was valuable nutritionally. One kilogram of soya beans was required for every five litres of milk. First the beans were soaked for 24 hours together with some sodium carbonate. Then they were cleaned, disinfected, and minced finely. Now the water was beaten together with the beans, boiled and sieved.

One of the worst medical problems was the lack of anaesthetics. On some occasions the medical personnel had to resort to virtually mediaeval techniques, hacking off limbs with hand saws whilst the patients remained fully conscious. Even out of this horror the doctors were able to bring something positive, for it prompted them to begin experiments with the use of hypnotism during operations. Sixty years later there are reports of the same thing being tried on patients who have no tolerance for drugs and gases with some instances of success.

Despite such remarkable efforts the total number of men from the regiment who ended their days in Changi Jail itself, rather than on work parties 'up country', is believed to be at least ten. In most cases the causes were linked to poor diet and lack of medical equipment. One who seems to have died indirectly as a result of negligence by the Japanese was Gunner G.E. Morris. Morris had been acting as a stage electrician on a production when called away by guards anxious to have an electrical fault repaired. Hurrying he slipped and fell onto some barbed wire. Though only slightly hurt the accident led to septicaemia.

'Binta' and the Outside World

Whilst the Japanese seemed to have little regard for their captives they demanded a great show of respect. Bowing and greeting was obligatory, and likely to be enforced with violence. Minor infringements of the code of servility were likely to be met with a thorough 'slapping', which although often served open handed, was usually delivered with tremendous force. A particular affectionado of this behaviour was a guard known to the 88th as 'Parrot Face'; one of whose victims was Captain Swainson. Lance Bombardier Haworth remembers being 'slapped' pretty harshly at the beginning and end of a particular work detail by the same guard every day for weeks. He never could work out why he had been picked on, but a fortuitous attack of dysentery took him out of harms way. Even in this unpleasantness the prisoners managed to find some twisted humour as on one occasion when a diminutive Japanese had to find a box to stand on before 'slapping' a particularly tall prisoner.

In the eyes of the Japanese, and the downtrodden Korean conscripts, 'slapping' was not accounted an abuse at all. The Emperor's men were regularly hit themselves during training, and in any case this 'slapping' or 'binta' as they called it was a 'light' discipline. Dealing with minor infringements in this way saved the bother of official reports, or involving the 'Kempeitei' or Japanese Military Police. Some therefore even reasoned, with twisted logic, that they were doing the prisoners a favour. More serious infringements or particularly sadistic guards would sometimes result in more dangerous beatings with sticks and pick axe helves. In such circumstances it was best to be a 'grey man', to conform quietly, and to do nothing which would mean being singled out.

Whilst overt and enforced politeness was in some form intelligible, other Japanese attitudes were difficult to fathom. Moustaches for example were a vexed question: Sergeant Rawlinson had it that a good growth of facial hair gained more respect; others have said that it could be a cause of envy or curiosity. Whether a man had children or not could also have some influence on his dealings with his captors; more children meant greater virility, and responsibility, and was therefore worthy of respect. One particularly puzzling punctilio from the prisoners point of view was the Japanese sensitivity to a man's height. On work details the prisoners first job was often to build a small mound, and on this the guard would take his position, his head safely raised above the 'inferior' prisoners. Some of the guards were Koreans rather than Japanese; but again opinion varied, some remember the Koreans as preferable, yet a good number were convicted for war crimes, and several were hanged as a result.

The 'cushy' job, so called after the Hindustani 'khush' meaning 'pleasant', had much allure in Changi as a way of improving one's position. Two of the best work details from this point of view were with the cookhouse and the trucks that ran outside the camp for collecting food and materials. Neither form of labour was quite as hard as the airport or the town, and both offered some opportunity for illicit trade, though this in theory was frowned upon by the British command. Gunner Bamber was one who struck lucky, partly through a gift for conversation, partly through a putative skill as a chef. As a diminutive figure working with a group of very tall Australians on a demolition site he attracted the attention of a Japanese Major, who took him on as a cook. His mentor showed civility, and an amazing knowledge of English which he spoke faultlessly, and he enjoyed describing to the gunner his travels in England. Bamber for his part found conversation and cookery, with a chance for better food including a little powdered milk and fruit, far more agreeable than beatings and hard labour. Even this apparently decent position had its nasty and unpredictable side: one day the Major threatened to decapitate a local for singing near his window, but moments later was giving his daughter a valuable can of condensed milk. This unpredictability was remarked upon by several men in the regiment: there were a few guards who would trade food, one or two who were noted as being passive or non vindictive, but even these could suddenly swing into a rage.

Clothing and footwear, regarded pretty much as necessities in European prison camps, featured nowhere in Japanese planning. Toshiyuki at least realised that lack of boots was going to limit the mens effectiveness as manual labourers, but since the supply department again had no intention of providing anything, he was reduced to raiding the stockpiles of discarded rubber tyres. These had to be painstakingly cut to shape and the results used for soling boots. To the lack of shirts and shorts there could be no real answer, and slowly but surely the prisoners began to wear less clothing. Toshiyuki rationalised that the sunshine would do them good.

As with food and clothes, so with washing and soap. The medical staff encouraged the making of brushes from coconut husk, and toothbrushes could be constructed with bamboo handles, but with poor diet and little chance to wash skin diseases would soon be widespread. Perhaps the least bearable of these problems was scrotal

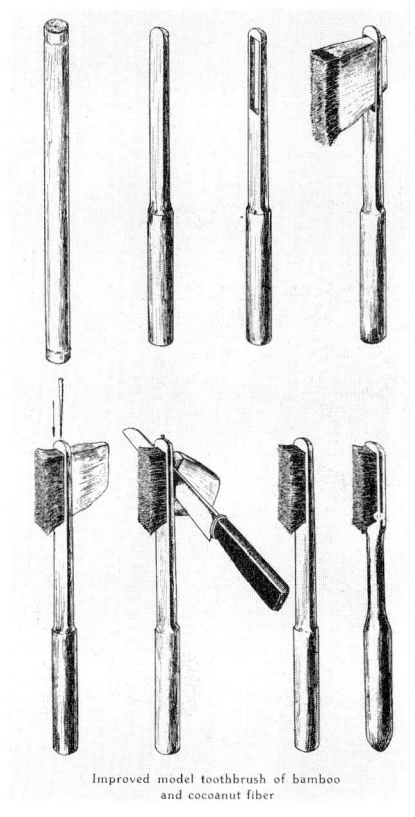

Improved model toothbrush of bamboo and cocoanut fiber

How to make a cocoanut fibre toothbrush, from the notes of 'Doc' Dickson RAMC.

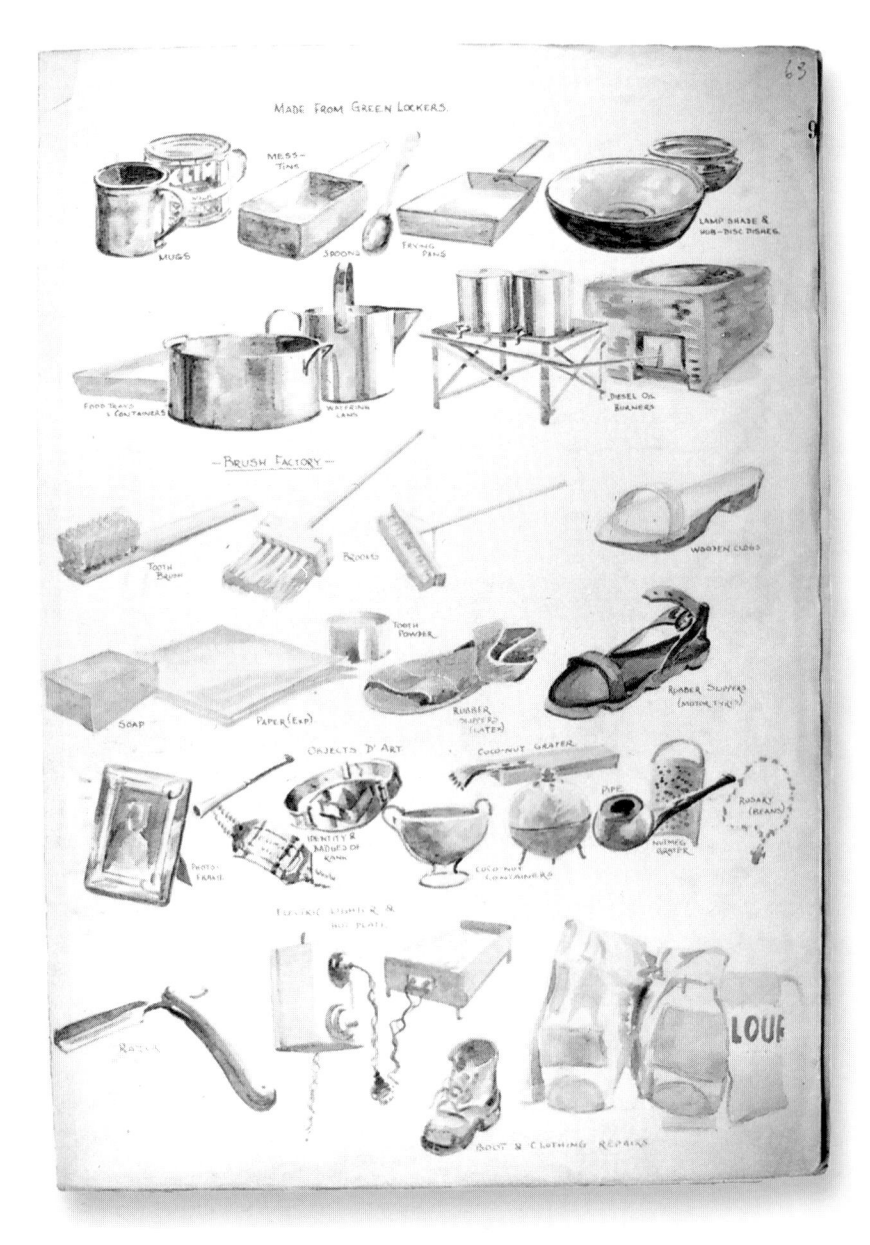

A selection of the many items manufactured by the prisoners at Changi: cooking vessels from old lockers; brushes from wood and fibre; sandals from old tyres; clothing repairs from old sacks. Desmond Bettany

dermatitis, which the prisoners irreverently nicknamed 'Changi Balls', or 'Shonan Scrotum'. The real answer to this would have been a balanced diet with plenty of fresh food, but with so little available palliatives were all that came to hand. One thing which may have helped marginally was the adoption of the 'Jap Happy', or loin cloth, which was apparently based on the traditional Japanese underwear or 'Fundoshi'. A surviving example worn by one of the

88th is of dark cotton cloth about 7 inches wide and 20 inches long with tapes sewn to one end; the tapes were tied around the waist and then the loose end was pulled up between the legs and under the tapes, in a manner which would have not seemed out of place in ancient Egypt. Early on there were still supplies of iodine available; which may also have helped, but it also stung. It is interesting that the term 'Jap Happy' was also applied to anything, or anyone, pro Japanese, and could also be used in the plural to denote Japanese rubber boots.

The deprivations of Changi were not merely physical: they could, and did, affect a man's moral and spiritual well being.

As one popular ditty put it,

> Leaves from the hedgerows in our grub,
> Never see a woman, never see a pub ...
> Its hard to be gay and its hard to be merry
> When you're sitting on the dub and you've got beri beri.

Mail from the outside world therefore became a valuable commodity, and one of the few rays of hope. Letters from the outside were scarce or non existent for long periods. Captain E.C. Dickson recorded that the first time he heard from home the letter from his parents was about a year old. It was therefore a double edged communication; he knew that they were alive and well a year previously, but with Britain subject to air raids this was no guarantee that they were still in good health. Major Denis Houghton actually received a letter from the octogenarian Honorary Colonel 'Paddy' Trimble whilst in captivity. This was uplifting not only for its message but also for the fact that the Japanese had no idea who the letter writer was.

Some prisoners were able to send or receive virtually nothing over a period of four years, but something which many did get to send at least once was the standard Imperial Japanese Army Field postcard. According to one account the first opportunity to send these came in June 1942. One version of the card announced in standardised text that the man was a prisoner; another acknowledged receipt of post or notified of illness. In theory these cards could be completed in only one way, crossing out irrelevant information, and leaving the relevant, and they were censored both by the British and the Japanese. Some men however found a way to make them say more than they were intended, often by crossing out things which were not supposed to be crossed out. Gunner Richard Ainscough of Deepdale, Preston, for example, sent three such cards and altered his last, in January 1944, to make it apparent that he was working in Thailand, without pay, was in good health, but had not received any letters. It arrived safely without comment. Major Houghton managed to get the message through to his parents on a card that he and three other officers were alive and well.

Postcards arriving in Britain were rare enough to be newsworthy, and the contents of several were published in the local papers so that relatives who had not been so lucky could also enjoy them. The *Lancashire Daily Post* also printed translations of the Japanese symbols and post marks which appeared on Prisoner of War Cards allowing the recipients to see where exactly they had come from. Something of the paucity of information is brought home by the fact that by August 1942 only 32,000 postcards had arrived in the United Kingdom from Far East prisoners, though 27,000 were declared destroyed in an air accident. It would appear therefore that over the first six months of captivity prisoners had averaged two communications each, although only about half got through.

The greatest success in obtaining messages and parcels from the outside was undoubtedly achieved by the Americans, for whom some packages were arriving in mid 1943. Some of these were viewed with utter incredulity by the British prisoners, for when opened were found to contain 'real luxuries', as for example polo shirts, mirrors, razor blades, flannels, cheese, vitamin tablets and ovaltine. Understandably these raised a certain envy, and left the British puzzled as to why they had got so little. One possible explanation appeared to be that information on the whereabouts of prisoners might be better in the US. Post marks and addresses on the little that did get through were therefore scrutinised over and over again, but to little avail since what had arrived included mainly messages with correct addresses, even to parties that had gone outside the camp.

It was all dreadfully frustrating, especially since prisoners were often aware that their relatives would have been without news of them for months. Bizarrely the latter part of 1944 saw a minor avalanche of mail arrive at Changi. According to one account this sudden improvement saw 95 bags of mail appear in July, 69 bags in late October, and 14 in mid November.

Though the prisoners were pretty well isolated from the world, their friends and relatives at home in Lancashire had certainly not forgotten them, and went to great lengths to do all they could to alleviate the situation. One of the main efforts was a 'Prisoner of War Welfare Committee' which raised funds in order to send food and comforts out to the Far East. Pitifully little was ever allowed through, but this did not stop those at home from trying. The results of the committees efforts were published frequently in the *Lancashire Daily Post*, and make fascinating reading. Colonel Trimble and other dignitaries, as might be expected, were regular contributors, but funds also came from many and unexpected sources. In June 1943 for example the local ARP wardens raised £11; the County Office Kitchen Staff came up with £1; Preston Steam Laundry collected £10; and St Andrews Infant School managed 10s. The 'Friday Night Whist Club' spared £1 1s., but all was dwarfed by the efforts of Mrs E. Wilkinson's Whist Drive which raised the then very substantial sum of £44 whilst providing entertainment for the benefactors.

In January 1944 there was a particularly successful month when the Guildhall raised £67, and the Knights of St Columba concert brought in £84 6s. 8d. Local business also did its share with collections raising various sums at Horrocks, E. Fisher Ltd., John Crook and Sons, and British Insulated Cable. There were numerous raffles, more school donations, and the results of Mrs Mercer's Christmas Draw 'for a Golliwog' were now finally totalled at £2 12s. 6d.

Donations listed that March included sums from the Firewatchers; the Fishwick Ramblers; the Girl Guides; English Electric; the Royal Army Pay Corps, and the 'vault rats' who drank at the Cemetery Hotel. Taken together the efforts of local people were considerable, and ran at hundreds of pounds per month for Preston alone: had the Japanese allowed all this effort to be translated into food and clothes for prisoners disease and starvation could largely have been avoided.

Perhaps the best morale raiser for the prisoners, though the most dangerous from the point of view of discovery, were hidden radios. Captain E. C. Dickson knew of at least two receivers, both ingeniously hidden. The first was in the bottom of a standard British army water bottle, and the only access to it was through two tiny holes in the base. The top of the bottle was given a false bottom, and as additional camouflage was still capable of holding a little water. The other set was equally well disguised in the head of a broom. Captain Bradley recalled that another set was concealed inside a wooden beam, and was operated by pushing a screwdriver into a tiny knot hole. Even this inconspicuous opening was thought risky and so the diameter of the hole was made smaller still to resemble a worm hole. Obviously it was not possible for a group of men to sit round listening to the radios and so a clandestine method of spreading the news was developed. One man was deputised to take the risk of actually listening in and later representatives from other parts of the camp would come and visit the listener, and he would pass on the news. Next the delegates would return to their own sections and repeat what they had heard to the remainder. It was a good system, but had some of the flaws of a game of Chinese whispers: if any of the couriers had bad memories the report would come out garbled, and corrections might have to wait until a later bulletin.

Religion, Art and Entertainment

Religion underwent something of a revival amongst the men in captivity. Many had been committed and practising Christians prior to their capture, but imprisonment gave worship a new edge, not only because of the danger of imminent death but because religion was at least tolerated by the captors, and could become a symbol of the prisoner's identity and spirit. One church in Changi frequented by men of the regiment was housed in a small former Mosque building, previously used by Indian troops and converted for Christian services. Now known as the 'Chapel of St George' the structure was provided with converted domestic furniture, and included a pulpit and altar. On the altar, stood the cross made out of an old brass 4.5 inch howitzer shell case. This was rescued by one of the chaplains at the end of the war, and would eventually be returned to Changi fifty years later. The 'Chapel of St George' was in fact just one of several places of worship at Changi. One plan showed a total of five religious establishments, of which, according to former inmates, two were for church of England use, two for Catholics, and one a synagogue.

Lance Bombardier Bettany's route to continued sanity was through his art, painting and drawing on scraps of paper, one source of which was old army forms from the now redundant British administration of Singapore garrison. Bettany had been an amateur artist for some years, and had recorded in realistic pen and ink sketches the progress of the regiment from its embarkation at Gourock in 1941. After capture, and contact with the Japanese, his work would become more escapist, with humorous cartoons and caricatures predominating. Paint was a more difficult commodity to find than the paper, and here his pre war training as a chemist would come in useful. His cell mate Lance Bombardier Geoffrey Haworth would later recall how, at every opportunity, Bettany would scour nearby plantations for natural things from which he could extract pigment. Green banana leaves for example produced an unexpectedly good blue dye; tree bark and roots provided other hues. Black came from lamp black and soot. Even so not all experiments were successful: some of the pigments produced were amazingly fugitive, others required much boiling to achieve the necessary hue. Brushes were also a problem, one which Bettany solved with characteristic inventiveness by the use of bamboo sticks with human hair pulled tightly down the middle.

Even this activity was not without serious risk: Bettany lent an early sketch book to a friend and it was discovered and taken by none other than Lieutenant General Saito Masatoshi, the commander of the Japanese garrison of Singapore who had arrived to replace General Fukuei in July 1944. Bettany was hauled before the Japanese Commandant and the British senior officer to explain himself, and never saw the book of drawings again. Humourless though his reception was he lived to tell the tale, but decided that as near total secrecy

Roman Catholic church at Changi, 1943, by Desmond Bettany.

as possible should now be employed. A quiet snook was cocked at the incident by the production of a cartoon depicting the confiscation.

Another secret subversion and support to morale devised by amateur artists of the 88th, and apparently employed quite widely, was the production of greetings cards with hidden messages. One such, given to Lieutenant P. Lane by 'the other ranks' of 464 battery, bore the inscription 'Wishing You a Merry Christmas – Singapore, 1942', yet careful examination reveals that the design is basically one large red 'V' for victory.

It is interesting to relate that Bettany was only one of several prisoners whose clandestine drawings and paintings have survived the war, and a number of regiments had their own 'resident artists'. Amongst these must be counted Leo Rawlings of Blackpool's 137th Field Regiment (author of 'And The Dawn Came Up Like Thunder'); Harry Kingsley, of 2nd Battalion the Loyal North Lancashire Regiment, and the somewhat better known Bernard Meninsky, George Old, and Ronald Searle.

All had their own methods of keeping their work quiet: Meninsky for example remembers working in the camp hospitals, often at night, as the Japanese tended to keep away through fear of disease. For use on the move a special haversack was made for him by a saddler with a false back which kept his drawings flat and dry. Some of Searle's work at least was done relatively openly when in Changi; amongst his sketches were drawings prepared for planned productions of the concert party, and of the improvised band which included Gunner Bamber of the 88th. Bombardier Stanley Warren was perhaps the most public, and probably the best known of the Changi artists, as his major works were large murals, on biblical themes, which decorated Barrack Block 151.

Some recreations were less artistic, yet helped equally to maintain a sense of purpose and kept men from dwelling on their predicament. Lieutenant Colonel D'Aubuz gave a series of lectures on the causes of the war; other officers and men gave talks on their own special subjects or hobbies. 18th Division as a whole had pretensions to running its own 'University' with experts 'lecturing', and for this purpose utilised many books which had been salvaged from Singapore's Raffles College.

Bombardier N.P. Embley of Preston specialised in bridge, and apart from ordinary 'rubbers' and competitions, organised advanced classes. Some of these activities required light at night, and so oil was stolen in order to make lamps. Later, in what was perhaps the ultimate version of naughty schoolboys reading under the blankets, Sergeant R. Outhwaite organised electric lighting. In order to do this signal wire had to be stolen from the Japanese and some rather alarming improvised fittings had to be produced.

Books were an important form of mental escape, but as might be expected were never plentiful, and some less interesting titles were sacrificed for their paper content: copies of the bible and Shakespeare for example smoked particularly well, due to their thin pages. Lance Bombardier Haworth, who also experimented with papaya leaves, had it that American *Life* magazine was the best smoke; its pages could be split laterally to the requisite thinness and the ink seemed to add little detrimental flavour to tobacco. Even so the books that were there were read and re-read. Camp libraries were formed from pooling privately owned volumes, and occasionally a few would find their way in, either by the scavenging efforts of work parties, or from the Red Cross. Amongst the inmates there were also men who knew bookbinding and laboured to preserve the valuable texts. What books there were had in theory to receive the approval of Japanese censorship, and be marked with a stamp or 'chop' to show that they were innocuous. Captain E.C. Dickson recalls that he had a book on wine entitled 'Stay Me With Flagons', which he re read so many times that he became something of an expert. Whilst there never was any prospect of wine in Changi it kept him, however tenuously, in touch with happier times and a more civilised world.

Sport and exercise also had their place, especially early on when the men had sufficient calories and energy to take an interest in football and games. Less welcome was the fact that the British administration would sometimes hand out exercise as a form of punishment to wrong doers. Americans, coming to Changi for the first time were speechless with amazement to find that British officers would give pack drill to their men. Yet there was some logic in this particular madness; it suggested that the men were still under orders, and that punishment, if need be, could be given out by their own kind and not inflicted with unnecessary barbarity by the Japanese. Whatever the theory British troops did survive marginally better in captivity, their death rate being a percentage point or two lower than that of the Americans. Those who had no organised exercise would usually take part in the so-called 'goldfish parade', milling about and walking around inside the wire for a while, after whatever had passed for their evening meal.

Entertainment of all sorts was at a premium and Changi soon had a concert party which included a tumbling act as well as an accordion player and a band. Indeed it was widely recognised that entertainers, of whatever sort, were a precious resource where tedium and depression were as much an enemy as starvation and cruelty. Thus it was that for plays and concerts great lengths would be gone to in order to provide costume or props: even when some men were lacking basic items of clothing it was felt worthwhile to attempt to dress the entertainers in at least a semblance of what audiences in Blackpool or London might expect. The quality of the entertainments was in fact surprisingly high, and amazed many who had been held elsewhere, as for example American troops who were transferred to Changi.

Many different groups put on plays and entertainments, in late 1942 Gunner E. A. Osman of the 88th produced *Jack and the Beanstalk* as a Christmas pantomime, and Lieutenant Fitzgerald and 'the officers' put on a less politically correct 'Nigger Minstrel Show' at Serangoon work camp. The 'Red Rose Players' of the 'Phoenix Theatre' did *Love on the Dole* in March 1944, whilst 'the officers', displayed their usual ebullient taste by producing a 'burlesque melodrama' called *Speakeasy* in September 1944, and the 'Coconut Grove' theatre did a *Christmas Review, Pygmalion,* and *Jupiter Laughs* in the winter of 1944 to 1945. In all these productions 88th Field Regiment's input was particularly significant, considering that the entertainers could be drawn from all regiments. The 'Red Rose' players however were special in that they were the 88th Field Regiment's own troupe, and their name was an allusion to the county of Lancashire.

Particularly noteworthy were the efforts of Lance Sergeant Martin R. English and Lance Bombardier G. Kenneth Dowbiggin who acted as producers on more than one occasion; also Gunner D.C. Reay, Gunner Eric Bamber, Sergeant S. Rawlinson, Bombardier G.V. Wakefield and Sergeant 'Bill' Potter who took various parts. The 88th were equally active behind the scenes with Gunner D.J. Meakin the set decorator, Lance Bombardier Milburn Foster who specialised in electrics, and thus became regular 'stage electrician', and lighting engineer to 'the Palladium', and Gunner/Fitter Joseph Silver of Preston who served as carpenter and handy man. Even Desmond Bettany, not known for acting skill, had more than one walk on role in productions, including that of a citizen in the comedy *Roman Rackets* which was staged in January 1944, and featured several members of the 88th.

Programmes and literature to accompany the productions were a particular problem, but one which was solved in a surprisingly professional manner. Programmes, as it would appear from surviving examples, frequently had cast lists properly duplicated, but there was no method of reprographics for the covers. These were provided, hand painted, by the artists like Bettany who produced original compositions, often in large numbers. The camp entertainers *pièce de résistance* came in 1945 when a ballet was mounted at 'the Playhouse' shortly before the end of the war. This however was viewed as so subversive by the Japanese and full of 'bad thoughts' that they not only interrupted the run, but put a stop to all such entertainment.

Straightforward music was another potential escape from the alternate terrors and tediums of Changi. Yet as radios were banned on pain of the severest penalty, and few men had the fortune to be captured with anything resembling an instrument, invention was again the order of the day. Nevertheless the 88th were central in the formation of the camp 'dance band' known as the 'Nitwits'. Captain Bradley was a good all rounder, Gunner Bamber played percussion, and Desmond Bettany somehow conjured both a mouth organ and a guitar. Particular leading lights were Bill Potter, and the Wilson brothers of Lancaster: many others proved to have decent singing voices. In the 88th Major Denis Houghton was the master of the art of making music from nothing and succeeded in making a practical and playable flute from parts of a bicycle, and washers cut from glove leather. This instrument was later presented to the Imperial War Museum, where it remained at the time of writing. So highly developed were the musical efforts within Changi that 18th Division would

Left: Major Denis Houghton as musician, by Desmond Bettany.

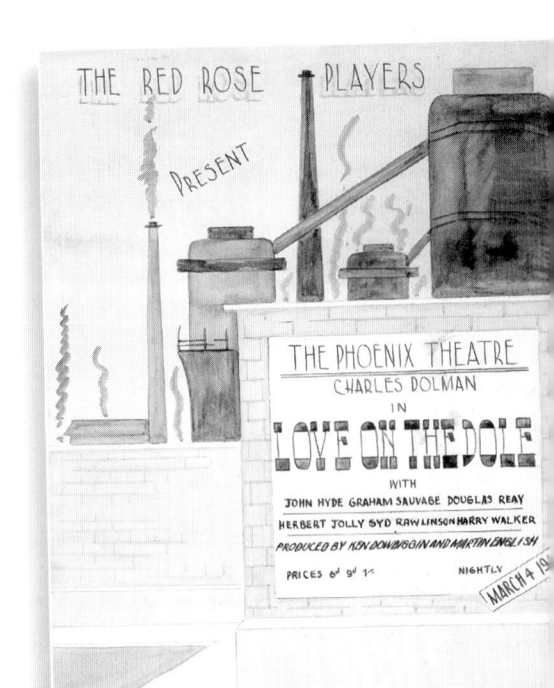

Above: Programme for 'Love on the Dole' by the Red Rose Players, march 1944. 'Red Rose' was an allusion to the 88th Field Regiment. The producer were Ken Dowbiggin and Martin English.

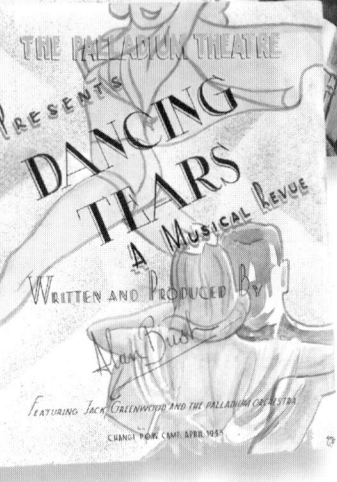

Entertainments programmes painted in captivity by Desmond Bettany.

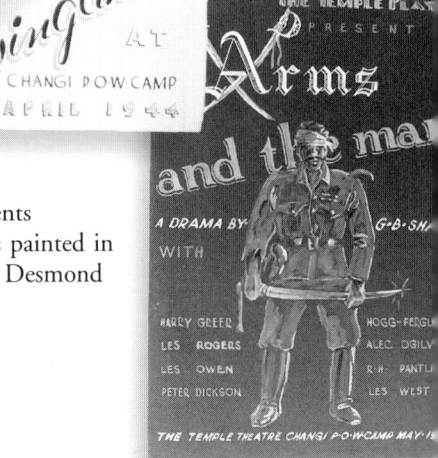

finally boast its own grandly titled 'Symphony Orchestra'. Music making generally did much to help uplift the spirits, so much so in fact that on one occasion a sentry actually handed his rifle over to an incredulous prisoner whilst he danced.

Nor was it only musical instruments which exercised the talents of the amateur craftsmen of the regiment. One particularly sought after item was a decent razor, and a good number were either made, or refurbished, in captivity. Two particularly good examples have survived, one of these, repaired and embellished for Captain E.C. Dickson, had as its point of departure an old blade, but was made to look rather better than new by the replacement wooden handle and ornamental box with sliding lid. Even more remarkable, considering the materials available, was that fabricated by Lance Bombardier Geoffrey Haworth. This had begun life as a standard army issue table knife, which was cut down, reshaped, and mounted in a metal handle. Its hand stitched leather case was cut and formed, rather cheekily, from the seat covering of a Japanese fighter plane. Less practical but equally absorbing creations included the model sailing ships of 'Jim' Parry, and the ever popular chess sets.

Possibly the most extraordinary thing to be produced by any member of the 88th, or anyone in captivity, was the lathe made by Captain Reg Bradley. So remarkable indeed was the final version that was later exhibited at the Machine Tool and Engineering Exhibition at Olympia in 1948, and a full description of its fabrication and mechanics appeared in the journal *Engineering* in January the following year. The methods by which the lathe was made, and its use established, were however tortuous in the extreme. In Bradley's first year in captivity he had made something of a speciality in stealing and using small tools taken from the Japanese for the benefit of the other prisoners; but by 1943 the difficulties and dangers involved in keeping his clandestine workshop activity going threatened to outweigh the benefits. The only solution appeared to be to bring the operation into the open and attempt to legitimise it. First Bradley and his colleagues engaged a Japanese NCO interpreter in conversation, and having gained some confidence, persuaded him to draw the Japanese characters for several words, amongst which was 'workshop'. Later the character was drawn onto a piece of wood, and the next time the guard was changed the sign was hung up in the officer's hut, with a selection of joinery tools arranged neatly nearby. The new guards did not question the fact that there was a small workshop functioning, nor whether it did indeed have official sanction.

Having set himself up as semi official workshop manager Bradley now turned his knowledge of other matters to good account. Prior to the war he had had an interest in both navigation and astronomy, and he had been the regiment's survey officer: in captivity he had begun to teach classes in these subjects to other inmates. A Japanese General who had learned of this activity and was particularly fascinated by astronomy came to Bradley, whom he addressed as the 'Captain of the Stars', for instruction. This Bradley turned to advantage, for he managed to insert into their discussions, such requests or complaints as had been passed to him. Perhaps most beneficially the General ensured that new tools and materials including some rivets, alloy sheeting, drill bits, and hacksaw blades, were passed on to Bradley. At about the same time he also managed to obtain a Chinese made six inch lathe; and a three and a half inch screw cutting lathe both of which had come from a repair shop which existed prior to the Japanese invasion.

With this new found wealth of material, meagre by peacetime standards, but miraculous in Changi, Bradley and 12 Royal Army Ordnance Corps technicians acting under him began work in earnest. Probably the biggest volume of work was for the camp hospital, which was starved of proper supplies. In this work Bradley co operated with Colonel Julian Taylor who was the senior consultant surgeon present at the camp. Amongst the jobs done were repairs to microscopes and the manufacture of splints, but the shop became best known for making artificial limbs, a project which appears to have been first pioneered by Sergeant Bill Kitchen, a Lancaster man serving with Regimental Headquarters of the 88th. Artificial legs were in demand from the moment fighting ceased, for more than one amputee had appeared in the ranks of the regiment. The position would later worsen as a result of those who had lost limbs to tropical ulcers.

The first 'Kitchen' design of leg used as its main raw material the redundant metal rods from mosquito netting. These long pieces formed the main structure of the limb, whether half or full length, and a metal ring padded with sorbo rubber accommodated the stump. Pieces of leather tied with a lace offered some measure of adjustment. First models were found to jar the hip somewhat, so later a spring attachment was fitted at the heel which acted as a shock absorber. Sergeant Atkinson and Bombardier Haworth were active in the design work. Effective though these legs were they bore little resemblance to a human leg, and the final versions perfected by Bradley were more naturalistically shaped, and incorporated an improved knee joint. Many men, who did not have the skill or opportunity to work in the workshop helped out by 'finding' material which they handed in to be transformed into something more useful. Amongst the most valuable of the scrap items were some instruments which had been used in conjunction with coast artillery guns: these yielded some gears and stainless steel shafts.

It was at this point that Bradley hatched his plan for the making of another lathe, small enough to be easily transportable, and 'unofficial' so that it could be kept a secret from the Japanese. This would have the advantage that should the full sized lathes be banned or confiscated work could continue: a contraband lathe would also have the benefit that it could undertake unofficial work on things like radio parts. Something like 600 hours went into the making of this new lathe, and apart from the artillery instruments a barrack room locker, some spares from the operating theatre emergency lighting set, a car dynamo, and a broken typewriter were sacrificed in its construction. Most remarkably

The main buildings at Changi, painted by Desmond Bettany, 1944.

it was electric powered, and could feed either from the building's power supply, or batteries. The clandestine lathe was set up in the 'office' of the workshop, but positioned so that in a matter of seconds it could be whipped off the bench and stowed in a wooden box inside the tool cupboard. Searchers were put off by the fact that the cupboard doors were usually kept brazenly open, and appeared to have nothing to hide.

Perhaps even more dangerous than Bradley's involvement in radio parts, was his work in making keys. His greatest coup came in helping those undergoing solitary confinement whilst manacled. One officer succeeded in briefly stealing the key to the handcuffs which were usually applied, and Bradley made a pattern from it. The workshop then made no less than five copies of the key, which sometimes enabled those being punished to slip out of their bonds.

One nagging doubt was what the Japanese would actually do if they were losing the war, and there was a possibility that the prisoners would be liberated. The precedents were by no means encouraging. When the Japanese garrisons on Wake, Tarawa, and Baldale had been threatened, their prisoners had been butchered. It therefore made sense that those in Changi should make an effort to break out when this danger threatened, but the only way that those in charge would have any way of knowing when this should be was by the clandestine radios. Lance Bombardier Haworth prepared against the day the Japanese would turn their machine guns on their prisoners by preparing a map of the camp, and attempting to ear mark potential weak spots in the perimeter through which he and his friends would exit. The map was itself a matter worthy of severe punishment if found, so it was rolled small and pushed down the centre of an innocuous piece of bamboo. If nothing else it was a symbol of hope.

The name Changi would become synonymous with harsh imprisonment; yet even here all things were relative, and set against some of the horrors awaiting the 88th in Burma and Thailand, some, especially after the passage of time, would come to regard Changi almost as a sort of haven. As one of the 88th who was there would later record,

> Looking back on the whole period, of course one tends to forget the worst and remember only those things which are worthy of a permanent place in the gallery of experience. First, of course the climate: hardly varying all the year round, day after day of wonderful blue skies, sometimes flecked with fleecy clouds, and sunsets which would seem unreal in England. One forgets that this same sun stabbed the eyes with a blinding reflected glare for long hours on the aerodrome, or blistered the skin from the shoulders again and again until there was no more skin to peel. One remembers again a particular night at the camp theatre, or lying on the grass at a gramophone concert listening to the breeze whispering in the casuarina trees above, forgetting the many nights when it was too hot to sleep and you tried in vain to forget your hunger and longed to escape from the arguing crowds around you.

> Changi was undoubtedly one of the best camps in Malaya though, and was always regarded as a home from home by those who had been sent away to other camps. It was headquarters of our own administration as well as the Japanese, and even though we lived in no more than shorts and clogs it had a faint air of civilisation.

Another thing that should be remembered about Changi was that it was not one camp, but several, and that for many the experience was one of prolonged uncertainty. Very few men spent the whole of their captivity in the Changi area, and it has been estimated that only about 80 of the 88th were never moved up country or overseas. The prisoner population of Changi therefore fluctuated wildly. The initial number may have been as many as 52,000 counting the Australians and first Americans, yet by mid 1943 this had shrunk to a mere 5,300. The following year saw the numbers rise to a little over 10,000, before falling again in mid 1945. About 12,500 were present at liberation. These changes in numbers were almost entirely the result of work parties being taken to work on projects further afield – and the most important of these was undoubtedly the railway.

6

The Railway

The episode which would cause the regiment its most catastrophic loss of the entire war was the building of the now infamous Burma-Siam railway, since often known as the 'Death Railway'. Despite its now well known macabre reputation, those who would toil and suffer on its 415 kilometre length, were, at the outset, largely unaware of what awaited them 'up country'. Major Denis Houghton, who was fortunate enough not to be selected to work on the project, recalled that the actual choice for men to do the task was carried out by British officers. Both they and their men, some of whom actively volunteered to be sent, were totally misled as to what the job would entail. Some believed the story put around by the Japanese that proper hospitals would be available for the sick: others thought that the work would be similar to that already carried out by smaller groups around Singapore. Whatever the story it would appear from surviving papers that D'Aubuz at least had some scepticism. He struck from the lists various personnel considered unfit to travel, and thereby attempted to prevent their departure. Some lives were doubtless saved, though unwittingly at the time.

The task of building the railway was huge and would use more prisoner labour than any other project in South East Asia, but in many ways was very poorly planned. The new track was intended to join up the existing lines in Burma and Thailand, and thus create a supply route to link Japanese conquests in Burma with the rest of the Empire. Such a link would also prove invaluable in the attempt to invade India. Surveys had been conducted in the 1920s, and some pieces of line, notably the Moulmein-Ye section, were already open in 1925, but here work had ceased. At the outbreak of war there was still a huge gap between the Burmese and Thai railways, which spanned vast tracts of inhospitable forest. Much of the proposed line would follow the route of the River Khwae Noi.

For work on the railway new parties variously known as 'Forces' or 'Battalions' were formed, mixing together members of the 88th with other units, each composite group being designated by a letter of the alphabet. Party 'A', made up of Australians, was exceptional in that it had already been formed before work on the railway commenced. It was used initially for airfield construction work in southern Burma, and was not transferred to the northern end of the line at Thanbyuzayat, Burma, until September 1942.

It was therefore party 'B', a body of 600 prisoners under Major R.S. Sykes of the Royal Army Service Corps, which became something of a trailblazing unit, and the first to find out the horrors which would claim the lives of

The beginnings of a macabre reputation: watercolour sketch of the Burma–Thailand railway, by Desmond Bettany.

approximately 16,000 allied prisoners, and a much greater number of locally impressed Asian workers. The regiment's contribution to this first tranche was 37 other ranks under Lieutenant Quartermaster W.J. Buswell. A gruelling four day train journey, completed on 24 June 1942 took them to the southern end of the proposed route, at Ban Pong, Thailand.

Here they discovered the truth of the supposedly better conditions, for there were no facilities at all, not even a hut for the guards. Therefore the first task was to build their own prison camp, starting with the guards accommodation, then a cookhouse, prisoner's huts, and finally sick quarters. There never would be anything that approximated to the modern idea of a hospital, yet the diseases and semi starvation which had galled and occasionally killed at Changi were present here in giant measures. To make matters worse heavy equipment was pretty well non existent: even wheel barrows were something of a rarity. After blasting by careless and sometimes incompetent Japanese engineers the men would therefore have to shift everything by hand, digging with picks and spades, and turn the ground with the 'chunkel' as the local form of hoe was known.

Earth was moved away in litters, in hods on mens backs, or on yokes and poles across the shoulder.

The first trace for the line was now begun, but it was not until late October 1942 that the biggest group of the 88th arrived on the scene as part of 'R' party, and track laying commenced. 'R' Party included 193 members of the regiment, 10 of them officers. Gunner J. Pemberton was one of those in this group, and vividly recalled how the journey 'up country' was made. About 30 men were put into each little rail carriage, and given a single mess tin of rice, and locked in: so apart from hunger they also had to cope with oppressive heat. From Ban-Pong to Tonchan 'R' party had to walk, abandoning heavy equipment, and, like many before them, they arrived to find not a camp with better facilities, but no camp at all. The first job was to build the accommodation.

A further 53 from the regiment, the most senior of which was Captain Pote-Hunt, were also shifted in October 1942, although it is not known whether this group had any specific designation. Next to go was 'L' force to which the 88th contributed 13 men, six of them officers, in early November 1942. A further 22 other ranks are also known to have been taken by the end of the year. Thus it was that by the start of 1943 roughly half of 88th Field Regiment was toiling on the railway, though widely spread, and often in ignorance of their comrades whereabouts.

Next to come out to the line were 'D' party in March 1943, of which 128 were men of the 88th, but accompanied by only one of their officers, the conscientious Lieutenant A. H. Raven of 464 Battery. 'F' force with Lieutenant J.W.B. White departed in April, and with him went 43 men. 'H' Force which left Changi at various dates during May included not only 'Doc' Dickson but six officers of the 88th and 26 men. More than three quarters of the regiment were thus employed on the line by mid 1943.

The debilitating effects of marching long distance between rail heads and camps were intensified both by Japanese attitudes, and by the rainy season. On the move men had to camp where they could, though 'camp' in this context was a misnomer since there was no cover at night. The sick got sicker and the reasonably fit became ill. Then men,

> who were absolutely unfit to march (owing to disease and weakness) were beaten and driven from camp to camp. Officers and Medical Officers, who begged and prayed for sick men to be left behind, were themselves beaten at many camps. In one particular case a Japanese medical officer (Lieutenant) ordered the Imperial Japanese Army Corporal in charge of Tarso station camp to leave behind 36 men who were too ill to move. The Corporal refused to obey this order though it was repeated in writing and a British officer (Major) Interpreter, and an Australian Doctor (Major) were severely beaten when they protested. A bone in the Doctor's hand was broken. Of the sick men who were compelled to march nearly all have since died.

Even so the initial pace of the actual construction was, for most, just tolerable. Officers were a little better off than the men, for at least in theory, they did not do manual labour at this time. Food was scarce, but survival remained possible since there were Thai villagers who would trade bananas, papaya, and watermelon for whatever the prisoners had. Sometimes the captives even had money to give, for whilst the men were entitled to receive a derisory four 'baht', the officers still had a few dollars, a quarter of which was given direct to help the feeding of their troops. Another vital aid to survival at one oasis on the line was the work of local businessman Boonpong Sirivejapandh, who, as village mayor, was given a concession to run a prisoners canteen. Later the work was made more lucrative for him, and more bearable for the prisoners, by the fact that some extra funds were smuggled in from the outside world. He, and the men he dealt with, certainly risked death for this humanitarian enterprise.

For 55 kilometres the line cut a great swathe through the forests, until it came to a place called Kanchanaburi, soon to be known universally amongst the prisoners as 'Camburi'. Despite the months of heavy labour the timetable of construction was now lagging, and the Japanese put into force the so called policy of 'Speedo', with increased work quotas for all, and long hours under threat of beatings or torture. To make matters much worse the original planned completion date of November 1943 was now brought forward four months by the Japanese Army High Command or 'Daihonei', in Tokyo. What had originally been merely a very arduous construction project in a disease ridden part of the world, was shortly to turn into mass murder.

Miraculously few deaths had occurred amongst the ranks of the 88th up to this point, but now the nature of the exercise changed. At first the prisoners had been regarded as a resource, albeit a sub human one entitled to no respect: but now they became an expendable commodity which the Japanese were totally prepared to expend. As it was put in a phrase overheard by Major Albert Eldridge of the South Lancashires, 'Let the men die, it doesn't matter'. Indeed if one looks at the manner in which individual 'parties' or 'forces' were taken out of Changi and systematically worked to death or exhaustion, this can be seen as a deliberate policy. With some justification this has been called by one American author, the 'biggest sustained POW atrocity in the Pacific war'. On the railway, as on some of the smaller slave labour projects, the conditions, and the death rates, would now parallel the situation of prisoners on the Eastern Front.

One of the factors in the equation was undoubtedly the Japanese realisation that victory was slipping away from them. Universal success in late 1941 and early 1942 would turn into an attritional struggle against the Americans at Midway and Guadalcanal, and ultimately to failure of the offensive against the British in India. No amount of sacrifice on behalf of the Japanese soldier, and no amount of 'Speedo' inflicted on the prisoners would change the nature of the calculation. Quick victory against the colonies and outposts of the Euro-

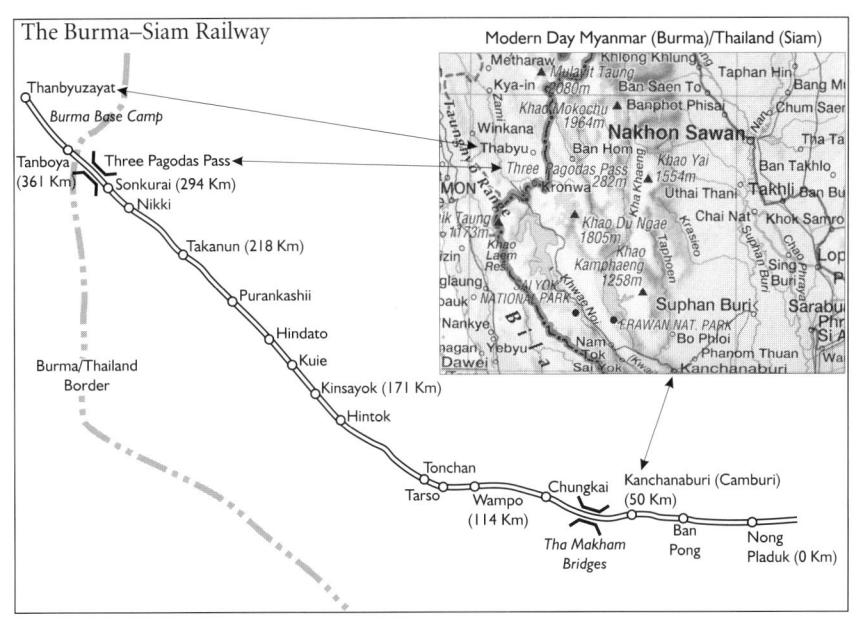

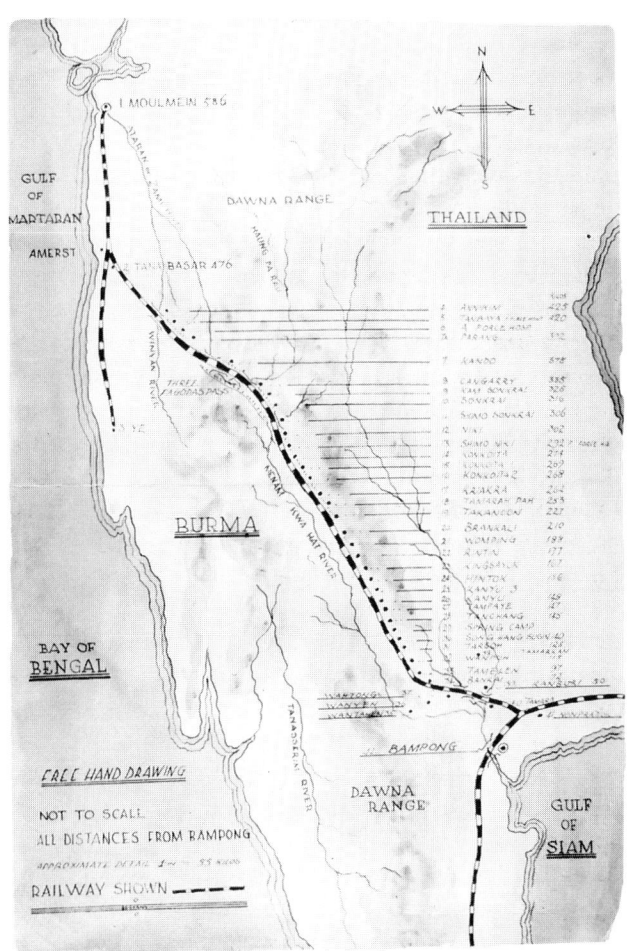

Right: Plan of the Burma–Thailand railway, by Desmond Bettany.

peans, and the lightning blow against Pearl Harbour had not finished the war in the Far East, and the Germans were now stalled in Russia. With each passing day the odds against a successful outcome for Imperial Japan were worsening.

Before long 14 hour days were commonplace on the railway, and men lifting heavy logs were literally being driven along with whips, sticks and fists. Dysentery, ulcerated feet, malaria, and cholera followed marches and exhaustion, and pneumonia was the natural result when men had to sleep in the rain in the open. In spite of debilitation the Japanese Engineers put the prisoners to work as soon as they arrived at the railway. The numbers 'allowed to be ill' were strictly regulated, so that even if a man could no longer stand he was often not permitted to report sick, since the 'quota' had already been filled. Sometimes the disoriented and the half dead were dragged off to the tragic farce of being forced to direct their feeble efforts at stone breaking.

At Songkurai under Engineer officer Lieutenant Abe conditions appeared to have reached their nadir: he specialised in emptying the hut which served as hospital personally, and seemed more than happy with the brutalities handed out by his men. As early as May 1943 1200 of his prisoners were dead, and another 200 were so ill as to be in threat of succumbing. In June the camp was populated by about 1900 prisoners, of whom over two thirds were so sick as to be useless.

By July half the remaining work force were without boots, and diseases of the feet multiplied; blankets were lacking, as were clothes and medicine. Allied medical officers and orderlies were reduced to using banana leaves, or rags cut from tattered shirts for bandages. Limbs that under normal circumstances could easily have been saved had to be amputated. That it was Lieutenant Abe's actions which added materially to the sufferings was demonstrated when he departed to be replaced by Lieutenant Wakabayashi that August. Things were not that much better, but the improvement was sufficient enough to be noticed. Wakabayashi duly acquired for himself the strange phonetic nickname of 'Rockabye Archie'. Eventually 16 men of the regiment died at Songkurai.

Japanese medical provision was well nigh non existent, and got worse the further one went up the line. At Hintok, where a further eight members of the regiment ended their days, the regime was especially peculiar. One Japanese medical orderly actually beat away any sick person who came near with a wooden sword. He was quickly christened 'Dr Death'. A number of men simply walked off into the jungle, perhaps less with the idea of escaping than with dying on their own and with some dignity.

An unpleasant, but by no means untypical, selection of railway camps were recorded in the diary of Captain E.C. Dickson who moved 'up country' as a part of 'H' Force in May, 1943. The transport was small rubber trucks about 18 feet by seven, and into his own little truck were jammed 27 men. Disembarking at Camburi his first impressions were of a 'filthy camp' with no shelter. The daily fare was, 'Hard work, and bad food, bad weather and dysentery'. If anything Tonchan in June was worse, buzzing with flies, and the roads a sea of mud: the men disliked it intensely, and met the enemy with a display of spirited booing. Dickson and his whole party were therefore 'bashed' to put them in their place. By 11 June the Japanese were so afraid of Cholera that they went around wearing face pads, and actually cancelled work details to keep down the risk of infection. British officers were sent to bury the bodies of Tamil workers who had died.

By this time Tonchan had little rice, no fish and no fats. The men were simply wasting away. Another party of prisoners who came into camp were quickly dubbed the 'Speedo Benjo's', pidgin Japanese for 'rapidly to the toilet', because they were so badly hit with dysentery. Another wit called these unfortunates the 'Tom Cats' because they were out all night, either working, or at the latrines. On 19 June Dickson allowed himself a little celebration because he had been able to buy some eggs, and there was a small issue of whitebait and soya beans. Nine days later he was moved on to Hintok: here the inevitable happened, for by early August he too went down with dysentery. Luckily he was one of those evacuated, and travelled back by barge and train to Camburi, to be placed in the primitive 'hospital'.

The hospital certainly had a nightmarish quality about it, and some of the most miserable sufferers were those afflicted with tropical ulcers. The Doctors could do little for them except scrape the putrefying matter from their wounds, or amputate in the most serious cases. Dickson noticed some Japanese come round with cameras and photograph the ulcers, but they did nothing to cure them. Against the odds Dickson slowly recovered: just as he was beginning to get better occurred one of the most sickening incidents. The railway line passed not far from his hut, and here, a Tamil worker, driven to despair, chose to end it all. He simply lay down with his head on the line and waited for the train. Finally, in December 1943, still weak, but answering to some Japanese description of fitness he was taken back to Singapore. The diabolical quality of the camps mentioned here is underlined by the fact that Tonchan claimed the lives of 17 men of the regiment, whilst Camburi took 11.

Near Camburi began the construction of what was destined to become the most famous bridge on the line, though actually there were many bridges, and this particular bridge was only one of two in the vicinity, and was not even strictly speaking, on the River Kwai. The main bridge, and its smaller wooden companion, later to inspire the film 'Bridge on the River Kwai', were actually at a place called Tha Makham, and, rather than spanning the Kwae Noi, were across the faster flowing waters of the Mae Khlaung. To the Japanese the bridges were known as the Futamatsu bridges, after the Japanese engineer who designed them. The smaller of the two edifices was a timber trestle bridge, about 220 metres in length, completed in February 1943. Its method of construction was similar to many of the others. As one eye witness put it,

> Japanese bridge making is simple and temporarily efficient. You first of all rig up the primitive pile driver on a scaffold worked by two teams pulling on

dozens of ropes, and then you drive great pointed stakes into the ground as the bottom uprights. When these piles are all driven well in, and are level, the entire wooden bridge is built on those wooden foundations. Some of us sat on the ground and cut the ends of the crude piles into sharp points; others on a rope and pulley hauled new teak timbers up from the river 30 feet below; others carried these enormous balks and stacked them; others broke stones and piled them; and then there was the hated pile driver.

A welcome ally in the really heavy work was the elephant, numbers of which were brought to work by their local mahouts. These beasts were capable of hauling much more than any man, and their broad feet were well adapted to soft going. They also caused the British relatively few problems, save that they had a tendency to hose down the prisoners whilst keeping themselves cool.

Thus, using techniques redolent of the construction of the pyramids, were built the majority of the bridges on the line. The larger of the two bridges at Tha Makham was however something of an exception in that it was much more permanent looking, and used both concrete and steel. Completed in April 1943 it reutilised components which had previously been part of a bridge in Java.

The senior British officer at Tha Makham camp was Lieutenant Colonel P.J.D. Toosey, a native of Birkenhead. Like the men of the 88th, he was a Territorial gunner who had seen service in France in 1940. It was undoubtedly due to Toosey's efforts that Tha Makham enjoyed a better reputation than most camps on the line. Yet charges that Toosey was more cooperative than necessary with the enemy were exaggerated, for his apparent compliance yielded concessions, and at the same time camouflaged his dangerous dealings with outside smugglers of medical supplies and currency. It was at least partly due to Toosey's obsession with hygiene, and his contraband supplies, that Tha Makham claimed so relatively few of 88th Field Regiment. According to Leo Rawlings of the 137th Toosey was a 'wonderful man', under whom the medical staff worked tirelessly for the sick, achieving such miracles as daily changes of dressings, and frequent shaves. His canteen was declared remarkable for its omelettes, tobacco and coconuts, luxuries seldom available at other camps.

It was not far from the famous bridges, at a point about 57 kilometres from the start of the line, that a major 'hospital' for the sick on the southern part of the line was established. The unenviable job of senior British officer at Chungkai fell to Lieutenant Colonel Henry Cary Owtram. This officer had begun the Malayan campaign as second in command of 137th Field Regiment, but had been promoted when the commanding officer had been killed. Since many, if not most, of those who came to Chungkai were already seriously ill, it soon became a more than usually popular place to die. As one Australian observed it was surprising that the Japanese 'had the gall to call it a hospital'. Drugs of any description were quickly exhausted, and even basics like bed pans and blankets had to be improvised from salvage. Dysentery and tropical ulcers were both major killers here. Thus it was that more than 30 members of the regiment succumbed at this camp, the majority of them during the latter part of 1943.

News of what was happening up country, or 'overland' as the official reports put it, gradually began to seep back to Changi, and here the remaining British officers took up the matter with the Japanese in a quite remarkable manner. They complained long and hard to the local representative of the Japanese Military Police. When stalled they protested again, and eventually he deigned to accept a 'frank' report on the conditions in Thailand, and how they could be improved. Given that they themselves were still prisoners, and equally at the mercy of their captors, what they dared to say was indeed significant.

First they pointed out that what was going on must almost certainly be contrary to the Imperial Japanese Government's policy, and that the Japanese Red Cross appeared to be in total ignorance of what was happening. They stated that some of the parties dispatched during the spring of 1943 were not 'working parties' at all, but had been sent with the agreement of British officials because they were going to 'better camps' where it was stated there would be a canteen and medical supplies. This was the only reason that unfit men had therefore been included in the transfer. In complaining about the conditions on the railway the British officers made it apparent that what was happening was not in the interests of the Japanese army, let alone the prisoners. As they put it to their captors,

> It was clear to all Prisoner Officers that if the Engineers continued to take all fit and convalescent men to work every day there would soon be no fit men at all to work. In fact that Engineers were rapidly destroying their only available source of labour, this aspect was explained to our own Imperial Japanese Army Headquarters who clearly agreed, but were apparently unable to prevent the Engineers from doing as they liked. The task in front of the Engineers and the need for speed were fully understood by us, but the destruction by the Engineers of their only available labour was just as bad from their point of view as ours. A little common sense on the part of the Engineers could, early in June, have saved the situation for us and for themselves. Unfortunately for us this short sighted policy continued and by the end of June only about 700 of the 5000 men north of Nieke were at work daily and of these at least half were unfit and useless for heavy work.

Though it bore little or no fruit this stance was doubtless the best that British officers who were trying to improve the lot of their men could have adopted. It linked their survival to the success of the project, but also blamed a segment of the Japanese command rather than making a blanket condemnation of the whole. It also made explicit appeals to the promises regarding life that had been made by Yamashita in accepting the surrender of Singapore in 1941. There was just a chance therefore, that if any had a will to do anything about the appalling conditions they could do so with minimum loss of 'face'. That so little was done by the Japanese command suggests very strongly that what

Japanese rail road truck, improvised from a six-cylinder diesel engine with lorry body. A surviving relic of the line photographed by Captain E.C. Dickson.

happened on the railway was official policy, rather than the whim of junior commanders.

Construction of the line finished in October 1943: according to Japanese figures the prisoners and the locally pressed 'romusha', or workers, had shifted three million cubic metres of rock and built four million cubic metres of earth works. They had also hauled 60,000 cubic feet of bridging timber and 650,000 cubic feet of timber poles, and built 688 bridges. The Japanese held a small celebration, struck a special commemorative medal for their men, and brought up 'comfort girls' in special brothel trains, but for the slave labourers the misery certainly did not end. The railway, as a strategic link for the Japanese army, served as an important target for the Allied air forces, who, by cutting it, could sever enemy supply lines and thereby shorten the war in Burma. Many labourers therefore stayed on in Thailand and Burma into 1944 and 1945, reacting to bomb damage by travelling up and down the line to make repairs. The prisoners were now at risk from their own bombers as well as illness and the Japanese.

In one raid against Nong Pladuk alone 95 prisoners were killed and a further 300 were wounded. The now famous Tha Makham bridge was attacked eight times, before both the new metal and the old wooden structure were destroyed on 13 February 1945. The prisoners were put to work on repairs immediately and had reerected the wooden bridge by 3 April when the Americans launched a new onslaught with B–24 bombers of 436th Bomb Squadron, 7th Bomb Group. The result of the attack, which carried anti personnel bombs to deal with the anti aircraft guns, and 'bridge buster' bombs for the bridge itself, was described by Lieutenant Colonel William Henderson;

As we neared the target the flak was light and we noted that the fragment bomb carrier that was to hit the sites had not yet arrived. For some reason only one of my bombs went away on the first pass at the bridge but it was a direct hit on the ten foot wide bridge, which looked like the thin edge of a knife blade even at this low altitude. My lone bomb destroyed a large part of the eastern section of the wooden bridge. The two bombs on the second pass were near misses; there was also a noticeable increase in ground fire. With three bombs remaining we began the final run as the flak suppression plane and the next bridge bombing aircraft arrived. When my remaining three bombs dropped everything looked perfect for another hit. The gunners reported flak getting heavier and closer but I requested the pilot to hold a steady heading for a few seconds longer so we could get photographs of the impacts. This move almost cost us our lives. I gave the 'OK to turn' when the bombs hit, and as the wings went nearly vertical in the turn we were hit by multiple bursts of flak.

Henderson managed to limp back in the riddled aircraft, which was indeed fortunate, since bomber crews were normally accorded even worse treatment than ordinary prisoners. Both bridges were now out of use, but again forced labour had them back in commission within a couple of months. On 24 June 1945 they were finally and definitively put out of action by a British raid, and not repaired again until after the war.

Dreadful though the building and maintaining of the railway undoubtedly was, it is worth noting that conditions were not uniform over time, nor from place to place. The worst camps were usually those furthest from civilisation, and from local people willing to barter with the prisoners. The worst camps had the most bestial of guards, and often suffered being cut off from supplies of food and medicine. In these places even rats were soon regarded as valuable food, a plain rat fetching 30 cents, and a curried one slightly more. Such of the inmates who were capable of standing would be worked all the hours of daylight and more, and without reason. Hell holes like this might well mean the death of two thirds of their prisoners. The worst time was undoubtedly mid 1943, with the height of the 'speedo' campaign and cholera and dysentery rife.

The better places were still bad, but had much lower incidences of mortality. Decent guards and camp commanders could mean the difference between life and death. At 'Camp 206', kilometre 206 on the line, one elderly Japanese Sergeant's nickname was 'Father Christmas', and for once the irony was only mild. For he earned his name by occasionally allowing extra 'Yasme', or rest, and the distribution of cigarettes. This was accounted extreme luxury.

At Chungkai at Christmas 1943 the prisoners even attempted to put on entertainments of the sort which were mounted at Changi. The 'playhouse' of course was more primitive being a draughty 'attap' thatched hut by the river, but the irrepressible thespians still managed to scrounge pieces of material to help the audience's imagination with costume. A band of sorts was also formed, which boasted a couple of clarinets, some violins and a home made guitar. That the extreme southern end of the line was better than the middle was acknowledged by the prisoners who referred to it as the 'egg belt', as here eggs could sometimes be traded from the locals.

It was remarkable that over much of the railway, prisoners continued to possess and operate radios. If anything however the dangers and penalties were greater than they had been in Changi. Isolation meant that punishment was likely to be summary and savage, and frequent movements made discovery more likely. It was also true that a makeshift hut or a tent offered fewer decent hiding places. The terrible risks were highlighted at Camburi in late August 1943 when the Japanese discovered not just one radio, but several under construction. Two British officers of other regiments were beaten to death, and others were handed over to the Kampeitai. Some had to face a particularly vicious punishment regime back at Outram Road Jail in Singapore, where malcontents were frequently sent for 'correction', or more likely an early death.

The total cost of the railway to 88th Field regiment was huge. At least 156 men died in the immediate vicinity of the line during construction, plus a minimum of a further seven of the attached signallers and engineers. It was the regiment's worst disaster, and one they could do nothing about. All parties which worked on the railway suffered badly, but 'F' and 'H' forces took the greatest losses. Of the members of the regiment attached to 'F' force only 12 lived. To what state the survivors were reduced can easily be imagined, and to add insult to injury most were now almost naked. At one base camp a survey was made of clothing which concluded that over half of the 4,804 prisoners present had no shirt, half had no footwear, a third had no hat. Even underpants were a noteworthy rarity.

Though it is the railway which has become by far the most famous slave labour project many troops were taken from Singapore to work on other details. The most unlucky toiled on the railway, and when this was complete were taken off to work elsewhere in similarly brutal conditions. It is believed that about a hundred members of the regiment were sent to other destinations overseas, for the most part to Formosa, or to Japan itself. Though they have received less than their fair share of attention the men who went with these parties fared scarcely better than those who worked on the 'Death Railway'.

By official Japanese statistics 10,800 of the 50,000 prisoners shipped from one area to another died even before they arrived. Some expired in transit, crammed like sardines, and neglected, but many more were drowned as a result of allied submarine and air attacks. The death rate was not helped by the fact that the Japanese did not mark ships which carried prisoners, so Allied air forces and navies had no way of knowing whether they were killing their friends. Eventually, by late 1944, it would seem that more Japanese transports were being sunk than arriving safely. 850 British prisoners were lost with the *Lisbon Maru*: the *Rakuyo Maru* and the *Kachidoki Maru* between them cost

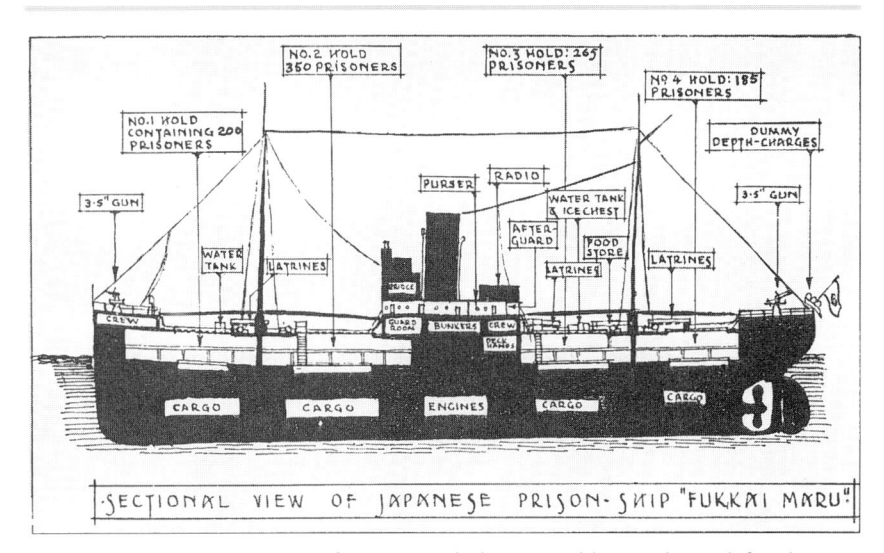

SECTIONAL VIEW OF JAPANESE PRISON-SHIP "FUKKAI MARU"

The Fukkai Maru, one of many similarly unsuitable vessels used for the transport of British prisoners. This particular ship, built at Yokohama in 1912, was used to take General Percival and other senior officers to Korea in 1942.

1,500 British and Australian lives; lesser numbers went with *Maros Maru*, the *Toyofuko Maru* and the *Junyo Maru*. It was all a deadly lottery, and the 88th lost particularly heavily on the *Rakuyo Maru*. In this one disaster alone 42 members of the regiment are believed to have perished.

Those that did arrive faced a selection of tough jobs. Arguably some of the worst were in the mines of Japan, Korea, and Formosa. One step up the prisoner's evolutionary scale were those who worked on, or mainly above, surface. These included workers in Japanese shipyards and docks, steelworkers, and those who laboured on building projects in Indo-China. In truth it is difficult to say whether, objectively speaking, such things were better or worse than the railway, but those who were transported 'overseas' from Singapore were presented with a different set of hardships.

In Japan diseases like cholera were rarely encountered, but on the other side of the coin it was often freezing cold. It was said that the Japanese believed that those with white skin could survive cold. Isolation could be as much of a problem as in the jungles of Thailand, for here one was an enemy alien, and very often single prisoners were held up to the ridicule and violence of the Japanese populace. The situation worsened with the degree to which the particular locality was subject to allied bombing. So it was that Indo-China, Formosa, Japan, and Borneo each claimed the life of one or more members of 88th Field Regiment.

Japanese officers lay down their swords.

British prisoners finally emerge from captivity in newly issued uniforms.

7

Coming Home

What would happen to the prisoners when the war finally ended was one of the great unknowns. One possibility was that the Japanese would simply massacre their captives in a last act of defiance. Another scenario, which must have appeared unlikely, was that the war would end so suddenly and catastrophically that the Japanese would immediately surrender outright. Even up to the beginning of August 1945 sudden surrender seemed an unrealistic hope. The prisoners continued to listen to Allied broadcasts, but the trickle of news in no way prepared them for the dropping of the atomic bombs or Japanese capitulation.

Even when the captives gleaned an inkling of the truth they had to show no sign that they knew of the progress that the Allies were making, since any celebration would not only have enraged the Japanese, but put the radio operators at dire risk. The final months of the war therefore passed with little obvious sense of anticipation. Gunner George Slater records that when the news finally did come through that the war had ended he was sitting mending his old 'Jap Happy' loin cloth, in the expectation that it would have many more months to serve. Immediate instructions were that the men remain in their camps until fresh orders should reach them from outside, but even so a few took off in search of food and excitement.

On 28 August 1945 Liberator bombers flew low over Changi and let fly a stream of small sheets of paper. Gunner Bamber was one of the first in the scramble to pick up a leaflet: on one side was a mass of unreadable Japanese pictograms. The text on the other face was in Roman letters, and began 'Tatam Ittahadi Jangi Qaidyon Ke Nam'; whilst a helpful note in English explained the meaning of the strange message. The war was definitely at an end, a surrender had been signed, and the air drop was designed to let the Japanese guards know. The erstwhile enemy were instructed to ensure that the prisoners also saw the leaflets, see that their charges were treated with 'every care and attention', and then withdraw to their own quarters. After a fashion the inmates of Changi were now free.

The end of the war did not mean instant repatriation to Britain for most of the shattered 88th, and for some time yet those who had endured almost four years incarceration would have to remain in the company of their former captors. The atmosphere at least was a little different, as was recalled by Russell Braddon in his *Naked Island*

Three days later even the Japanese themselves admitted that we need no longer

Just after the enemy surrenders, British prisoners travel in style in a Japanese lorry, 1945. The former guards, left, seem somewhat bemused.

work. But the war had not been won: nor lost. It had simply for the moment, stopped. They ceased to bellow 'Currah' and instead bowed politely when we passed. The food which they had recently declared to be non existent, they now produced in vast quantities so that we might eat our fill. Likewise drugs appeared from everywhere and in profusion.

A little while later British parachutists arrived at Changi where the bulk of the prisoners were gathered. The Japanese greeted the incredulous paratroops politely. Desmond Bettany was one of those who could see a funny side to the situation: the strapping British troops were by no means all tall men but they seemed to tower above emaciated prisoners and diminutive guards alike. It served naturally enough as the inspiration for a cartoon. There were those of course who lacked Bettany's sense of humour, some of the Japanese committed suicide, some were killed by local people who now had the chance to settle old scores before order was fully restored. Count Terauchi the Japanese Field Marshal responsible for the whole area suffered a stroke from which he would never recover.

A few men set out for home very quickly. These were packed without ceremony into the bomb bays of bombers which now had no targets, and flown homewards. In one particularly sad incident Sergeant A.E. Arthur of 351 Battery, was killed in a crash. Another group of about 600 of the most fit men, from assorted units, including Lance Bombardier Haworth, were also

Lord and Lady Mountbatten examine Captain Bradley's ingenious contraband lathe, made from odds and ends scavenged in Changi.

sent off quite rapidly from Singapore in the Harland and Wolf built New Zealand troopship, *Monowai*.

Soon afterwards Lord Louis Mountbatten the Supreme Commander of South East Asia Command demonstrated that even if transport home was slow in coming he had not forgotten Singapore, the captives, or their sacrifices. In Singapore town on 12 September 1945 he took the Japanese surrender, a brief ceremony which a few prisoners managed to attend by begging rides, or even by walking, from Changi. The man who handed over a samurai sword, on behalf of the sick Count Terauchi on the steps of the Civic Hall, was General Seishiro Itagaki. This man had been an officer in the Imperial Japanese Army since 1904, and by 1945 had become Commander in Chief of the 7th Army area which included Singapore and Malaya. His submission betokened the surrender of 738,400 men. Mountbatten later described it as 'the greatest day of my life'.

On the same visit Mountbatten and his wife also managed to see and talk to a number of the prisoners. Amongst them was Captain Bradley of the 88th who had been given a new uniform and cap for the occasion. The main topics of conversation were Bradley's remarkable lathe, and the artificial limbs which he had helped to make for amputees. For some prisoners though the main pleasure of the occasion was not the recognition of Bradley's ingenuity, nor the presence of the dignitary, but merely the chance to see his wife, the first European woman that some had seen for years.

There were many who were too ill to contemplate surrender ceremonies or any form of celebration. A substantial minority of the 88th were in the hospital at Woodlands on the north coast of Singapore Island; a few who had made it as far as India, were hospitalised there. A handful were so debilitated that they would not live long, many others would be permanently incapacitated by the effects of tropical diseases and parasites. Malaria and kidney ailments were a particular problem, and it would prove very difficult to predict recurrences. Other men had blood vessels weakened, or heart conditions which would remain with them for the rest of their lives. There were also of course the amputees and the blind, their long term livelihoods permanently damaged. Even those who were relatively fit could be startlingly thin: Desmond Bettany records that he weighed about six stone on liberation.

The bulk of the regiment finally started out for home in late September 1945, aboard the transport ship *Almanzora*, on which Lieutenant Colonel D'Aubuz was 'Officer Commanding Army Details'. This vessel carried not only men of the 88th, but of 137th Field Regiment, and various other units. The ship was still very much under military discipline, yet the shipboard routines were varied in consideration of the condition of the passengers, and special medical inspections were held. Large doses of vitamins were handed out, and although the men still had to rise early permission was granted, 'as a concession', for them to take to their hammocks between lunch and 4 p.m. Sergeant Rawlinson enjoyed this 'fattening up' process, as he later called it, and managed to climb from seven to nine stone.

During a very pleasant stop at Colombo, the local Ceylon garrison did their best to make the ex-Prisoners feel at home. There were also shipboard entertainments, which though very limited by the standards of a modern cruise liner, were good by the yardstick of a troopship. These included concerts, a library, bingo or 'housie-housie', quizzes, and an 'other ranks' treasure hunt. Regular pay was resumed, and for once this was money which really could buy food and drink, even bitter and Guinness being readily available. One unusual highlight was an exhibition of 'works produced during internment', including a wireless, chess pieces, sketches and clothing, with prizes for the best exhibits.

On 7th October all ranks received an issue of new clothes during a short stop at Adabiya. This diversion was heralded by the issue of a Middle East Command booklet entitled 'Information for those on their Way Home from the Far East and Who are Stopping at Adabiya, Suez, En Route'. Having welcomed all and sundry this publication informed the ex-prisoners, somewhat apologetically,

> Clothing of thousands of people of all sizes and sexes is no small job. We have not had much information about your size and shape before you arrive, and you will realise that the quality of clothing has not got any better in the past four years of war.

However the ex-prisoners of war, and civilian internees alike, were pretty well fully re-equipped, and whilst ladies and children in other queues received garments like corsets and nappies the men of the 88th exchanged whatever tropical gear they had for European winter kit. In the case of an 'other rank' this included not only battle dress, gloves, shirts and greatcoats, but sundries like brushes, razor blades, new badges, and medal ribbons which anticipated the actual issue of medals themselves. All this took quite some time, and whilst this was going on there were various other possibilities on offer. Some were able to take advantage of a trip to the beach, or swimming pool, or send letters home. Others were able to catch an 'Ensa' entertainments performance, or visit a restaurant for the first time in years. Even so everything was still controlled, everyone had to be back aboard at dusk, and some areas ashore were marked 'out of bounds'.

Some of those to have the most convoluted journeys home were those who had been sent on, after the construction of the notorious railway, to other slave labour projects. Amongst these was Driver Jim Pemberton who had finally washed up in Indo-China digging shelters. A total of 36 bouts of Malaria had done nothing to improve his humour, yet he was as anxious as any to be in England. First came a gruelling drive to Bangkok, where he slept in his first proper bed for three and a half years whilst at the aerodrome. European food, including coffee and cakes, was a similar delight. Next came a flight to Rangoon, and the much appreciated ministrations of the Womens Voluntary Service who dispensed 'Players Cigarettes and a feed of fruit and cream'. It was also in Rangoon that he paid a visit to the cinema, but what was most impressive was not the main feature but the news, which brought him 'a little more up to date'. Some basic hospital checks were also carried out and he was handed a pamphlet on his malaria, before at last he too was on a ship for home. The last leg, Liverpool to Preston, was on the bus.

What the released prisoners did not get, and in retrospect they really needed, was advice or help on overcoming the mental scars which they had sustained during their captivity. Counselling was in its infancy, and perhaps more significantly the prisoners did not receive the general recognition which some thought might be forthcoming. With the war now over, and both VE and VJ days come and gone, they were no longer the news headlines that they would have been in the summer. There was also little consideration given to long term support, and whilst there were small disability pensions to claim, most who were 'demobbed' would go on their way with just a token gratuity and a new suit. This would go some way to explaining why military and ex-prisoners associations would continue to be so important to so many.

The entitlements and responsibilities of ex-prisoners were outlined in a somewhat anonymous looking publication entitled 'To All Ex-Prisoners of War', first issued in September 1945. Whilst by no means generous it did offer certain provisions which the well informed at least would have done well to take up. Amongst other things any who required hospitalisation were entitled, for the time being at least, to remain in the army, and therefore to be paid whilst sick. A provision was also made for 42 days leave, or 56 days 'terminal leave'. For six weeks ex-prisoners were allowed double the ration coupons of civilians, giving them some chance to regain their bulk. On the other hand servicemen were strictly enjoined not to give any interviews without permission, nor to pass on 'casualty information' to next of kin as it was intended that this should go through official channels. Nevertheless worried parents and wives did ask, and in some cases men had news which was not on official forms. For the most part the men of the 88th were as helpful and tactful as they could be, and later their information was vital in listing the dead.

It is believed that 278 men of the regiment never did come home. For these were the ones who lay in improvised cemeteries, or were simply 'missing' over a vast tract of Europe and South East Asia, their bodies scattered from France, Germany, and Belgium, to Burma and Thailand, to Malaya, Singapore, and across the sea to Japan and Formosa. The Japanese kept few records, and despite the great pains that Lieutenant Colonel D'Aubuz, Major Houghton, and others had gone to document their comrades' last resting places, not all would ever be found. In a few cases individuals had buried their friends with as much dignity as they could under the circumstances, and noted the location on scraps of paper which they kept with them until they could put them in the hands of the relevant authorities.

Bombardier N. Edwards of 464 battery was one such who performed this service for his late friend Harry Gardner in the depths of the Thai jungle in July 1945. He not only made sure that the location was dry and the grave deep, but manufactured with his own hands a 'good stout cross' with a name plate. He then wrote directions, drew a tiny map, and not only delivered it, but kept a copy ever afterward. Sergeant J. Singleton of 464 Battery was similarly buried in obscurity, but at least had died a free man, as he had succumbed to illness during an escape. One researcher who later attempted to thoroughly document the subject of burials would locate no less than 41 last resting places for members of the regiment along the Burma-Thailand railway route alone.

Sergeant S. Rawlinson's personal effort to keep a permanent record was a tiny notebook just a little over two inches square, wrapped in canvas, in which he maintained not only a nominal role, but notes of deaths, and which men had gone 'up country' with which party. He was however well used to keeping records under trying circumstances. He had been responsible for the regimental archive at Dunkirk, and had already rewritten many of the records from memory after they were lost during one of the moves at Changi. His notes would still be intelligible fifty years later when deposited with his local museum.

Though the regimental scribes had done a marvellous job under almost impossible conditions, the headache which faced the Commonwealth Wargraves Commission in the post war years would be a major one. The job of correctly identifying, marking, and maintaining the graves of all Empire servicemen in the area was bedeviled by political instabilities and sensibilities, as well as the magnitude of the task. The Japanese alone had no less than 170 main prisoner of war camps, and 214 temporary or branch establishments over South East Asia, and prisoners had died at most if not all of them. In the light of the scale of the problem it is perhaps more remarkable that so much was achieved, rather than that there were occasional and regrettable ommissions or mistakes.

The first effort to do something about this chaotic situation came as early as September 1945, even before many of the living prisoners had been evacuated. Records were collected at Sathorn House in Bangkok, and from here a party was organised to take immediate action. This consisted of a 'Graves Commission' expedition of 16 men along the route of the 'Death Railway' designed to report back to Britain, the Netherlands, and Australia, the locations of cemeteries along the line. Another of their duties was to recover records which the prisoners themselves had buried or kept hidden in the cemeteries. The leaders of the party included Lieutenant Eldridge of the South Lancashire Regiment, several Australian officers, and a Chaplain, some of their activities being filmed for posterity by Captain Nicholson of the Australian Army Military History Section. Undertaking this 'expedition' so quickly had advantages since memories were fresh, and some members of the party had themselves been prisoners. Somewhat bizarrely however there were still Japanese troops in the vicinity, some of whom were kept armed in order to maintain order, and guard against bandits. Good use was also made of them to dig out secreted containers of records and films, and to tend graves. Orders were then issued for the erection of signposts pointing to the cemeteries, some of which were well preserved, whilst others were overgrown or ill-documented. All in all this preliminary work proved invaluable: of 10,549 known graves which were being sought, all but 152 were located.

Fairly quickly there was a decision to attempt to rationalise the position by gathering together the dead in a relatively few places, where cemeteries could be effectively maintained to a high standard: a practice which had already been established after the Great War. Singapore posed particular problems because of the pressure of population, and the intended expansion of the airport at Changi. The Army Graves Service therefore relocated all the remains from here, and from Buona Vista, and other smaller cemeteries, in 1946. The site chosen for the new consolidated cemetery was at a site on a hill at Kranji, where there were already some graves, and which before the war had been a military camp and ammunition store. There are 16 regimental burials here, and, on a remarkable memorial which dominates the skyline, are inscribed the names of those who have no known grave.

Along the path of the 'Death Railway' the plots were consolidated to just three major locations, Thanbyuzayat in Burma covers the northern end of the line, Chungkai and Kanchanaburi in Thailand cover the south. At Thanbyuzayat a base camp and 'hospital' camp had existed since late 1942, and a cemetery had been set up at the foot of the hills which separated Burma from Thailand, on the Moulmein Amhurst Road. As it is now laid out the graves form a semi-circle around a stone of remembrance, and amongst the dead are 24 members of the regiment, together with at least one of their attendant Royal Corps of Signals signallers.

Chungkai in Thailand is essentially a forest clearing about 200 yards from the bank of the river Kwai Noi, three miles south of Kanchanaburi: there are 35 members of the 88th buried here. At Kanchanaburi (or Camburi) itself, not far from the station, is the largest of the war cemeteries with its great oblong blocks of interments centring on a cross of sacrifice. Here is located the biggest concentration of burials relating to 88th Field Regiment anywhere in the world. Amongst the 79 laid to rest here are Lieutenant Adrian Anthony Huxtable, aged 23 at the time of his death, and the Regimental Sergeant Major, Eric James Busby.

Malaya contains several Commonwealth war cemeteries, of which two have particular significance to 88th Field Regiment. At Taiping about 60 miles south east of Penang have been gathered the graves of many casualties of the campaign of 1941–1942. These include four members of the 88th who fell or died of wounds at Gurun and Kampar. Kuala Lumpur Cheras Road cemetery contains just one regimental burial, that of Gunner R.F. Wilson who died of wounds at Parit in December 1941. It has proved possible to at least name all but one or two of the regiment's war dead in the roll of honour at the end of this volume.

Probably the oddest monument in the Far East with regimental connections was erected by the Japanese. This was put up near the bridge at Tha Makham using prisoner labour in March 1944, and consists of a concrete pillar set on a large plinth with four corner buttresses. A notice nearby, placed by the 'Japanese Association in Thailand' after the war proclaims in English:

> This monument was erected by the Japanese Army in World War II in memory of the personnel of the allied forces who helped in the construction of the Burma-Thailand railway and died through illness during the course of the construction. Once a year in March the Japanese residents in Thailand assemble here in a ceremony to commemorate this memorial.

As might be expected it prompts distinctly mixed reactions from the veterans of the railway.

When the brown card packets stuffed with star shaped campaign medals began to reach the deserving hands of the survivors, the members of the regiment were at last able to ponder the weird and wonderful workings of the 'Committee on the Grant of Honours, Decorations, and Medals'. The first surprise was that unlike medals of former wars these new devices were unnamed, recipients marking them with their names if they so wished. The second point worth noting was that no one was entitled to more than five campaign stars, plus the War and Defence Medals. No special medal was struck for Dunkirk, and the commemorative piece later given to veterans by the town was to be regarded as purely unofficial, and not to be worn on the bar with official awards. Perhaps the biggest surprise however was that those who had toiled on the Burma railway were not entitled to the Burma Star, since as prisoners they were not regarded as 'on service'. Instead those who had fought in the Malayan campaign were awarded the Pacific Star. It was therefore unusual for anyone who was in the 88th to be entitled to wear the Burma Star, the main exceptions being those, like Gunner G.R. Pemberton, who had left the unit after Dunkirk, and joined another unit which was redeployed to Burma.

Some felt slighted at the omission of the Burma Star, but happily most members of the general public perceived that to have been a prisoner of the Japanese was every bit as exacting as to have served with General Slim's 14th Army, and probably even more dangerous. The main practical distinction drawn seems to have been the different associations which the veterans of the Malayan campaign, and those who fought in Burma, tended to belong after the war. Whilst the latter were frequently members of the 'Burma Star Association', the 88th tended towards the 'Far East Prisoners of War Association' and the '18th Divisonal Association', in remembrance of the last fighting division to which they were attached. The 'Far East Prisoners of War' or 'Fepows', had as one of their figureheads General Percival, who, although authorised to leave by the Supreme Commander when he surrendered Malaya, stayed and endured captivity.

There were many who never wished to be reminded again of their terrible captivity. Some who would never speak, but there were also those who wanted to speak of little else. It would be fair to say that most felt a sense of distance when they returned, if not downright alienation. In many instances former soldiers fell back on the support of former comrades. Leo Rawlings of the 137th stated that he spent a good part of the first year back in the company of Gunner Eric Newman of the 88th, much of it in 'an alcoholic dream', though he declared it 'worth it, every second'.

Those who saw army 'rehabilitation officers' who were supposed to ease the passage back to civilian life sometimes felt that it was those who were trying to help rather than they who needed rehabilitating, because they simply could not understand the experience. In this respect at least the veterans of the war in the Far East, and the prison camps, had something in common with their fathers who had fought in the trenches in the Great War. One of their biggest problems was their unwillingness to subject their families to the details of their ordeal, and this trait could be identified even before the war was over.

The 88th provided more than one concrete example of this phenomenon. Major Cornish's father, understandably very concerned about his son's welfare in captivity, had managed to track down a gunner who had been in Thailand in 1942 and 1943 and had then been sunk aboard a Japanese transport, and finally rescued by the Allies. The account of the railway that he was given was optimistic in the extreme and was designed more to save the enquirers feelings rather than to give a candid picture. Mr Cornish was told that although the climate had at first been 'a heavy strain' the men had become 'acclimatised' to living and working 'as natives do'. The health of everyone he was reassured was 'very good'. As far as food went fish, rice, and bananas were all available, and although there was no beer, wines, or spirits, there was water, tea, and coffee. According to this version of events football was the common recreation, often played against the 'Japanese Staff'. Conditions had certainly been bad initially due to poor organisation and there had been some 'harsh treatment' but this had been 'gradually put right'. On the whole it was concluded 'the men were not badly treated'. The gunner obviously had his heart in the right place when it came to dealing with anxious relatives, but it was hardly surprising that people at home could not grasp what had really happened when presented with such a sanitised version of events. It was indeed the Second War equivalent of the letters which had come back from the trenches to assure grieving mothers that their son had died 'instantly'.

A memorial service for the war dead of 88th Field Regiment was held in Preston Parish church on the morning of Sunday 3 February 1946. Hymns were sung, and the very relevant text included the passage which stated that 'Greater love hath no man than this, that he lay down his life for his friends'. The address was given by the Reverend T.G. Beer 'lately Chaplain to 88th Field Regiment'; and a collection was made. Appropriately enough the proceeds were directed to the Royal Artillery Orphans and Widows Association, and to the Preston and Fulwood Victory Thanksgiving Fund.

A rather happier event for the benefit of the living was a reunion dinner in the old Preston Guildhall in November of the same year. Amongst those attending were over 200 former members of the regiment including Colonels Simpson, Stanford and D'Aubuz. Also present was George Howson who had joined 2nd West Lancashires in 1910 as a boy trumpeter. An official photographer was on hand to record the event. It was, as one veteran put it with remarkable understatement, 'very nice'. One who sadly missed the dinner was the old Honorary Colonel Trimble who had recently died whilst the regiment was still in captivity.

On 8 June 1946 was held the great victory parade which marched through London from Buckingham Palace, to Oxford Street, Charing Cross, along Whitehall, and finished with a salute on the Mall not far from where it had started. Included were not only army units but the other services, Empire troops, industrial workers, the Civil Defence, tanks, and a fly past of most types of combat aircraft. The intention was that all army units should be represented, and in the case of 88th Field Regiment the choice fell on two particularly worthy other ranks, Sergeant S. Rawlinson, regimental record keeper, and Military Medal winner Bombardier H. Walker. Fittingly the first came from Preston, whilst the latter was from Lancaster.

One other duty would be carried out by Sergeant Rawlinson before the chapter could be considered closed, for he was one of those who had to go to Tokyo to attend the trials of War Criminals. The task facing the allied prosecutors was huge; many thousands had died as a result of Japanese atrocity or neglect, and although many of the perpetrators had been identified, many

The 88th Field Regiment reunion at Preston Guild Hall, November 1946. The two figures standing on the left of the room are Lieutenant E.W. Sowerby, and Sergeant Syd Rawlinson. Immediately in front of them is the officers' table with Colonel S. Simpson at its centre, flanked by Lt Col. S.C. D'Aubuz and Lt. Col Stanford. About two hundred members of the regiment attended, many of them still in uniform.

would also escape justice. Some slipped away for lack of evidence, others because their names were easily confused by non Japanese speakers who knew them only by nicknames. Later, and especially after 1951, some would be freed in the interests of maintaining Japanese support for the west in the Cold War. Those who were tried were divided into 'A', 'B' and 'C' class suspects: 'A' class were determined to be the most important, influencing the conduct and policy of the war, like Prime Minister Tojo himself; 'B' and 'C' class were the smaller fry, of the type encountered by the 88th. Some of these lesser people were tried in batches: perhaps with unseemly haste. Eventually 927 Japanese were executed; 32 of them for incidents on the Burma-Thailand railway. Amongst those executed was General Itagaki, the man who had finally surrendered Singapore to Lord Mountbatten. The crimes of which he was found guilty included the death and maltreatment of both prisoners of war and civilian internees. He was hanged in Tokyo in December 1948. Another who went to the gallows was the man who had captured Malaya and Singapore in the first place, General Yamashita. In his case the evidence had been less clear, but eventually he too had been condemned.

One of the trials of greatest interest to the regiment was that surrounding the ill fated 'F' Force, who had been force marched, starved, beaten, worked, and then allowed to die in droves at Songkurai. This incident alone had led to the unnecessary deaths of 31 members of 88th Field Regiment, and a further 15 with 'H' Force. Seven men were collectively arraigned for trial by a joint British and Australian court in September 1946. The most senior of those tried was Lieutenant Colonel Banno Hirateru commander of 4th branch Malaya Prisoner of War Camp, and with him were a medical officer, two Engineer officers, a more junior camp commandant, and two Korean guards. As one Australian academic has since put it, 'in no trial was the atrocity so obvious but the attribution of responsibility so difficult'.

Perhaps surprisingly, although the court heard evidence that Banno was 'incompetent', 'doddering' and 'fatuous', most witnesses agreed that he had not intentionally caused suffering. The task he had been set was well beyond him, if not impossible. Under his direct command he had just three Japanese officers and 50 guards to cope with 7000 sick men; but with this unpromising material he was supposed to help build a railway in double quick time. He received only three years imprisonment. Captain Tanio the medical officer was similarly found to be without any great malice, and had at least one prisoner speak up for him, so he was sentenced to five years. It was different for Captain Maruyama and Lieutenant Abe, the two Engineer officers primarily responsible for driving the sick captives to work. Both were found to have used great brutality, and both were sentenced to death, although this was later commuted to 15 years. Similar considerations applied to Captain Fukuda who was found to not only have ordered many beatings, but to be both 'lazy' and 'callous', he was sentenced to death, but then reprieved to serve a 'life' sentence.

Of the two guards on trial one admitted beating prisoners, including, on one particularly horrendous occasion, the use of a golf club. Again a death sentence was handed down, and again it was commuted to life. The other guard's actions were deemed far less serious, and he escaped with a token 18 months in prison. Considering that many hundreds of prisoners in their care had died the Japanese and Koreans in charge on the Songkurai section of the line had got off very lightly. In the final analysis none had paid with their lives, and most were out of prison in a comparatively short space of time. The court appears to have accepted that the men in the dock were actually relatively insignificant, as the greatest fault lay at a higher level: with those who had planned the line, with those who had decreed an impossible time table, and with those who had allotted ludicrously little or no food and medicine. Lieutenant Abe would later bitterly protest that it was the Emperor and the 'Top Brass' in Tokyo who were responsible. Others however were actually hanged, notably several officers from the camps in the Hintok area These included Lieutenant Colonel Ishii Tamie, Lieutenant Usuki, and Lieutenant Hirota: 'Dr

Death' whose real identity was Sergeant Okada Seiichi, was sentenced to ten years. The Military Police or 'Kempeitai' were found to hold responsibility for some of the worst incidents, and members of that unit received about a third of all the death sentences.

As Colonel Wild summed it up at the Tokyo tribunal,

> We told the Japanese that the way they were treating their labour, both Asiatic and military, was, from a soldiers point of view, worse than a crime; it was a blunder. We told them, and I consider now, that if they had treated their labour properly and fed it and housed it and given it reasonable working hours, they would have finished the railway by the time they wanted to. We told them ... that as a result of the way they treated their labour they were months later than they intended in finishing that railway, and as a consequence lost a campaign that it was intended to supply in Burma.

The experience of war would mean very different things to the men of the 88th. Several had their health so shattered by Japanese imprisonment that they died within a year of reaching home. Most suffered some symptoms of anxiety, with recurrent nightmares, or an inability to adjust to civilian life, and this applied in some cases as much to those who had fought in Europe as well as the Far East. The experiences they had been through would never quite fade away: as some veterans put it, they might forgive eventually, but they could never forget. This remembrance was often felt as a duty to their comrades. Moreover the events of the post war half century often seemed to turn history on its head from the veterans point of view. It was never quite clear what they were supposed to make of a Britain full of Japanese electrical goods; or of the Queen meeting with Hirohito; or of the little things like Japanese restaurants and exotic Far Eastern dishes. Nevertheless there were many veterans of the 88th however who would prove their resilience by going on to new challenges and new careers, or by readapting and managing to pick up the threads of an old life.

One of the most remarkable in this respect was Roy Marshall who had worked for Colmans Limited but joined the 88th at Preston as a Territorial gunner in 1938. He showed early promise, was a Lance Sergeant at the outbreak of war, and was awarded the Military Medal with the regiment during the retreat to Dunkirk. He was commissioned in 1942 and therefore was not captured in the Far East, but landed on D-Day to fight in North West Europe where he also won the Military Cross. He stayed in the army thereafter and had meteoric promotion, reaching the rank of Major General by the 1960s. Finishing his army career as Deputy Master General of the Ordnance, he was awarded both the C.B. and O.B.E. He then went on to become an advisor in the dynamics group of British Aerospace.

Denis Houghton stuck with the Territorials, and in 1947 when the regiment was reformed as 288th (2nd West Lancashire) Light Anti Aircraft Regiment R.A. T.A. he became its Commanding Officer. He steered it through the mysteries of anti-aircraft work with Bofors guns, and camps at Bude, Towyn, Castlemartin and Stiffkey. He retired from this post in 1952 after two decades with the regiment, but still this did not mean that all connection was lost for he would serve as Deputy Lieutenant of the County, and as High Sheriff. Houghton also did more than almost anyone to help heal the scars of war. One effort he made on behalf of the families of the dead and missing was to interview members of his battery in an attempt to discover what had finally happened to a number of men who had been unaccounted for at the war's end. Another service he performed required extreme discretion. At least one soldier's wife, believing her spouse to be dead, had taken a new husband and given birth to another child. Divorce, bastardy, and bigamy, even of an accidental kind, were extremely difficult subjects in 1945, and Houghton did his best both as officer and as legal practitioner to help sort out these problems.

Desmond Bettany, who described his exit from the army as 'a suit, a mac and a goodbye', had discovered his aptitude for art in the adversity of war, went on to make it his peacetime occupation. He attended the Storey Institute Lancaster in 1946 to obtain professional training, and one of his pictures appeared in the Royal Artillery War Commemoration Book. In the 1950s he emigrated to Australia, prompted perhaps in part by his close association with Australians during captivity. Here he would eventually rise to become principal of Adelaide School of Art.

Geoffrey Haworth, survivor of the Alexandra hospital massacre, went home for a rest. He was technically still a soldier but had leave until his demob in 1946. He had only been at home a day or so when his old employer the proprietor of the local garage came to call. He had been short of mechanics, and would he like his old job back? Haworth gave the matter careful consideration, and said that he would, but only if his wages were raised to £5 a week, a considerable increase on pre war days. The garage owner agreed immediately, but at the end of the first weeks' work Haworth found £5 5s 6d in his pay packet. Querying the mistake the man said he had not the heart to give the ex-prisoner short measure: over the years he had been in captivity the mechanics usual wage had gone up about 50 percent.

Gunner Eric Bamber was still young enough to readapt to the upheavals which war had wrought. He would eventually be elected as a Lancashire County Councillor, and serve on the museum, arts and library committee. Many years later he would return to Changi as a tourist, and, greeted as an honoured guest, got to see a new generation of prisoners. Whilst Changi is still a byword for strict conditions he was pleased to see men at least properly fed and in far better health than had been the case fifty years before. In the 1990s he would give public talks on his wartime experiences, bringing a fresh awareness of the war in the Far East to new generations with a refreshing lack of bitterness. Another member of the 88th connected with local government was Bombardier C.G. Millward who went to work for Preston Borough Council. He would be there for the remainder of his career, and serve as Mayor's secretary.

The Pemberton brothers Jim and George ('Bob'), both of whom had served with the 88th, were reunited on Preston station in the early hours of a chilly morning in February 1946. One had been a prisoner of the Japanese, the other had been fighting for the prisoner's liberation. They went home and took up their lives just where they had left off, in the newspaper distribution business. After they retired from active running of the firm their sons took over 'Pemberton's' which was later renamed 'North West News', which perhaps more accurately reflected its coverage of Preston, Chorley, Leyland and Southport. Jim Pemberton made copious notes on his experiences and read widely on the war in the Far East and would eventually give talks to local societies on the subject. He never again ate rice if it could be avoided.

Veteran George Howson who had joined the Territorials in 1910, fought in the Great War, rejoined the 88th in 1920, and risen to bandmaster by 1938, had again served in the Second World War. He was discharged in 1954, but even this was not the end, as in 1958 when official sanction was given for the reformation of the band he rejoined as bandmaster. Even outside drill hours he would spend much of his free time coaching members of the band at his own house in Preston. He retired for the last time with the rank of Warrant Officer in August 1965. His service with the 88th, its predecessors and successors therefore spanned 55 years, and his dedication was marked by the award of a silver tea service and a well earned British Empire Medal. The notes given as a prompt to the 'presenting officer' observed that 'he has found no task too difficult, too arduous or too irksome for him to undertake'. It was a statement which could have been applied to many of his comrades.

As a regiment it can scarcely be denied that 88th Field Regiment R.A., T.A., had been a good example of its type: at least as efficient as its peers, and on occasions worthy of distinction. Despite reorganisations and losses it had retained a character and cohesion of its own. In adversity its men had shown a willingness to stick together and help each other. It is also apparent that those adversities were not normally of the regiment's own making. At Dunkirk they had been very much part of a bigger picture, and withdrawal with the majority of the men was as much as could be realistically expected.

In Malaya the odds were more heavily weighted, and it is arguable that Lieutenant Colonel D'Aubuz had been handed a more ticklish problem than his predecessors. Malaya and the Japanese were essentially a mystery, and the early orders received by the regiment were both exacting and sometimes confusing. At times the various batteries were widely separated, and air cover was seldom in evidence. From this debacle there would be no escape, save for a fortunate handful. The Malaya campaign had been a debacle in which the commanding officer and the regiment had made every effort to make the best of an irretrievably bad job. As Lieutenant Alexander of the Hertfordshire Yeomanry observed there were occasions when the officers held men of other units to their posts at the point of a pistol.

After the regiment was reformed as 288th Light Anti-Aircraft Regiment in

1947 its headquarters was moved to Kimberley Barracks in Deepdale Road Preston in 1958. The Old Sessions House on Stanley Street, the old headquarters which had been falling into disrepair, was converted between 1958 and 1961 for use as a motor vehicle licensing office. Extensive alterations in the 1980s led to the opening of the building in 1987 as the 'County and Regimental Museum', a title since changed to 'The Museum of Lancashire'. Many veterans have visited the new museum to see exhibits relating to the 88th. The year 1995 saw the fiftieth anniversary of the end of the war, and a special exhibition of Desmond Bettany's pictures of his time in Malaya and in captivity. Even when all the veterans are gone, some time in the new millennium, the building will continue to remember the 88th Field Regiment R.A., T.A. For where paint wears thin, or renovations are carried out, ghostly signs bearing messages like 'Orderly Office' or 'Magazine' appear.

The grave of Captain A.C. Dickson, killed in action at Gurun, December 1941, aged 25 years.

8

Roll of Honour, 88th Field Regiment, 1939–1945

The following lists of names have been compiled using contemporary records kept by the regiment, and Commonwealth War Graves cemetery registers. They are also heavily reliant on personal notes compiled by Lieutenant Colonel S. D'Aubuz; Major D.A.S. Houghton; and Sergeant S. Rawlinson. Given that the regiment was involved in two major campaigns, in which it had its records destroyed on more than one occasion, and that missing men were sometimes not properly accounted for, total completeness cannot be claimed. Apologies are therefore made in advance for any inadvertent errors or omissions. However, it may be claimed that the list which follows is the fullest and most up to date yet published.

As far as the surviving information permits, the names have been grouped alphabetically according to campaign, or area where prisoners died. Wherever possible the following data has been listed: name; rank; number; battery or HQ etc.; home town; cause and place of death; date of death; place of burial or memorial. For sake of brevity attached Royal Engineer, Royal Corps of Signals, and Royal Army Medical Corps personnel have not been included, and the following abbreviations have been adopted.

(B)	Bombardier
BB	Beri Beri
(BSM)	Battery Sergeant Major
(Capt)	Captain
CH	Cholera
d.	Died
(DR)	Driver
DW	Died of wounds
DY	Died of dysentery or similar diseases
(G)	Gunner
KA	Killed in action
(L/B)	Lance Bombardier
(L/S)	Lance Sergeant
(LT.)	Lieutenant
(M)	Mechanic
Mem.	Memorial
(QM)	Quarter Master
(sig)	Signaller
(S)	Sergeant
(T)	Temporary or acting

Than   Thanbyuzayat, Burma
(W)   Warrant Officer
+   Buried

The Campaign in France and Belgium, 1939–1940

Chalker, F.V. (S) 273178, KA, Dunkirk, 1.6.40.
Fox, G.W. (G) 1073911, DW, 8.6.40.
Gregson, G.D. (Major) Preston, KA, France, 27.5.40.
Grinham, E.G. (G) 943152, KA, Dunkirk, 28.5.40.
Ridley, F. (G) 906880, KA, Dunkirk, 2.6.40.
Tyrer, A. (G) 878648, DW, Belgium, 16.5.40.
Woodworth, A.D. (B) 858580, DW, Dunkirk, 31.5.40.

Died in, or escaping from, German captivity, 1940–1945

Foulkes, J. (G) 885183, d. POW camp, 4.8.44.
Sturton, — (LT) Shot while escaping from train.

Killed or died in the United Kingdom, 1940–1941

Bell, C.R. (G) 941150, d. 6.3.41.
Duckworth, G.H. (G) 910786, d. 18.6.41.
Gardner, G.B. (BSM) 3702720, d. Oakhampton, Devon, 9.6.40.
Heasmere, T.J. (G) 6757089, killed London, 8.9.40.
Jerome, G.H. (G) 904385, d. 26.1.41.
Orr, J. (BSM) 815346, killed Southend, 30.6.41.

Killed or died of wounds, Malayan Campaign, 1941–1942

Bartlett, R.W.E. (G) 974427, 352, Dewhurst, Gloucs, KA Kampar, 1.1.42, + Taiping.
Bennett, J. (G/DR) 1458187, RHQ, KA Ipoh Station, 23.12.41.
Collier, F. (G/Sig) 902157, 351, DW Blanga Bridge, nr Pusing, 23.12.41.
Collins, W. (G) 828382, 464, KA Singapore, 14.2.42.
Connor, D. (G) 1077702, 352, Malaria, 15.1.42, + Kranji.
Dawes, F. (G) 862151, 464, Skerton, Lancs, KA Singapore, 15.2.42.
Dickson, A.C. (Capt) 70153, RHQ, Preston, Lancs, KA Gurun, 15.12.41, + Taiping.
Gardner, L.S. (S) 818591, RHQ, KA Gurun, 15.12.41.
Graves, H.J. (G) 805068, RHQ, KA Gurun, 15.12.41.
Hare, H.T. (L/B) 800790, 352, DW Batu Anam as a result of anti-tank mine, 19.1.42, + Kranji.
Heath, E.J.W. (G) 34106, 351, KA Gurun, 15.12.41.
Heaver, A.E. (G) 956624, 352, DW Kampar, 2.1.42, + Taiping.
Ingram, J. (G/DR) 855368, RHQ, KA Ipoh Station, 23.12.41.
Ingram, W. (G/DR) 901484, 351, KA Gurun, 15.12.41.
Kelly, J.E. (Major) 464, KA Buloh Kasap when armoured car turned over, 19.1.42.
McGillicuddy, P.T. (G) 982814, 464, Nunthorpe, Yorks, KA Singapore, 10.2.42, + Kranji.
Miller, J. (G) 1096709, 352, DW.
Murray, J. (G) 858916, RHQ, 15.2.42.
Shaw, A. (Battery QMS) 1021736, 352, South Ruislip, Mdex, KA Singapore, 15.2.42, + Kranji.
Shield, G.E. (LT) 464, Eastbourne Sussex, DW received in campaign, 18.3.42, + Kranji.
Stevens, G.F. (S) 882179, RHQ, KA Ipoh Station, 23.12.41.

Trethewy, R.G. (LT) 351, DW Kampar, 2.1.42, Tavistock, Devon, + Taiping.
Walsh, J. (G/Sig) 1113242, 351, Manchester, DW 17.2.42, + Singapore Hospital.
Whitley, J.H. (G) 896409, believed killed Alexandra Hospital, 15.2.42.
Wilson, R.F. (G/DR) 941676, 351, DW Parit, 23.12.41, + Kuala Lumpur (Cheras Road) Civil Cemetery.

Died in Japanese captivity, Changi Jail, Singapore, of causes other than wounds received in battle, February 1942–August 1945

Carlisle, S. (S) 768941, 464, Preston, Lancs, pleurisy, 13.8.42, + Kranji.
Ellis, J.A. (G/Sig) 1085761, 464, peritonitis, 22.9.43, + Kranji.
Gregson, J.E. (G/Sig) 892643, 351, Preston, Lancs, DY, 10.7.45 (sometimes given as 11.7.45), + Kranji.
Grover, J. (G) 987481, 464, DY, 10.11.42, + Kranji.
Gumsley, W.S. (G) 1085567, 351, ulcers, 17.5.42, + Kranji.
Jay, J.F. (G) 990199, 464, DY, 11.6.42, + Kranji. (some sources state d. Thailand)
Lamplugh, J.S. (G/DR) 941331, 352, Thornaby-on-Tees, Yorks, DY, 31.7.42, + Kranji.
Maxwell, A.V. (L/S) 915429, 464, Lancaster, burns, 21.5.42, + Kranji.
Morris, G.E. (G) 930754, 464, septicaemia, 1.5.44, + Kranji.
Worsley, T. (L/S) 885409, 464, Preston, Lancs, DY, 21.4.42 (also recorded as 30.4.42), + Kranji.

Died in Japanese captivity on, or near, the Burma–Thailand Railway, 1942–1945

Archibald, A. (G) 1109050, 351, Glasgow d. Camburi 4.6.43, + Camburi.
Atherton, H. (L/B) 890965, RHQ, Preston, d. Kinsayok, DY, 31.7.43, + Camburi.
Atkinson, N. (G/Sig) 1123200, 352, Bingley DY, 27.2.43 (or 28.2.43) + Camburi.
Baker, M.J. (B) 820222, 352, Lancaster, DY, 1.12.42, + Chungkai.
Banks, J. (L/B) 3856638, 351, Preston, d. Sonkurai, DY, 13.7.43, + Than.
Barley, W.E. (G/Sig) 1119923, 352, Lowestoft d. Tonchan, BB, 26.7.43, + Camburi.
Bartle, D.E.C. (L/B) 980377, 351, Lambeth, d. Tonchan, BB, 11.3.43, + Camburi.
Bate, G.H. (G) 1089095, 464, Wolverhampton, Malaria and DY, 17.7.43, + Chungkai.
Beale, E. (G/DR) 890868, 464, Blackpool, 25.6.43, + Chungkai.
Bergin, N. (G/Sig) 1119452, 464, Salford, d. Tonchan, BB, 27.3.43, + Camburi.
Bills, W. (G) 1092339, 351, Stockbridge d. Kinsayok, DY, 25.6.43, + Camburi.
Bishop, G.M. (G) 980264, 351, Aberdare, d. Tanboya, DY, 31.8.43, + Than.
Briggs, H.W.J. (G) 965840, 352, Northampton, d. Sonkurai, DY, 15.8.43, + Than.
Bull, A.J. (L/B) 938509, 351, Leyton, d. Sonkurai, CH, 1.6.43, + Than.
Burns, F. (G/DR) 941143, 352, Manchester d. Sonkurai, CH, 15.7.43, + Than.
Busby, A. (L/S) 841682, 351, Abbey Wood, d. Hintock Valley, CH, 19.7.43, + Camburi.
Busby, E.J. (W) (Regimental Sergeant Major) 6607404, Gt. Linford, Bucks, d. Thailand, 1.7.43, + Camburi.
Cable, E.W. (G) 959203, 352, Merthyr Tydfil, d. Tonchan, CH, 24.6.43, + Camburi.
Carter, J.T. (G) 867069, 464, Hereford, d. Hintock Valley, CH, 3.8.43.
Cates, A. (L/B) 1044488, 351, Guildford, d. Kinsayok, CH, 26.7.43, + Camburi.
Clarke, A. (G) 1041730, 352, d. Thailand, 26.10.43, + Camburi.
Clayton, H.N. (G/Sig) 1119437, 351, Southport, d. Tha Makham, DY, 16.7.43, + Camburi.
Clayton, W. (G) 891813, 464, Great Harwood, d. Tarso, DY, 7.2.44, + Camburi.
Codd, D.E. (G) 980799, 352, London, d. Tanboya, ulcers, 29.9.43, + Than.
Cole, C.T. (G) 1092360, 351, Cadley Heath, d. Chungkai, 11.6.43, + Than.

Cole, J.R. (G) 1108488, RHQ, Lancaster, d. Tanboya, DY and Malaria, 10.9.43.
Cooper, F.C. (B) 835223, 352, b. Matlock d. Camburi, BB and DY, 15.12.43, + Camburi.
Cornall, C.V.C. (S) 903421, 351, Preston, Lancs, encephalitis, 15.9.43, + Chungkai.
Corns, F.R. (B) 906313, Blackpool d. Tanboya, 3.9.43, + Than.
Darwen, C.R. (BSM) 749224, 351, Lancaster, d. Tarso, BB, 20.8.43, + Camburi.
Davison, J.C. (G) 849027, 351, Preston, Lancs, d. Tarso, CH, 5.8.43.
De Santi, L. (G) 855893, 351, Preston d. Tarso, CH, 1.12.43, + Camburi.
Dent, F. (L/S) 885043, 351, d. Tarso, Malaria and DY, 26 (or 28).11.43, + Camburi.
Downes, W.H. (G) 1085753, 352, Birmingham, killed, 29.11.44.
Duddle, J. (L/B) 852314, 464, Preston, d. Sonkurai, Malaria, 10.7.43, + Than.
Dunn, W.A. (G) 857688, RHQ, Birmingham, d. Camburi, 20.5.43 (attached from 9th Coast Regiment).
Dyke, H.G. (G) 961313, 352, Lynton, Devon, d. Tonchan, CH, 8.7.43.
Eccleston, J. (S/Sig) 801303, 351, Preston, Lancs, CH, 27.8.43, + Chungkai.
Farnsworth, J.E. (G/Sig) 903403, Langley, Notts, d. Kinsayok, 16.7.43, + Camburi.
Fields, H. (G) 1017912, 351, Sheffield, d. Nakompaton, 8.9.44.
Fish, H. (L/S) 908413, 352, Blackpool, d. Tanboya, BB, 26.9.43, + Than.
Fletcher, W. (G/Sig) 891732, 351, Preston, d. Camburi, 29.6.43.
Fox, C. (L/B) 902169, RHQ, Preston, Lancs, CH, 18.6.43, + Chungkai.
Gale, A.M. (L/S) 830400, 351, Kensington, London, 22.6.43, + Chungkai.
Gardner, H. (L/B) 855810, 464, Lancaster, d. Thailand 11.7.45, + Camburi.
Goadbey, E. (G) 1085566, 352, Portsmouth, d. Tonchan, CH, 21.6.43, + Camburi.
Greenbank, H. (B) 849664, 352, Lancaster, d. Sonkurai, CH, 30.7.43, + Than.
Griffiths, A.G. (L/B) 821960, 351, d. Tha Makham, ulcers, 8.9.43.
Groves, H.A. (G) 1504966, 352, Doncaster, d. Kinsayok, CH, 11.7.43, + Camburi.
Halston, S. (G) 1115275, 351, Derby, d. Kinsayok, CH, 25.7.43, + Camburi.
Hallworth, F. (G/Sig) 1119444, Poynton, Cheshire, 351, d. Tarso, DY, 17.11.43, + Camburi.
Harper, G.H. (G) 1092437, 352, Chesterton, Staffs, 19.12.43, + Chungkai.
Harrison, J.N. (L/B) 871220, 464, Grimsargh, Lancs, d. Camburi, DY and ulcers, 6.10.43, + Camburi.
Harvey, L.W. (G) 974417, 352, Hednesford, CH, 4.7.43, + Camburi.
Harwood, L.C. (G) 984112, 352, London, d. Tarso, 6.11.43.
Haslam, W. (T/S) 910912, 464, Bolton, d. Kinsayok, DY, 12.8.43, + Camburi.
Henden, A.W. (G/Sig) 980350, 352, Norwich, d. Tarso, DY, 17.10,43, + Camburi.
Hermon, E. (G) 876354, 351, Yateley, d. Thailand, 12.8.45.
Heward, J.K. (G) 967440, 351, Stanhope, d. Sonkurai, CH, 8.6.43, + Than.
Hill, G.S. (L/B) 1072232, 351, Whitby, d. Kinsayok, CH, 17.7.43, + Camburi.
Hindley, H. (G/Sig) 1119414, 352, d. Thailand, 18.7.44.
Hirst, L. (B) 861253, 352, Blackpool, d. Tarso, DY, 20.6.43, + Camburi.
Hitching, J.E. (G/Sig) 1108929, 351, Kendal, 7.4.44.
Hodgson, R. (G) 1083660, 464, Lancaster, d. Sonkurai, CH, 3.6.43, + Than.
Hodson, F. (G) 858164, 351, Fulwood, Lancs, 24.11.43, + Chungkai.
Huckle, F. (G) 1085702, 464, Conberton, d. Thailand, 14.11.44. + Camburi.
Hudson, A. (G) 946428, 464, Stapleford, Notts, Avitaminosis, 12.7.43, + Chungkai.
Hutchinson, M. (G) 1085585, 351, CH, 2.6.43. Sonkurai.
Huxtable, A.A. (LT) 351, Preston, Dorset (b. Kuala Lumpur) d. Tonchan, DY, 5.7.43, + Camburi.
Ingham, K. (G/DR) 1115070, 352, d. Tonchan, CH, 21.6.43, + Camburi.
Ingham, T. (G) 894613, 351, Preston, d. Sonkurai, DY, 29.7.43, + Than.
Jackson, L. (G) 1115069, 352, Methley, d. Thailand, 29.4.43, + Camburi.

Jenkins, C. (G) 11050431, 464, Leytonstone, 24.7.43.
Jenkinson, G.M. (G) 897895, 351, Bamber Bridge, d. Kinsayok, DY, 14.8.43, + Camburi.
Johnston, J.I. (G) 845275, 352, died in US air raid, 15.12.44, + Camburi.
Johnstone, W. (G) 967512, 351, Edinburgh, ulcers, 3.9.43, + Chungkai.
Jollie, J. (L/B) 915323, 352, Kettle, d. Sonkurai, CH, 1.6.43.
Keegan, F.J. (B) 955192, 351, Seaham, Durham, starvation, 2.3.44, + Chungkai.
Keogh, T. (G) 1118178, 464, Hull, d. Tonchan, DY, 16.6.43, + Camburi.
Lamb, B.T. (G) 923920, 352, Lancaster, d. Sonkurai, CH, 3.6.43, + Than.
Lambert, D. (G) 954236, 351, Liverpool, d. Hintock River, CH, 27.7.43.
Lawrence, E.F.J. (G/Sig) 2029978, 351, Enfield d. Tanboya, 6.10.43, + Than.
Lawton, K.W. (G) 1113481, RHQ, Hull, d. Camburi, ulcers, 22.1.44, + Camburi.
Lea, R.P. (G/DR) 111578, 352, Fristone, Yorks, 9.10.44.
Leack, W. (G) 923907, 352, Lancaster, d. Kuie, 24.9.43.
Lewis, H.B. (G/D/M) 845665, Lancaster, d. Tarso, BB, 29.9.43.
Lloyd, G.W.R. (G) 1094249, 464, Chester, d. Kinsayok, DY, 1.6.43, + Camburi.
Lockyer, J.H. (S) 1072570, 352, Bristol, d. Hintock Valley, CH, 16.7.43.
Lowndes, E. (G/Sig) 1119397, 351, Bradford, d. Sonkurai, CH, 9.8.43, + Than.
Lyon, J. (G) 896992, 464, Preston d. Sonkurai, DY, 24.6.43, + Than.
McDonald, G.T.C. (G) 893063, 464, air raid, 21.9.44.
MacKellar, J. (G/DR) 1112544, 351, Inverness, d. Tonchan, Malaria, 10.6.44.
Marshall, C. (G/Sig) 1085605, 351, Old Batsford, Notts, d. Kinsayok, DY, 9 (or 4).7.43, + Camburi.
Martin, M.G. (G/Sig) 1119447, 352, Dublin, starvation, 26.4.43, + Chungkai.
Mason, G.D. (G/DR) 1417074, 352, Bradfield, d. Tonchan, CH, 27.12.43, + Camburi.
Maynard, C. (G/Sig) 1108826, 351, Crowborough Sussex, Malaria, 31.5.43, + Chungkai.
Mayor, A. (G) 855752, 351, Preston, d. Transit camp Kendo, DY, 30.9.43, + Than.
Mills, R.M. (G/DR) 843934, 464, d. Thailand, 7.2.44.
Mitchell, W. (L/S) 902158, RHQ, Burslem, d. Tarso, 8.10.43, + Camburi.
Moore, A.V. (G) 958330, 352, Chiswick, 9.4.43, + Chungkai.
Moss, J.R.S. (G) 891727, 352, Austwick, d. Camburi, 20.6.43.
Moule, S.H. (G/DR) 1118278, 351, Shoreditch, 26.4.43, + Chungkai.
Muir, J.L. (T/S) 394195, 351, Preston, d. Kami-Sonkurai, 21.10.43, + Than.
Munro, R.A. (G) 1105842, 352, Goatbridge, d. Tonchan, CH, 6.7.43, + Camburi.
Munson, W.E. (L/B) 980356, 351, Spalding 19.6.43, + Chungkai.
Nash, A.S. (G) 964198, 351, Walworth, d. Tonchan, 24.6.43, + Camburi.
Nelson, T. (L/B) 861704, 351, Preston, d. Kra Peninsula camp, 3.7.45, + Camburi.
Newman, R.A. (G/Sig) 941946, 351, Halesowen pneumonia.
Newton, D. (L/B) 900352, 464, South Shore, Blackpool, DY, 19.2.44, + Chungkai.
Nickson, C. (S) 871224, 351, Preston, d. Sonkurai, Malaria, 26.8.43, + Than.
Nickson, F. (G) 903463, 352, Blackpool, DY, 28.8.43, + Chungkai.
Noblett, W. (G) 898749, 464, Preston 18.5.43, + Chungkai.
Noyce, G. (G) 963069, 352, Christchurch d. Camburi, Ulcers and DY, 6.10.43, + Camburi.
O'Connell, J.G. (G) 1087680, 352, Cricklewood, Mdex, 20.8.43, + Chungkai.
O'Connor, D. (G) 1087681, 352, St Leonards, Sussex, Starvation, 16.10,43, + Chungkai.
O'Dowd, C. (G/DR) 1090819, 352, Doncaster, d. Thailand, 1.8.44.
Ord, W.C.S. (G) 898795, 351, Preston DYS, 6.10,43, + Chungkai (sometimes incorrectly listed 85th Field Regiment).
Overton, A.E. (G) 1094275, 464, Cobham, Surrey, Malaria and DY, 2.8.43, + Chungkai.
Palmer, J. (G) 990055, 352, Blackheath, Birmingham, d. Kinsayok, BB, 15.9.43, + Camburi.

Parry, G.W. (B) 1068791, 464, Liverpool DY, 30.12.43, + Chungkai.
Poole, H. (L/B) 891094, 464, Out Rawcliffe, Lancs. 9.6.43, + Chungkai.
Rand, F.H. (G/Sig) 1123224, 352, b. Southampton, d. Tanboya, Ulcers, 9.9.43, + Than.
Read, E. (G/DR) 1118303, 464, Hull, d. Tarso, peritonitis, 4.4.43, + Camburi.
Reeves, W.E. (G) 947563, 351, d. Hintock River, CH, 13.7.43.
Richardson, E. (G) 888776, 351, Lancaster, d. Tonboya, DY and Malaria, 6.11.43, + Than.
Riggall, E. (B) 950030, 351, Skegness, d. Tarso, Malaria, 1.10.43, + Camburi.
Roberts, C.H. (G) 1459938, 351, Peckham, d. Hintock River, DY, 28.8.43.
Roberts, S. (G) 1092527, 351, d. Tanboya, BB and DY, 13.10.43, + Than.
Robinson, J. (G) 779733, 352, Liverpool, d. Kinsayok, DY, 16.7.43, + Camburi.
Robinson, W.S. (L/B) 956653, 464, Birkenhead, d. Kinsayok, DY and BB, 25.7.43, + Camburi.
Roscoe, J.A. (G/Sig) 878898, 464, South Shore, Blackpool, Cholera, 29.9.43, + Chungkai.
Rourke, B.T.R. (G) 1321440, 352, Winton, d. Kuie, BB, 23.7.43, + Camburi.
Ruffell, R. (G) 959667, 464, Tiptree, d. Kinsayok, 7.8.43, + Camburi.
Saunders, W.F. (G) 951255, 352, Weston-S-Mare 14.8.43, + Chungkai.
Seed, H.N. (L/S) 857392, 351, Preston d. Tarso, BB, 29.1.44, + Camburi.
Sibilia, A. (G/Sig) 1119424, 464, London, tree felling accident, 20.12.42, + Camburi.
Simpson, S.G. (B) 930712, 351, Bowes Park Middex d. Camburi, 31.7.43, + Camburi.
Smith, H. (G) 982262, 464, Sutton Coldfield Warks, Pneumonia, 24.8.43, + Chungkai.
Smith, J.A. (G/Sig) 1119228, 351, Westcliff on Sea, Essex, d. Kinsayok, BB, 20.7.43, + Camburi.
Singleton, J. (S) 885723, Preston, Died whilst escaping Thailand, 13.9.43, buried by (S) Bradley 85 Anti-Tank regiment.
Singleton, W.J. (G) 921518, 351, Preston d. Thailand 22.6.44.
Stevenson, G.T. (L/B) 910785, 351, Wigan d. Tonchan, CH, 16.10,43.
Stewart, J.P. (L/B) 799003, 352, Glasgow d. Tanboya, 5.12,43, + Than.
Stones, G.S. (G/DR) 1120606, 352, Grainthorpe Lincs, d. Tarso, 21.10.43. + Camburi.
Storey, S.G. (G/Sig) 1113108, 351, Plumstead D. Kinsayok, BB, 14.7.43, + Camburi.
Summersgill, T.R. (L/S) 895372, 352, Blackpool, Starvation, 19.6.43, + Chungkai.
Swinhoe, H. (S) 1070583, 352, d. Tha Makham, Ulcers and DY, 25 (or 24).9.43, + Camburi.
Thomas, G. (G) 869998, 352, Lancaster DY, 28.8.43, + Chungkai.
Thorne, A. (G) 908392, 351, Aston 29.4.43, + Chungkai.
Titchner, J.J. (G) 948399, 351, Camberwell d. Kinsayok, CH, 25.7.43, + Camburi.
Tolley, F.C. (G) 899388, RHQ, Preston d. Camburi, 8.7.43, + Camburi.
Tonks, J. (G) 1092571, 464, Birmingham d. Tonchan, DY, 3.12.43, + Camburi.
Wade, C.E. (G/Sig) 1108596, 351, Stoke Newington, BB, d. Thailand 23.7.43, + Camburi.
Wall, G.E. (G) 968257, 352, Moreton d. Tanboya, Ulcers, 15.8.43, + Than.
Wallis, G.W. (G) 1092600, 352, Birmingham, Malaria, 5.7.43, + Chungkai.
Wallis, L. (B) 895038, 464, Preston d. Nieke, DY, 18.8.43, Camburi Mem.
Walsh, J. (G/DR) 896408, 352, Blackpool, Pellagra, 28.9.43, + Chungkai.
Ward, J. (G) 906164, 351, d. Tanboya, 28.1.44.
Waterhouse, A. (G/Sig) 1119454, 464, Manchester d. Tarso, DY, 15.7.43.
Watson, J.L. (G) 908197, 352, Fleetwood d. Tonchan, Pellagra, 30.5.43.
Watts, J.F.E. (BSM) 1055199, 352, Edinburgh d. Hintock River, CH, 19.7.43.
Whatling, E. (S) 816592, 352, Preston d. Tha Makham, Jaundice, 20.9.43.
Whittle, E. (G) 879115, 351, Bamber Bridge Lancs. BB, 30.11.43, + Chungkai.
Wilkinson, C. (G/Sig) 1119426, 464, Moston Manchester, Ulcers and BB, 20.9.43, + Chungkai.

Wilkinson, J.N. (B Fitter) 870012, 352, Preston d. Thailand, 18.7.45.
Winder, H. (L/B) 912216, 352, Lancaster d. Kinsayok, Ulcers and BB, 16.8.43.
Wolfe, H.E. (G/Sig) 899258, 464, Birkenhead d. Hintock Valley, CH, 26.7.43.

Died in transit to Japan when the transport ship *Rakuyo Maru* was sunk 12.9.44

Armstrong, H.B. (G) 1082000, 351, Newcastle.
Bennett, G. (G/DR) 861804, 351, Islington.
Berry, J.T. (Capt) 351, Preston.
Cadman, A. (G) 1085742, 352, Madeley Salop.
Condon, D.A. (G) 926807, 464, Castletown, Isle of Man.
Corless, F.J. (G) 801494, 351, Preston.
Dacre, W. (L/S) 359284, 351, Workington.
Drake, D. (G) 984350, 352, Leeds.
Dyer, C.H. (BSM) 828358, 464, Eastbourne.
Eley, J.F. (G) 923904, 464, Lancaster.
Fox, F. (G) 894779, 351, Preston Lancs.
Grice, C. (G) 1115636, 352, Stoke.
Hewitt, C.W. (G/DR) 904257, 464, Dunkinfield Cheshire.
Hodkinson, J.B. (G) 871410, RHQ, Lancaster.
Jackson, J. (G) 905032, 352, Preston.
Joyce, A.B. (G) 900180, 464, Liverpool.
Kennedy, S. (G) 867514, 351, Irvine.
Lambert, L. (L/B) 885349, 464, Lancaster.
Lavey, G.E. (S) 3384670, 464, Leyton.
Lea, J. (G/DR) 1115657, 464, Wigan.
Lewis, P. (L/B) 1068953, 351, Swansea.
McGlennon, J. (G) 912217, 464, Whitehaven.
Malam, N. (G/DR) 1115661, 464, Stoke.
Marsh, J.A. (L/S) 2730252, 464, Lambeth.
Miller, E. (G) 1119448, 351, Manchester.
Mitchell, L. (G) 895985, 351, Blackpool.
Mount, R. (G/DR) 870971, 352, Lancaster.
Mulrennan, M.T. (G) 955631, 351, Woolwich.
Newman, F.W. (G) 6405401, 352, Battersea.
Ormerod, R. (G/D/M) 834824, 464, Preston.
Parkinson, G.R. (G) 905582, 464, Preston.
Robbins, W.F. (G/Sig) 1098348, 351, Lambeth.
Rudd, J.J. (L/S) 812509, 351, Whitehaven.
Rudd, J. (G) 966543, 351 Whitehaven.
Simpson, E. (TS) 923114, 352, Coventry.
Sumner, A.M. (TS) 887115, RHQ, Preston.
Vaughan, H. (G/Sig) 891729, 351, Preston.
Whitehurst, J. (L/S) 905756, 351, Bolton.
Wilson, H. (G/Sig) 905586, 464, Preston.
Wintersgill, E.W. (/DR) 953953, 464, Warmfield.
Woodward, P.N. (L/B) 953824, 464, Wolverhampton.
Worden, R. (L/B) 851723, 464, Preston.

Died elsewhere in South East Asia, or missing presumed dead, 1942–1945

Arthur, A.E. (S Artificer) 788861, 351, Kingsbridge d. air crash returning home, 9.9.45.
Atkinson, A.V. (Staff S) 1415917, 351, York d. Kranji, 16.4.45, + Kranji.
Boyle, H. (S) 900034, 352, Newmills Derbyshire d. Taichu Formosa, 5.4.43.
Burgin, A.G. (L/B Fitter) 955218, 352, Kensington d. 20.8.45 after release.
Edwards, P.G. (G) 1089614, 464, Shoreditch d. French Indo China, 9.4.45.
Green, W.J. (G/D/M) 1058664, 351, Leyont d. accident in Manilla, 10.9.45.
Grice, J.W.K. (G/DR) 880649, 464, believed drowned July 1944.
Hanlon, W. (G/Sig) 968413, 352, d at sea, 21.9.44.
Harrison, L.R. (G) 108569, 351, Bovington Dorset d. Formosa, 28.10.44.
Kennedy, E.G. (G) 977397, 464, Captured and disappeared.
Middleton (L/S) 810148, 352, Kirkudbright d. Japan.
Malbon, S. (G/DR) 1085811, Chesterton d. after release, New Zealand 30.10.45.
Oliver (G) 944973, Captured and disappeared.
Quinn, J. (G) 889345, 352, Newcastle d. at sea, 19.1.45.
Rendell, G.W. (G) 1061045, d. Malaya, 7.8.43.
Smith, D. (G) 1525417, d. Borneo, 1944.
Willmott, J.J.W. (S/Sig) 1073133, 464, London d. Kra Peninsula camp (also stated to have died French Indo-China) 19.6.45.
Walker, T.W. (G) 855388, 464, Preston d. Kra Peninsula camp, 6.8.45.

Commanding Officers 88th Brigade and 88th Field Regiment, 1920–1945

Lt. Col S. Simpson Appointed June 1920
Lt. Col S. Smith DSO MC Appointed June 1922
Lt. Col J. Hudson MC Appointed June 1930
Lt. Col H.C.H. Eden MC Appointed July 1936
Lt. Col R.D. Marshall Appointed September 1938
Lt. Col H.M. Standord MC Appointed September 1939
Bevt. Major G.M. St Leger (Temporary) July 1940
Lt. Col R. Hilton DSO MC DFC Appointed July 1940
Lt. Col H.S. MacDonald DSO MC Appointed September 1940
Lt. Col S.C. D'Aubuz Appointed June 1941

Brief chronology of Regimental War Service, 1939–1945

1939
31 August	Regiment embodied for service.
27 September	'Road Party' leaves for France.
4 October	Main body disembarks at Cherbourg.
14 October	Regiment arrives at Gondecourt.

1940
1 March	Regiment moves to Lille area.
12 May	Advance into Belgium.
15 May	In action for the first time.
21 May	Battle on the Escaut River line.
27 May	'F' Troop overrun and captured.
28 May	Defence of the Dunkirk perimeter.

Roll of Honour, 88th Field Regiment, 1939–1945

1 June	Main body evacuated from Dunkirk.
6 June	Reassembly begins at Okehampton.
14 June	Used as infantry Bournemouth area.
July	Equipped with 75mm guns in Kent.
4 August	Deployed in defence, Brighton area.
21 October	Redeployed to Chichester.

1941

16 January	Reorganised into three batteries.
19 February	Moved to Essex.
18 May	Equipped with new 25 pdr guns.
29 September	Embarkation on *Empress of Canada*.
28 November	Arrival at Singapore.
8 December	Japanese attack on Malaya.
11 December	464 Battery deployed Kuantan.
14–15 December	Battle at Gurun (351, 352, RHQ).
20 December	Retreat from the Krian River line.
23 December	Under air attack at Ipoh.
27 December	Battle at Kampar commences.

1942

7 January	Batang Bajunti bridges defended.
15–16 January	Firing in defence of Gemas.
19 January	464 Battery engaged Buloh Kasap.
22–24 January	Actions around Yong Peng.
31 January	Singapore causeway blown.
4–8 February	Defence of the straits.
9 February	Enemy invades Singapore Island.
15 February	British surrender.
16 February	Prisoners ordered to Changi.
22 March	Regiment to Farrah Park.
25 April	Main body to Towner Road.
May	Main body to Serangoon Road.
19 June	First party to Burma railway.
7 December	Opening Bukit Timah memorials.

1943

March	Start of railway 'Speedo' period.
April	Completion Tha Makham bridges.
May	Start of Changi airfield work.
June	Cholera in Thailand camps.
17 October	Completion of Burma railway.

1944

May	Construction of new billets.
12 September.	*Rakuyo Maru* disaster.
5 November	Start of air raids on Singapore.

1945

24 June	Tha Makham Bridge destroyed.

15 August   Japanese final capitulation.
12 September   Singapore surrender ceremony.
15 September   Main body embarks on *Almanzora*.
17 October   Arrival at Southampton.

Organisation of a Three Battery Field Regiment (from beginning of 1941)

Regimental Headquarters

6 officers; 54 men.

Three Batteries

Each battery – 10 officers; 194 men divided into two troops and battery HQ (Battery HQ 4 officers; 74 men).

Six Troops

Each troop – 3 officers; 25 men.
Total personnel Royal Artillery: 36 officers; 636 men.
Attached: Royal Corps of Signals, 1 officer; 37 men.
Royal Engineers, 1 officer; 12 men.
Royal Army Medical Corps, 1 officer.

Equipment

24, 25 pdr guns; 683 rifles, machine guns, and pistols; 13 anti-tank rifles; 42 motor cycles; 36 tractors; 48 trailers; 10 cars; 9 armoured observation posts; 45 trucks; 29 lorries; 1 water trailer.
(NB During the 1939–1941 period the organisation was two rather than three batteries per regiment, though the total number of guns was the same).

Bibliography

Primary sources, memoirs, journals and interviews

Bradley, R. 'An Engineer's Work in Japanese Prison Camps' in *Engineering* (Vol 167, 7.1.1949)

Bull S.B. & Read F *Notes, Interviews, and Correspondence with Veterans of 88th Field Regiment Including: Major D.A.S. Houghton, Captain M.C. Dickson (RAMC), Captain E.C. Dickson, Lieutenant P. Lane, Sergeant S. Rawlinson, Lance Bombardier G. Hawarth, Lance Bombardier J.E. Lyon, Lance Bombardier D. Bettany, Gunner E. Bamber, Gunner G. Slater, Gunner F. Race, Gunner F. Parkes, Gunner/Signaller L. Livermore, Driver G.R. Pemberton, Driver J. Pemberton* (Unpublished Lancashire County Museums)

Commonwealth Wargraves Commission. *The War Dead of the British Commonwealth and Empire. Cemetery Registers* (Maidenhead 1950s, reprinted and updated Maidenhead 1980s).

D'Aubuz S. *History of the 88th Field Regiment R.A. in Malaya 1941–1942* (Unpublished Typescript, Lancashire County Museums).

Boyle J. *Railroad to Burma* (Sydney, 1990).

Coast J. *Railroad of Death* (London, 1946).

Dickson E.C. *The Diary of Captain E.C. Dickson* (Unpublished manuscript, Imperial War Museum).

Eldridge A. *First Reconnaissance of the Burma-Siam Railway* (Bangkok 1945, reprinted Lytham, 1995).

Fletcher-Coke J. *The Emperor's Guest* (London, 1971).

Gordon E. *Miracle on the River Kwai* (London 1963).

Gort Viscount. Despatches from the B.E.F. in *The London Gazette* 17.10.41.

Hardie R. *The Burma–Siam Railway* (London, 1983).

Lomax E. *The Railway Man* (London, 1995).

Mitchell R.K. *Forty Two Months in Durance Vile* (London, 1997).

Percival A.E. 'Operations of Malaya Command, From 8th December 1941, to 15th February 1942', in *The London Gazette* 26.2.1948.

Percival A.E. *The War in Malaya* (London, 1949).

Rawlings L. *And the Dawn Came Up Like Thunder* (London, 1972).

Rawlinson S. *Papers Salvaged from Changi* (Unpublished typescripts).

Rollo D. (ed.) *88th Field Regiment 1939–1945* (Unpublished typescript, Royal Artillery Institution, 1996).

Tsuji M. *Japan's Greatest Victory, Britain's Worst Defeat* (1951, English edn, Staplehurst, 1997).

U.S. Army *Handbook on Japanese Military Forces* (Washington, 1944).

War Diaries *War Diary of 88th Field Regiment R.A., T.A. in France and Belgium 1939–1940* (Public Records Office, WO 167/499, and 166/1511).

War Diary of 88th Field Regiment in Malaya 1941–1942 (Public Record Office WO 172/41).

War Diary of 9th Indian Division, 1941 (Public Records Office WO 172/41).

War Diary of 18th Division, 1942 (Public Record Office WO 172/91).
War Office *Artillery Training, Advance, Withdrawal, Attack, Defence and Position Warfare* (Vol. 1, Pamphlet no. 6, 1938).

Secondary sources

Allen L. *Singapore 1941–1942* (London, 1977).
Atkin, R. *Pillar of Fire: Dunkirk 1940* (London, 1990).
Brooke G. *Singapore's Dunkirk* (London, 1989).
Collier B. *The Defence of the United Kingdom* (HMSO, London, 1957).
Corfield J.J. *Bibliography of Literature Relating to the Malayan Campaign and the Japanese Period* (University of Hull, 1988).
Davies P.N. *The Man Behind the Bridge: Colonel Toosey and the River Kwai* (London, 1991).
Daws G. *Prisoners of the Japanese* (London, 1995).
Ellis L.F. *The War in France and Flanders* (HMSO, London, 1953).
Elphick P. *Singapore, The Pregnable Fortress* (London, 1995).
Elphick P. & Smith M. *Odd Man Out, the Story of the Singapore Traitor* (London, 1993).
Fuller R. *Shokan: Hirohito's Samurai* (London, 1992).
Gelb N. *Dunkirk* (London, 1990).
Gilchrist A. *Malaya 1941* (London, 1992).
Hogg I.V. *British and American Artillery of World War Two* (London, 1978).
Hughes B.P. (ed.) *History of the Royal Regiment of Artillery Between the Wars, 1919–1939* (London, 1992).
Kirkby S.W. *The War Against Japan: Volume 1* (HMSO, London, 1957).
Lee C. *Sunset of the Raj, Fall of Singapore* (Durham, 1994).
McCormack G. & Nelson H. (eds) *The Burma-Thailand Railway* (St Leonards Australia, 1993).
Pallud J.P. *Blizkrieg in the West Then and Now* (London, 1991).
Simpson A.W. *288th (2nd West Lancashire) Light Anti-Aircraft Regiment Royal Artillery, Territorial Army, A History* (Published by the Regiment, Blackpool, 1960).